INFORMING CULTURAL POLICY

INFORMING CULTURAL POLICY

THE RESEARCH AND INFORMATION INFRASTRUCTURE

J. Mark Schuster

Transaction Publishers
New Brunswick (U.S.A.) and London (U.K.)
A Center for Urban Policy Research Book

Supported by
THE PEW CHARITABLE TRUSTS

Second printing 2015, by Transaction Publishers.
Originally published in 2002 by The Pew Charitable Trusts

This book is printed on acid-free paper that meets the American National Standard for Permanence of Paper for Printed Library Materials.

ISBN: 978-0-88285-174-7
Printed in the United States of America

Cover photograph: Quadracci Pavilion, Milwaukee Art Museum, Milwaukee, Minnesota
(Architect: Santiago Calatrava)
Photograph © J. Mark Schuster

Typesetting: Arlene Pashman

à Augustin Girard

mon maître, mon collègue, et mon ami

CONTENTS

II. RESEARCH AND DOCUMENTATION CENTERS

III. RESEARCH AND DOCUMENTATION CONSORTIA

APPENDIX

FOREWORD

In 1999 The Pew Charitable Trusts launched an initiative to foster broader public appreciation of nonprofit arts and culture and its role in American society. This initiative, *Optimizing America's Cultural Resources*, was largely premised on the idea that the development of supportive cultural policies depended on providing more and better information on arts and culture to policymakers. Developing new sources of credible, easily accessible, policy-relevant information became a key objective of our work. We knew that many other countries had already built information structures for this purpose and believed that learning how those nations collected, maintained, and made this information available could inform our efforts in the United States. In June 2000, we commissioned a report from J. Mark Schuster on international models for the gathering, sharing, and archiving of information relevant to cultural policy development.

Professor Schuster has long been internationally recognized as a leading cultural policy researcher and had both the knowledge and contacts to develop his report quickly. We asked Dr. Schuster to describe how other nations manage policy-relevant information on arts and culture and to suggest whether an existing model could be effectively emulated in this country or whether uniquely American circumstances would require the adaptation of elements from several models.

Professor Schuster's report, *Informing Cultural Policy, A Consideration of Models for the Information and Research Infrastructure*, suggested that no one model can adequately serve as a template for the United States. His observations on the strengths and weaknesses of other nations' efforts were so perceptive and helpful that the Trusts wanted his report to be disseminated to others who work in this field. In September 2001, the Trusts made a grant to the Center for Urban Policy Research (CUPR) at Rutgers University to accomplish two objectives. First, CUPR would convene experts to discuss Dr. Schuster's findings. Second, CUPR would publish the report in book form.

In an appendix to this book the reader will find the proceedings of a December 2001 meeting held at Rutgers to stimulate conversation around U.S. interest in international models of cultural policy information development and exchange. At this meeting, representatives from U.S. research institutions, cultural organizations, and government and private funders, along with international experts, considered the premise put forth by Professor Schuster that an effective information infrastructure is critical to policy formulation and implementation in culture as much as in other fields. Among other things, the discussion pointed out the probable limits on adopting designed elements into a unique U.S. system that has mostly developed ad hoc and without consideration for how the pieces worked as a whole.

This publication completes Professor Schuster's and CUPR's efforts for the Trusts. We are grateful to Dr. Schuster for his superb work on the report and on opening up these ideas to discussion among stakeholders in the United States. Thanks also go to the organizer of the December 2001 meeting, Ruth Ann Stewart, research professor at the Center for Urban Policy Research at Rutgers' Edward J. Bloustein School of Planning and Public Policy, for her work to stimulate conversation around these ideas. Our appreciation also to Robert W. Lake and Arlene Pashman at CUPR Press for their cooperation in preparing the publication.

We hope that the report will assist cultural policy researchers and policymakers in understanding better the risks and, importantly, the significant rewards of working to strengthen the U.S. cultural policy information infrastructure.

MARIAN GODFREY
STEPHEN URICE
SHELLEY FEIST
NATIONAL CULTURE PROGRAM
THE PEW CHARITABLE TRUSTS

MARCH 2002

ACKNOWLEDGMENTS

The origins of this book lie in a series of conversations that I have been privileged to have had over the years with the staff of the Culture Program of The Pew Charitable Trusts. These conversations always seemed to find their way back to two central questions: how best to inform their own policies and programs in the cultural arena and how best to make a lasting contribution to the evolving debate surrounding government support for the arts and culture in the United States. In both cases, attention to the research and information infrastructure underlying cultural policy seems to be warranted. Hoping to find clues and insights elsewhere, Pew provided me with a grant under the umbrella of its *Optimizing America's Cultural Resources* initiative, asking me to look at how this infrastructure had developed and how it was operating in a number of other countries. I thank especially Marian Godfrey, Director of the Culture Program; Stephen Urice, Program Officer; and Shelley Feist, Program Associate, for their support in this endeavor.

This book would not have been possible without the cooperation and candor of the many individuals who were interviewed during several research trips. Many of them put up with quite a bit of e-mail from me, arranging my visits, checking my facts, and filling in the holes after the interviews. All of them were very generous with their time and with their opinions. I am extremely grateful to these friends and colleagues, many whom I have known for a long time, others whom I met for the first time during this project. Today, scattered throughout the world, is a strong and committed group of individuals who have made it their life's work to assure that cultural policy is well informed. I celebrate all that you have accomplished, and I hope that this document is a modest tribute to your work.

A number of individuals have read and commented on various components of this book. Christopher Gordon, former head of the English Regional Arts Boards, provided a particularly complete set of comments; Julia Lowell of the Rand Corporation asked a number of probing questions on earlier drafts; and Andreas Wiesand of ERICArts and the *Zentrum für Kulturforschung*, and Claire McCaughey of the Canada Council for the Arts, provided detailed comments on certain sections. Thank you one and all. My thanks also to Erin McNeece, who served as my research assistant and editor for the final revisions, and to Arlene Pashman, senior editor at the Center for Urban Policy Research at Rutgers, who nurtured this manuscript through to final publication. As is customary, the views expressed and any errors committed in this book are mine alone and do not represent the individuals or the institutions on whose contributions this book is based, nor do they necessarily reflect the views of The Pew Charitable Trusts.

The field of cultural policy research is changing quite rapidly. We have made every effort to ensure that names of organizations and individuals, contact information, and Web site addresses are up-to-date as of April 2002, but the accuracy of this information will no doubt erode over time. Indeed, the organizational structures and programs that are described herein continued to change right up to the moment at which we fixed the text for publication.

The circle of researchers who are working in the field of cultural policy is quite small. Consequently, it is incumbent upon me to reveal my own professional ties to the organizations discussed in this book where they go beyond the realm of normal collegiality. CIRCLE, Cultural Information and Research Centres Liaison in Europe, has recently opened its membership to individuals in addition to its traditional institutional members, and I have become a member in order to maintain better contact with its work. Similarly, I have agreed to become a member of ERICArts, signaling my willingness to participate in its collaborative research projects. And, finally, I have agreed to become a member of the board of International Intelligence on Culture as it emerged from the former International Arts Bureau. I trust that these relationships have not clouded my perceptions too much, but my readers ought to be aware of this potential.

The opportunity to shape my original report into the current book was provided through additional support from The Pew Charitable Trusts. The final work was completed at The Cultural Policy Center of The Irving B. Harris Graduate School of Public Policy Studies at The University of Chicago, under whose auspices I received sabbatical support from The Franke Family Charitable Foundation and The Harris Foundation.

One of the great pleasures of this project was that I was able to return to France and interview Augustin Girard, my mentor in the field of cultural policy research. In 1979–80, Augustin welcomed me, on a postdoctoral fellowship, to the Research Division of the French Ministry of Culture, where I had my first real introduction to the emerging cultural policy research and information infrastructure. Augustin headed the

Research Division for many years, shaping it into the leading such research office in the world. Now in (semi) retirement, Augustin heads the *Comité d'Histoire du Ministère de la Culture*, where he is overseeing a large and comprehensive project to document the history of this ministry. I dedicate this volume to him.

J. MARK SCHUSTER

THE CULTURAL POLICY CENTER
THE IRVING B. HARRIS GRADUATE SCHOOL
OF PUBLIC POLICY STUDIES
THE UNIVERSITY OF CHICAGO

APRIL 2002

INFORMING CULTURAL POLICY

I

The Research and Information Infrastructure

INTRODUCTION

In any policy arena, the crafting of appropriate and effective policy depends on the quality of the information infrastructure that is available to the participants in that arena. Such an information infrastructure does not develop on its own accord. Rather, it is designed, developed, and managed as a critical element in policy formulation and implementation. This should be no less true in cultural policy than in other policy arenas.

In the twenty-five years that I have been doing research in the field of cultural policy, various pieces of such an infrastructure have begun to develop in the United States. The National Endowment for the Arts has had a research division, which has supported a growing volume of research, most notably the Surveys of Public Participation in the Arts. Princeton University, Columbia University, and the University of Chicago, among others, have created university-based cultural policy research centers. Many of the major arts service organizations have added research directors to their staffs. But, while various attempts have been made to map the extent of the existing cultural policy information infrastructure in the United States—encompassing the mix of government offices, university research centers, research staff within arts service organizations, individual researchers, and consulting firms of various types—no structured attempt has been made to conduct a cross-national analysis intended to draw on the more highly developed models already in operation elsewhere.

What are the important models for a cultural policy information infrastructure that have been developed in other countries during the last thirty to forty years? What are the lessons most applicable to the United States? A cross-national comparative look can provide valuable information on how this infrastructure has evolved, on what has succeeded and what has had less success, on what is sustainable and what is not, and on how the range of interests of the various individuals and institutions involved in the cultural policy arena can best be accommodated through careful design (or, at the very least, reflective adaptation) of the information infrastructure.

This book focuses on examples drawn from the European and Canadian contexts. This selective emphasis makes sense for two reasons. First, these are the models most accessible by virtue of the involvement and visibility of these countries in various international research networks, as well as by virtue of their relationship with multinational agencies. I did uncover other models during the research, and where they are particularly relevant I have cited them, but the budget and timing of the project on which this book is based did not allow for their full exploration. Second, the models discussed here tend to be those that are the most highly evolved, suggesting that they are particularly good examples to consider when one is interested in the track record of various forms of the cultural policy information infrastructure. The evidence of accumulated experience is key to understanding the various models and their properties.

Research Questions

This inquiry was designed around a set of research questions that included the following:

- What is the structure of the cultural policy information infrastructure? Which individuals and which institutions contribute most to its operation?
- How is the infrastructure funded?
- How are comparability, continuity, and stability built into the system?
- How are the various research-related activities of data collection, data analysis, generation of statistics, information development, documentation, cataloging and archiving, dissemination, and communication handled?
- What is the relationship between the private and the public sectors in providing the infrastructure?
- How (and how well) are the interests of the various parties in the cultural policy arena met by the system? What is the nature of their relationship with the system?
- To what extent does the cultural policy information infrastructure involve parallel structures operating simultaneously? How do they work together? Is there a division of labor in the system that allows it to function better?

- How do demands for new types of information and new forms of inquiry enter into the system?
- How does the system allow for multiple interpretations of the data it is collecting?
- To what extent is the system motivated by a data collection and documentation mentality as opposed to a research mentality?
- What is the balance between basic research and applied research? How is that balance managed?
- To what extent is the system designed and managed as an element of public policy toward the arts and culture? To what extent has it simply evolved?
- To what extent and in what form does the system generate information that is used for advocacy purposes?

These questions set forth an ambitious research agenda for this inquiry. It was not always possible to get clear answers to all of them, but the contents of the interviews that were conducted were incredibly rich, often leading in directions not imagined by this original set of research questions.

The Structure of This Inquiry

This book is organized in three parts. Part I provides an introduction to the inquiry and summarizes the main crosscutting themes that have emerged from the research. Note, however, that Part I is not entirely separable from the rest of the document; it draws heavily upon the analysis and the further detail of the case studies presented in Parts II and III. In Parts II and III, each case is summarized using a standardized format in which the significance of the case is explained, the background and evolution of the case are documented, and an assessment of the case is offered. Each description includes the Web site address, a list of key contacts, and a list of the documents that were consulted in the compilation of this book. Part II focuses on individual research and documentation centers, organizing them by country so that one can get a sense of the ecology of the information infrastructure by reading consecutive cases. Part III focuses on research and documentation consortia, including research projects involving multiple institutions.

Institution-Based Models

At the outset of this research, I identified several different models for the organization of cultural policy research and information, and I have made every attempt to include several examples of each model among the cases that were ultimately investigated. A description of each model follows.

Research Division of a Government Cultural Funding Agency

The archetypal model in which the research and information function in cultural policy is assumed by the central government agency is the *Département des Études et de la Prospective* of the French Ministry of Culture and Communication. This office administers what is probably the most extensive national-level research and information capability in cultural policy. It commissions research on a regular basis, administers ongoing work in the development of cultural indicators, maintains an extensive documentation service, and provides policy-based research on a one-off basis.

The Strategic Research and Analysis Directorate of Canadian Heritage; the Cultural Policy Directorate of the Dutch Ministry of Education, Culture and Science; the Planning and Research Section of the Public Affairs, Research and Communications Office of the Canada Council; and the Statistics and Social Policy Unit of the British Department for Culture, Media and Sport also turned out to be similar in intent and in structure, if not in scope.

In some ways, this is the model that one would most expect to find: the central governmental agency taking its mandate seriously and maintaining an in-house research capability to document the field in which it is operating and to inform the making of policy in that field.

National Statistics Agency

In some cases, the national statistics agency has a specific mandate to collect, maintain, and disseminate government statistics on the cultural sector. This is true for Statistics Canada and will also be true with the creation of a new cultural statistics observatory at the provincial level in Québec. The Social and Culture Planning Office in the Netherlands provides an interesting variation on this theme. (Not considered in this study, the National Centre for Culture and Recreation Statistics in the Australian Bureau of Statistics is another premier example of this type.)

This model responds directly to the need to establish a foundation of statistics as a way of understanding the profile and parameters of the field toward which policy is being directed.

Independent Nonprofit Research Institute

On occasion, the research function is delegated to an independent nonprofit institute. The *Boekmanstichting* in the Netherlands is perhaps the best-known example of this model. Even though its emphasis is on information and documentation, it also provides a variety of research services.

This model offers the possibility of insulating research and information from the political pressures that might be brought to bear within a governmental agency.

Government-Designated University-Based Research Center

The model of creating government-funded research centers based in universities is used extensively in France by the *Centre National de la Recherche Scientifique* (a rough equivalent to the National Science Foundation in the United States). Several of these research centers are discussed in Part II.

Another clear example of this model, not included in the current study, is the Australian Key Centre for Cultural and Media Policy located at Griffith University in Brisbane. This center is part of the Australian Research Council's Research Centres Program, through which research centers are established in a particular policy field and a specific university with expertise in that area is designated to host the center.

This model has two particularly interesting properties: It, too, allows the research function to be insulated from day-to-day political concerns and machinations, perhaps fostering research of a more social-scientific nature than would occur in centers that are linked more closely to policymaking institutions; and it makes it possible for the cultural policy information infrastructure to be more closely linked to university training and teaching programs than would customarily happen under other models. The relationship between the *Centre de Recherche sur le Politique, l'Administration, la Ville et le Territoire* (CERAT) at the Université Pierre Mendès France, and the *Observatoire des Politiques Culturelles*, both in Grenoble, France, illustrates well this latter point.

Private Consulting Firm

In some cases, the cultural policy information infrastructure has evolved so that it has become primarily the province of a private, profit-making (or at least profit-seeking) consulting firm that specializes in the field. Many private consulting firms have conducted cultural policy–related research on a one-off basis and have moved into and out of the field as projects have become available, but there are some that have made a longer-term commitment to building up expertise in this field. International Intelligence on Culture (formerly the International Arts Bureau) in London is a case in point. Originally formed when the international information and research capacity of the Arts Council of Great Britain was privatized, International Intelligence on Culture is now involved in providing a wide variety of information and consultation services to the field. EUCLID International is a more recent example, but there are many other examples in the increasingly complex cultural policy research and information environment.

The *Zentrum für Kulturforschung* (ZfKf) in Germany might also be placed in this category, but its structure and intent perhaps distinguish it from more traditional consulting firms. Although it is set up as a private company (with provision of up to twenty-five percent participation by public or nonprofit bodies in its ownership and governance), it functions more as a research institute than as a consultancy. Admittedly, this boundary is not entirely clear, but ZfKf has functioned primarily on the basis of contractual research relationships with the German federal government, with joint federal/*Länder* bodies, or with various European and international agencies. These contracts, which typically are for multiyear research projects, often rule out the possibility of realizing any "profit." Perhaps the "private research firm" deserves a category of its own, but ZfKf may be unique in this regard.[1]

Cultural Observatory

When I began this inquiry, I was aware of several institutions that called themselves "cultural observatories." What I discovered is that there has been a recent proliferation of cultural observatories beginning with the *Observatoire des Politiques Culturelles* in Grenoble and the European Audiovisual Observatory in Strasbourg, both of which are frequently cited as the archetypes for the others. They have been joined by INTERARTS (INTERARTS Foundation: European Observatory for Cultural Research and International Cultural Co-operation) in Barcelona,[2] the *Observatoire de l'Emploi Culturel* within the Ministry of Culture and Communication in Paris, the Regional Observatory on Financing Culture in East-Central Europe in Budapest, and many others. Two new observatories are under development in Canada: the Canadian Cultural Observatory at the national level and *L'Observatoire de la Culture et des Communications* at the provincial level in Québec. This proliferation of observatories eventually led UNESCO to convene a meeting to discuss this phenomenon and to consider the creation of an International Network of Observatories in Cultural Policies.[3]

In a strictly taxonomic sense, these observatories do not constitute a separate pure type. Instead, they combine a variety of hybrids of the different models under a common rubric. Nevertheless, because of their recent popularity, it is worth considering cultural observatories as a separate phenomenon. Accordingly, they are considered separately in the next section of this book.

Non-Institution-Based Models

My research has suggested that there are at least three other categories of models not tied to a single institution that also need to be considered in any survey of the research and information infrastructure for cultural policy.

NETWORKS

In recent years, a variety of cultural policy research and information networks have been created, and they should be considered as important actors in their own right. Arguably, the best-known example, at least in Europe, is CIRCLE. A program of the Council of Europe, CIRCLE (Cultural Information and Research Centres Liaison in Europe) is an international nonprofit association that brings together cultural policy researchers and users of the results of cultural policy research. It organizes roundtable discussions and conferences, publishes reference works and a newsletter, carries out research, and works to facilitate the circulation of policy-relevant information. Originally organized around independent research institutes, as well as the research offices of cultural ministries and arts councils, it has recently been restructured to include interested individuals as members, regardless of their institutional affiliation.

Other examples exist as well. In Canada, a Canadian Cultural Research Network has been formed. As mentioned above, UNESCO convened a meeting to discuss the creation of an International Network of Observatories in Cultural Policies. The field is even beginning to see the formation of networks of networks: The Council of Europe has established the Forum of European Cultural Networks (*Forum des Réseaux Culturels Europeens*), a network of networks in the cultural field, and UNESCO has funded Culturelink, the Network of Networks for Research and Cooperation in Cultural Development.

ERICArts, the European Research Institute for Comparative Cultural Policy and the Arts, was originally established as an association to be a provider of comparative cultural policy research. It brings together interdisciplinary teams of researchers from throughout Europe (and elsewhere), involving them in projects of common interest. Although it currently has some of the characteristics of a network, it was actually created as a reaction to the perceived failure of networks to accomplish truly meaningful and useful comparative research because they must rely heavily on volunteers who have little investment in long-term yet timely research performance. The eventual goal of ERICArts is to create a permanent European-level cultural policy research institute that would function as a "managed consortium" with nonprofit or foundation status, run by major cultural observatories and research bodies.

Program Models

Some of the most interesting research work in the field has been organized around research *programs* rather than research *institutions*. The most interesting and most visible of these has been the Council of Europe's Program for the Evaluation of National Cultural Policies. The council has offered its member states the opportunity to participate in this program for the past fifteen years. Each state that participates commissions a study of its own national cultural policy, the so-called National Report. The Council of Europe then commissions a panel of outside experts who evaluate and react to the National Report, eventually filing an Examiners Report. The result has been a fascinating and valuable series of reports documenting and debating national cultural policies in Europe.

Journals and Periodicals

While there are a number of academic journals that operate in the field of cultural policy—the *Journal of Cultural Economics*; the *International Journal of Cultural Policy*; the *International Journal of Arts Management*; the *Journal of Arts Management, Law and Society*; *Media International Australia* (incorporating *Cultural Policy*); *Nordisk Kulturpolitisk Tidskrift* (the Nordic Journal of Cultural Policy); *Economia della Cultura* (the journal of the Italian Association for Cultural Economics); and *Boekmancahier*, among others—several journals have been developed to serve more specific data, information, and research dissemination needs. Two in particular are considered here: *Cultural Trends*, published by the Policy Studies Institute, University of Westminster, London, and *Culturelink*, published by the Institute for International Relations in Zagreb, Croatia. Note that many of the institutions discussed in this book publish their own newsletters and journals and thereby contribute to the dissemination of cultural policy–relevant information in this way.

The Ecology of the Information Infrastructure

While I have used the names of various organizations and institutions to illustrate the archetypal models above, the truth is that one does not observe pure types in the field. As is often the case in public policy, pure types simply do not exist in the world of cultural policy practice. Rather, most of these examples combine elements from several models. Research divisions of ministries of culture commission research from private consulting firms, participate in research networks, and publish newsletters and, occasionally, journals of their own; nonprofit research institutes team up with university-based research centers to conduct research and conferences on behalf of public agencies. The combinations are endless.

Moreover, each of the examples discussed at length in Parts II and III must be understood in the context of the research ecology in which they operate. The research division of the French Ministry of Culture and Communication works in the context of the wide variety of social science research units supported by the *Centre National de la Recherche Scientifique*; one cannot appreciate the work of the *Observatoire des Politiques Culturelles* of Grenoble without understanding its relationship to the *Centre de Recherche sur le Politique, l'Administration, la Ville et le Territoire*; the Australian Key Centre works in collaboration with the research office of the Australia Council; the *Boekmanstichting* works alongside the Dutch Social and Cultural Planning Office; and so on. Often the ecology of the cultural policy information infrastructure involves four or five main organizations and many other smaller ones.

Given this complexity, it is inevitable that the information infrastructure has evolved differently in different places, not only with respect to the sharing of research responsibilities across public agencies but also with respect to the balance between public provision and private provision of the research infrastructure. From the national level, one can clearly see that the division of research labor differs from place to place depending on how this infrastructure has evolved.

In this book I have focused on the cultural policy research and information infrastructure in four different countries—France, the Netherlands, Great Britain, and Canada—but I have also introduced other cases where they seem particularly interesting and germane. While it would be rash to characterize my representations of the research and information infrastructure in these four countries as complete, I am confident that they are sufficiently comprehensive to demonstrate the different ways in which the ecology of this function has come to be structured.

A Personal Reflection

In the pages that follow, I have tried to write with a point of view. This has meant making judgments and saying things that some of my interviewees might have preferred be left unreported. But I interviewed real people with real opinions as to what works well and what works less well. If one works only with the official material that one can glean from a Web site or from a set of official brochures and publications, one can document a view—the official view—of what is going on, but that is hardly a useful picture of what is actually happening. Nevertheless, the judgments and reactions recorded here are personal ones, informed by my view of the information and data that I gathered. Others might well have come to rather different conclusions based on the same information and the same data. In the end, what is important here is not the evaluation of the various initiatives and institutions that have been considered. Rather, it is the promotion of a discussion about those initiatives and institutions in order to surface the salient issues that underlie the provision of a rich and policy-relevant information infrastructure for the arts and culture.

At the same time, it was not within the scope of the current project to document or evaluate the existing information infrastructure in the United States. (Nor has there been any attempt to design a complete cultural policy information infrastructure for the United States.) Suffice it to say that, in comparison to the many foreign examples considered here, there is considerable room for development. As part of the process of bringing the current report to publication, The Pew Charitable Trusts sponsored a meeting at the Center for Urban Policy Research at Rutgers, The State University of New Jersey, on December 7, 2001, to discuss the implications of this research in the American context. The appendix to this book, coauthored by Ruth Ann Stewart and Catherine C. Galley, is an essay based on this meeting.

THEMES, FINDINGS, AND CONCLUSIONS

The bread and butter of this study is presented in Parts II and III, in which each of the cases is discussed in considerable detail. For a complete understanding of how each research institution, documentation center, information service, or research program operates, the reader should turn to those pages. In this section, I attempt to do something rather different. I extract the major themes, conclusions, and findings that emerge from those detailed discussions with an eye toward generalizing beyond the individual cases. The process of generalization is, itself, an interesting one. When one generalizes, one departs from the idiosyncratic details of the individual cases, squinting a bit in order to see the overall profile of the landscape, the lay of the land. As a result, it becomes difficult to track any specific one-to-one relationship between the attributes of a particular case and the generalizations to which it contributes. And that is not only appropriate, it is desirable, as one puzzles through the applicability of these cases to the American context.

The Resurgence of Cultural Policy Research

Perhaps the most important finding to emerge from this research is that there has been a dramatic resurgence of investment in policy-relevant research and information in the field of cultural policy. Government agencies in many countries are rebuilding their research capabilities after periods in which that research capability lay fallow (cf. particularly the Arts Council of England and the Canada Council); in other countries, research capabilities are being built for the first time, often under the rubric of cultural observatories; and the rise of transnational governmental organizations (e.g., the Council of Europe, the European Union, and the reentry of UNESCO into the field of cultural policy through the window of "cultural development"[4]) has, to some degree, created a demand for comparative research and information sharing as a prerequisite for collaborative, cross-national projects.

At the same time, the mantra of "value for money" and the call for "policy-relevant advice" have permeated cultural funding agencies, making them much more conscious of the effectiveness of the programs they oversee. The reorientation of some of the major arts-funding bodies toward strategic action rather than grant making has also contributed to this trend. And the creation of new cabinet-level umbrella agencies (Canadian Heritage in Canada and the Department for Media, Culture and Sport in England, for example), while raising the profile of the field, may well impart a new importance to coordinated policy initiatives informed by applied comparative research. Here the clearest example is the International Comparative Research Group of the Strategic Research and Analysis Directorate of Canadian Heritage.

It is useful and informative to contrast the development of cultural policy research within ministries of culture to its development within arts councils, whose relationship to government is typically at arm's length. When a coherent research policy has evolved, it usually has been within ministries of culture, which are less reluctant to be seen as exercising central control while monitoring the field. Arm's-length arts councils traditionally have been less subject to central government's expectations for explicit policy and planning, so it is perhaps not surprising that arts councils' commitments to research have fluctuated considerably over time.

Recently, however, as central governments have applied increased pressure on arm's-length arts councils in an attempt to ensure that they are operating within the general direction of government policy, there has been a marked rise in the call for *evidence-based* policy and planning, a call that arts councils are finding difficult to resist. To the extent that the call for organizational restructuring of arts councils leads to an internal structure focused on transversal issues that have a close link to perceived public interests, a direction that many arts councils are taking, the relevance and utility of research might become more clearly perceptible, and one might well expect additional resources to be invested in research. To the extent that the reorganization of arts councils leads to a strengthening of more traditional, discipline-based structures (perhaps as a backlash), one might expect considerable resistance to an investment in research that is not clearly linked to the health of one or another of the artistic disciplines.[5] Indeed, it probably would be quite easy to construct an account of the waxing and waning fortunes of the various cultural policy research divisions in both ministries and arts councils as a direct function of such shifts in relative internal power and influence.

Not surprisingly, this resurgence of research has once again brought to the forefront the debate between basic research and applied research. Much of the new investment in cultural policy research has been targeted at very applied projects with a direct relevance to (short-term) policy decision making. It is less clear that the new investment in research has benefited basic research in the traditional social science mode. The one place where the basic research tradition continues to be strong is in France, through the parallel system of university-based research centers funded and staffed through the *Centre National de la Recherche Scientifique*. While there are a number of university-based research centers working on cultural policy questions in the other countries that I visited, particularly in Great Britain and the Netherlands, these research centers tend to be evidence of a rather different trend—the attempt to create profit centers at universities by establishing research centers that function essentially as consulting firms, producing very applied work and, arguably, paying attention more to the bottom line than to the construction of knowledge in the field. They, in turn, are being judged on their publications and measurable outputs, often within relatively short time horizons that militate against long-term longitudinal studies. In Great Britain, for example, the University Higher Education Funding Council now makes use of a "research assessment exercise" as the primary basis for allocating public funds to higher education.

It may well be that we should not expect the professional cultural agencies to engage in basic, blue-sky research; the internal pressures of the various art-form departments that consistently push to devote every available resource to short-term, direct assistance to their particular art form rather than to the building of a knowledge base are simply too strong. If this type of research is to happen, a parallel state research structure may need to be deployed (as in France), as it is unreasonable to assume that private support for basic research would suddenly turn in the direction of cultural policy and away from health policy, science policy, or education policy.

What Constitutes Research in the Field of Cultural Policy?

While it is relatively easy to argue (and document) that there has been a resurgence of interest in cultural policy research, if only in its applied form, it is more difficult to actually place a coherent boundary around that research. In this project, I have taken a very broad view as to what constitutes *research*, including various library, documentation, statistics-gathering, and publication functions as well as the more traditional research question–driven research projects. This reflects how the field itself conceptualizes cultural policy research. With respect to *cultural policy* research, I have taken a middle ground, looking for policy research that goes beyond the arts to other forms of cultural policy but stopping somewhat short of the fullest, most anthropological conception of culture.

Frédérique Patureau, of the *Département des Études et de la Prospective*, French Ministry of Culture and Communication, argues that cultural policy research has three essential elements: (1) studies, (2) statistics, and (3) documentation. She is correct in her assertion that all three are necessary components of a well-integrated research infrastructure, but, as I have already suggested, it would be useful to distinguish a bit further by separating applied policy studies and basic research studies. Nevertheless, it is difficult to imagine that a research system whose goal is to inform policy and decision making can function without each of these elements.

Various countries have responded to these elements differently by dividing the research labor in their own signature way. The clearest division of labor is in evidence in the Netherlands. The Dutch Central Bureau for Statistics (Statistics Netherlands) provides the main source of data collection for the state; the Social and Cultural Planning Office uses these data and others to write a series of interpretative reports depicting various aspects of the cultural life of the country; the *Boekmanstichting* provides the library and documentation function while facilitating conferences and seminars and conducting some limited desk (secondary) research; and the Cultural Policy Directorate of the Ministry of Education, Culture and Science supports these ongoing efforts financially and commissions research projects from time to time depending on the policy needs of the Ministry. Yet, despite this highly evolved division of research labor, support for basic social science research in the arts and culture in the Netherlands is perhaps not as developed as it is elsewhere.

In France, the *Département des Études et de la Prospective* of the Ministry of Culture and Communication combines several elements under one roof: It provides substantial library and documentation services to the field; it commissions and oversees a wide variety of research projects; and it serves as the primary collector of statistical data through its function as the Ministerial Statistical Office of INSEE (*Institut National de la Statistique et des Études Économiques*), the national statistics office. Basic social science research in the arts and culture is separate, though not neglected. The *Centre National de la Recherche Scientifique* maintains an extensive system of university-based research centers, a number of which conduct research of importance to cultural policy.

In some countries, the division of labor in cultural policy research is still being worked out. The Arts Council of England, for example, has announced its intent to invest substantially in a rejuvenated research capacity, but the documentation and information capacity of the Arts Council was partially privatized when the International Arts Bureau (now reconstituted as International Intelligence on Culture) was spun off from the Arts Council. That function is now being challenged by EUCLID International and other profit-making entrepreneurs who have entered the field. Thus, it is not entirely clear to what extent the Arts Council will actually be able to or want to recoup all of these research activities under its umbrella. In addition, the Department for Culture, Media and Sport is currently reevaluating its own role in research and information, which heretofore has been quite limited.

In Canada, the research work of the Strategic Research and Analysis Directorate of Canadian Heritage has been relatively hidden from the view of the field, the Canada Council is just beginning to rebuild its research capacity with a new emphasis on strategic policy and advocacy, and two new cultural observatories are planned, one at the national level and one at the provincial level in Québec.

The resurgence of cultural policy research has contributed to the evolving interest in cultural policy as a field of academic inquiry. The Council of Europe has made a major contribution to this interest with the publication of reports from its Program for the Evaluation of National Cultural Policies[6] and of many other booklets and ancillary documents related to this program. In November of 1999, an International Conference on Cultural Policy Research was held in Bergen, Norway. A second was held in Wellington, New Zealand, in January 2002. In the United States, the Research Center for Arts and Culture at Teachers College, Columbia University, in cooperation with the Washington, D.C.–based Center for Arts and Culture, convened a seminar on the teaching of cultural policy in June of 2001.[7]

Cross-national differences in how the boundary of the cultural field itself is construed are not trivial. In some countries (most notably the United States), the boundary has implicitly been drawn quite narrowly to include the performing arts and the visual arts, perhaps extending to museums and art galleries. But note that even those agencies that are responsible for clearly delimited arenas within the arts and culture have begun broader research programs, in part because they believe that the more general government agency to which they report has neglected research across a broader definitional boundary; this has clearly happened in England, where the Arts Council has taken on research that one might have thought more appropriate for the Department for Culture, Media and Sport. In some countries, the boundary has been enlarged to include heritage policy, and, increasingly, the media and the cultural industries. Variations in the boundaries of the field as defined by each agency and as practiced by government are both having an impact on the research agenda being pursued.

Numbers versus Analysis

Much of the cultural policy research being undertaken around the world today might be better thought of as the development of a statistical base of data. Many of the institutions that I studied see the development of basic statistics on the cultural sector as their highest priority. All of these institutions seem to be operating with the conviction that if such numbers were available, they would prove useful. Of course, separating statistical data gathering from a well-posed research question can be a frustrating as well as illuminating exercise in any attempt to map the current research and information infrastructure of the field.

Over the years, many of the research organizations in the cultural field have been criticized because they have appeared to be more interested in generating numbers than analysis. Among the publications produced by the organizations described in this document are hundreds if not thousands of statistical reports documenting one or another subsector of the arts and culture. Perhaps the purest example in this vein is *Canada's Culture, Heritage and Identity: A Statistical Perspective*, the biennial report of the Culture Statistics Program of Statistics Canada (along with the "shelf tables" it also produces), but there are many other examples of such reports in which interpretation is nearly nonexistent.

The reason for the emphasis on numbers over analysis may, in part, be politically rational. Research divisions in arts-funding agencies have had a hard time justifying their existence in the face of demands for providing more support directly to the arts and culture, and they have protected themselves by retreating to the perceived safety of neutral statistical presentations, though, as the example of Jack Lang's reaction to the publication of *Pratiques Culturelles des Français* demonstrates,[8] even "neutral" statistics can prove threatening.

Yet it would be a mistake to suggest that it is possible to separate completely statistics gathering from statistics interpretation. It is clear from the criticisms that one hears of even those statistics collected by the indisputably reputable national statistics agencies that interpretation begins at the data-gathering stage when categorization schemes are designed and used to collect data. What one sees is shaped by the framework through which one chooses to view the world. This points to an old dilemma in data gathering and analysis, a dilemma that is very much in evidence in the arts and culture. To ensure comparability over time, one is reluctant to make changes in data-collection instruments; yet, to ensure that data collection is keeping up with changes in the field under consideration, data-collection instruments and concepts must be revised. It is rarely economically feasible to do both. Consequently, many of the criticisms that one hears about time-series data argue that one or the other of these desirable attributes—comparability or responsiveness—has been sacrificed.

One of the most interesting themes that echoes across the countries considered here is the recognition that it is not so much the shortage of data that should command one's attention; rather, it is the lack of use of those data that needs to be addressed. In most countries, a considerable quantity of data on the arts and culture *is* being collected, often on a regular basis as part of the submission requirements of the grant-making process—though little of this mass of data is ever used in any organized fashion by the arts-funding agency that requires it. Collection and assumed availability substitute for research and inquiry. Alan Peacock has raised this issue in his own inimitable way in a recent critique of arts funding in Scotland:

> The major museums and galleries and the major companies supported by the Scottish Arts Council do produce accounting data as legally required, but this is not analysed, or at least for the public's benefit. Detailed examination of them reveals striking differences in the grants per attendance at arts events which require explanation. One can hardly blame Scottish Executive officials who are hard-pressed as it is to churn out a succession of policy documents, for not offering evidence of statistical literacy, if their masters have no wish to be confused by the facts.[9]

Moreover, the data collection that does exist is uncoordinated, involving many different government agencies, service organizations, research centers, and industry groups. Terry Cheney, in his recent review of available data for the Publishing Policy Group of Canadian Heritage,[10] found that each sector had its own constellation of data sources, a constellation that includes Statistics Canada, the program office within Canadian Heritage that deals with the sector, and service organizations and associations operating within the sector. In other words, a considerable volume of data is already available, but the institutional capability for mining those data is limited. Cheney's first and most important conclusion was to pay attention to using the data sources that already exist (even though he also recognized that these sources are incomplete, inconsistent, and of varying quality).

Several of the countries I visited have recognized the importance of encouraging other governmental agencies and statistical services to analyze from a cultural perspective the data that they collect as part of their routine operations. In some cases this requires financial support from the arts council or the ministry of culture (as is the case in the Netherlands, with the relationship between the ministry and the Social and Cultural Planning Office); in other cases, this is simply viewed as part of their customary charge.

As research organizations, cultural observatories, networks, and private profit-making entrepreneurs proliferate, the sheer volume of available data will only increase—though much of it may simply be repackaged, distributed, and marketed via the new information technologies. Consequently, there will be a need for data mediators who can make informed judgments about the quality and applicability of data and who can analyze their meaning. Much of the impetus behind cultural observatories seems to be inspired by this need for data mediation.

Instances in which the available statistics have been fully explored, interpreted, and debated are rather rare. Here, once again, the model of the Dutch Social and Cultural Planning Office is instructive. The mandate given to this office by the ministry is to mine and interpret the available data on the arts and culture according to several main themes of interest in the cultural sphere—themes that change from year to year—and to publish regular reports. The authors of these reports are encouraged to give their own interpretation and spin to the data in order to provoke comment, reflection, and debate.

Some interviewees actually expressed a concern about being too successful. If the research function is successful, they asked, will demand grow and expectations become unrealistic, particularly with respect to speed and to the political necessity of arriving at rosy findings?

All of the countries considered here rely on a basic repertoire of studies to develop the statistical base of information. Typically, the first studies are descriptive, documenting the supply of art and culture. How many arts and cultural organizations of what type are located where? How many heritage sites have been officially designated, and where are they located? How much money are local, regional, or national governments spending on each type of cultural organization? How many artists and cultural workers of various types are there? Where do they live? What are the economics of their lives? More recently, these studies have been expanded to include the demographics of the cultural industries.

But, increasingly, attention is turning toward studies of the demand for the arts and culture as another element in the basic statistical repertoire. Most countries now conduct participation studies of their adult population to gauge what percentage of various demographic groups attends or participates in various cultural activities. Many countries also conduct time-use surveys to ascertain the relative amounts of time their population spends engaged in various types of activities. Some conduct expenditure surveys.

For each of these studies the methodology has become sufficiently refined over time and sufficiently similar across countries that, for the first time, it has become possible to envision truly cross-national comparative studies. Indeed, the hope of many of the individuals involved in the Council of Europe's Program for the Evaluation of National Cultural Policies was that it would eventually result in the adoption of a standardized set of methodologies for gathering information that could then be compared across countries. Many of the research organizations considered here are just beginning explicitly comparative research of one sort or another. The data now exist; the work remains.

In the last several years, the issue of cross-European data comparability in the field of culture has been taken up by Eurostat, the statistical agency of the European Union. Several leadership groups on cultural statistics have been formed with representatives of the various interested countries in the European Union as members: a Task Force on Methodology, a Task Force on Employment, a Task Force on Cultural Spending and Cultural Funding, and a Task Force on Participation in Cultural Activities. The initial report of the leadership groups has been published.[11]

In the end, of course, it would be foolish to think of numbers and analysis as being two ends of the same spectrum. To borrow an idea from public policy analysis, the key is to figure out how best to transform data into information and information into evidence. Data must be given meaning by being interpreted through analysis. Those meanings and interpretations must then be given policy relevance and turned into the grist of policymaking debates and decisions. At each step in this process—the collection of data, the massaging of data into information with meaning, and the transporting of that information into the policy process—value is added by the cultural policy research and information infrastructure. Whatever system evolves, that system must pay attention to all of these stages to be maximally effective.

Quality Assurance

With the proliferation of data from a wide variety of sources has come the issue of how to assure the quality of the data. Historically, the field of cultural policy research has suffered from the widespread distribution of data collected and manipulated with the self-interest of the collecting agency in mind. Terry Cheney's point about the existence of usable data notwithstanding, one does need to be conscious of the advantages and drawbacks of each of the data sources being cited. This issue has been exacerbated by the quick and easy sharing of information electronically. It is now quite common to find many different Web sites making reference to the same data or information, but without attribution or explanation. As more and more sites are linked to other sites, it will become increasingly difficult to verify the quality, the applicability, and the timeliness of the data. Thus, evaluation of and commentary upon existing data is another role that might be played by some form of intermediary institution or data mediator.

A second problem with quality assurance arose during the interviews. The research posts in cultural policy research divisions are not necessarily occupied by trained social science methodologists. Many people in these jobs recognize that, although they are not trained as researchers, they are being asked to contract for, supervise, summarize, and occasionally conduct research. This has been exacerbated with the spread of research budgets throughout the departments of ministries of culture and arts councils as the various subcomponents of the ministerial system recognize the usefulness of data to their operations and the desirability of having more direct control over the collection and dispersal of those data. At the very least, the central research division should have an oversight role with respect to the research activities taking place throughout the organization, but that is not always the case. Short-term, low-budget research projects can often be commissioned with very little internal oversight of the contracting process and even less of research design and implementation. Clearly, this compromises the quality of the work. Thus, the role of research divisions may change; they may need to become more involved in giving advice to other offices within the ministry concerning research design and methodology and perhaps less involved in direct commissioning, supervising, and conducting of research.

Policy Shifts: Decentralization

Some of the more substantial changes in the cultural policy information infrastructure have come about because of fundamental shifts in policy direction. One of the most dramatic such shifts over the last ten to fifteen years has been the degree to which decentralization and devolution policies have finally taken hold within cultural ministries and arts councils. The degree of decentralization has greatly complicated the delivery and design of the research function. Indeed, much of this book focuses on the proliferation of centers of research, information, and documentation, a proliferation that has been greatly fueled by this policy shift.

The experience of the *Département des Études et de la Prospective* (DEP) of the French Ministry of Culture and Communication is instructive, if not entirely typical. In recent years there has once again been a major shift toward decentralization in the cultural policy of the French Ministry of Culture and Communication. The ministry has turned over a considerable amount of authority and responsibility to its *Directions Régionales des Affaires Culturelles* (DRACs)—the regional cultural affairs offices. But the DRACs do not yet have access to the information they need to promulgate informed policies and programs on the regional level, so they often feel that they are flying blind. This change has resulted in a debate between the DRACs and the central administration of the ministry, a debate with substantial research implications. The DRACs, exercising their newfound independence and authority, refuse to respond to the information and research demands of the disciplinary offices at the ministry that deal with the various artistic disciplines across the country, presumably because they perceive these disciplinary offices as policy competitors. But the DRACs themselves have neither the information they require nor the means to analyze it, nor the information needed to implement policy at a more local level. The result is that the regional offices demand a lot of information from the central research division, which is not perceived as a policy competitor, but DEP does not have the staff or resources to undertake, for example, twenty-seven studies of regional employment in the arts and culture (one of the most pressing issues for the regional offices). However, DEP can and does attempt to provide advice at the level of methodology and research coordination.

This dilemma has been "resolved," if unsatisfactorily, by providing the various offices of the ministry with resources to do research themselves, thereby creating multiple research budgets within the ministry rather than just one. These budgets are then typically used to contract with the many exterior consulting agencies and research firms that have developed (or are intending to develop) expertise in a particular subfield. As a consequence, the field of cultural policy research in France is becoming much more diverse with many more actors, fueled in large part by this change in national cultural policy, which renders centralized policy and centralized research less attractive, less feasible, and perhaps even less relevant. This pattern may well be replicated elsewhere as decentralization policies take hold.

Policy Shifts: The Cultural Industries

As has already been mentioned, the field of cultural policy has also shifted from areas that have traditionally been rather closely allied with the state and state intervention toward more of a relationship with, and dependence upon, industry. This shift is revealed in a change in vocabulary; government cultural agencies have begun to present themselves as responsible, for example, for "Creative Britain,"[12] or even to restructure themselves as "Creative New Zealand."[13] One result of this shift is that the center of gravity in research is moving away from research offices with a general mandate to more specialized research groups and centers that are familiar with the terrain of various segments of the cultural industries. Some of these centers are clearly linked to the industries that they observe, raising issues of confidentiality and reliability and encouraging rivalry among competing centers of expertise.

Because of the multiple government agencies that come under the umbrella of cultural policy when the cultural industries are explicitly included, this shift also means that this part of the field is actually moving toward the bread and butter of the mainline governmental statistical agencies, whose relative expertise resides in counting firms and measuring trade, employment, and labor markets. The statistical methodologies for studying these entities are much more highly developed than the statistical methodologies for studying artistic and cultural activities in the nonprofit and governmental sectors. The difference in quality between these two sets of statistics may well provide the pressure finally needed to improve statistics gathering on the nonprofit and governmental sides.

This development is nicely depicted in a recent British report. In 1997, Chris Smith, the Secretary of State for Culture, Media and Sport, established a Creative Industries Task Force to assess the value of the creative industries, to analyze their needs with respect to government policy, and to identify ways of maximizing their economic impact. The creative industries were broadly defined to include "those activities which have their origin in individual creativity, skill and talent and which have a potential for wealth and job creation through the generation and exploitation of intellectual property," a definition that is much more inclusive than the concept of the "cultural industries," which has been present in cultural policy debates, particularly outside of the United States, for some time. One of the first activities of the Task Force was to compile the *Creative Industries Mapping Document*, a report that drew on a wide variety of statistical sources to map and document the dimensions of each of the creative industries.[14]

Another way to frame this shift is to notice that in the years since many of the research organizations and institutions studied here were created, the boundaries of the field of cultural policy have expanded beyond the boundaries of the traditional ministries of culture and arts councils. Multiple governmental agencies have always been involved in cultural policy—the early work of the *Département des Études et de la Prospective* (DEP) demonstrated this clearly in France—but that multiple involvement is now much more explicit. Culture is no longer the sole domain of national ministries and arts councils, and the research portfolio has changed to reflect this shift. François Rouet of DEP describes the shift in this way: "Twenty years ago we had a monopoly on numbers and statistics. Now you find expertise in all parts. We are no longer the sole place. Therefore it is necessary for us to have a new role. . . ."

Policy Shifts: Buck Passing and Defensive Research

As it has become more common to talk about cultural policy and to recognize it as a separate, identifiable domain of government involvement, more attention has been paid to the necessity of informing that policy through documentation and research. One aspect of this increased attention has been a dramatic rise in the number of commissions to carry out short-term research projects with very particular political ends: "Give me something to back up the policy I want to pursue." The clearest example of this dynamic, albeit in a slightly different form, came up in interviews with the International Comparative Research Group of the Strategic Research and Analysis Directorate of Canadian Heritage. Dick Stanley describes its work as "defensive"; it wants to be able to answer "Yes" to the Minister when asked if it has checked on what other countries are doing with regard to any particular proposed policy initiative.

Not surprisingly, the turn to this type of research is viewed cynically by those who have argued for a long time that the cultural policy system ought to pay more heed to research—and researchers. These cynics describe the politicians and agency bureaucrats as wanting to pass off responsibility for their decisions; they are seen as wanting to have someone else to blame if things go wrong. This poses a dilemma for the more traditional research institutes that take a narrower view of what constitutes acceptable research. Many of them have resisted short-term, politically motivated commissions with the inevitable result that the contracts go elsewhere, to other non-research offices within the ministry or to outside consultants—"guns for hire"—who are seen as being less concerned about politically motivated research.

Ironically, despite their reputation on the pure research side of the ledger, it is these short-term projects, driven by the heat of the policy moment—"I need an answer yesterday"—that have provided much of the impetus for building cultural policy libraries and documentation and information centers. It is relatively easy to see their value when they are consulted time and again. It is also driving, to some degree, the development of regular statistical reporting mechanisms. But the fact that there is pressure in these directions does not mean that they have been adequately funded; the restricted access to a number of the libraries and documentation centers studied here suggests otherwise.

Evaluation and Research

Combining the research function and the evaluation function into the same cultural policy research division seems eminently logical. After all, these functions require many of the same methodological skills. But they do not involve the same political skills.

It has not been uncommon for research divisions within ministries of culture and arts councils to be asked to take on the evaluation function. Reasonable and responsible public policy implementation requires an informed look at which programs and projects are succeeding, which are failing, and why. But when research divisions have taken on this function, they have often found themselves in jeopardy. Ministers begin to wonder, Why are we spending money so that someone within our agency can criticize us? Wouldn't it be better to spend that money on the arts? Why should we be spending money on research at all?

For these reasons, Harold Horowitz, the founding director of the research division of the National Endowment for the Arts, resisted merging the then existing evaluation office with the newly created research division. The evaluation office has long since disappeared. Similarly, the research office of the Canada Council has managed, for the most part, to steer clear of the shoals of evaluation. Except for one year in which two evaluations were completed, there has never been an evaluation program at the Canada Council; and when evaluation-like activities are undertaken, which is rare, they are undertaken under another name. The lack of success of the French *Comité Ministériel d'Évaluation* is another case in point.

Some of the interviewees drew a distinction between two types of evaluation. The first is *ex ante evaluation*: the assessment of potential grantees to establish whether they are deserving of support (and to see what they have accomplished with their support in the past). The second is *ex post evaluation*, asking the question of how effective a particular project, program, or policy has been. A number of the research offices I visited participate in the former, hardly any in the latter.

For the moment, the Arts Council of England seems to be the exception to the rule with respect to program evaluation. Evaluation has been explicitly included in the mandate of the newly rejuvenated research department. Perhaps this will come to entail only the documentation of what is happening in the field with the implementation of the projects and initiatives of the Arts Council and its clients. But Peter Hewitt, the chief executive officer, seems to be determined to use council research to put a number of questions on the table for debate and wants the council to be much more proactive in putting out material that might be seen as critical in one way or another, even of itself.[15]

Another distinction drawn in the area of evaluation is between *evaluation of policies* and *evaluation of programs and projects*. Interestingly, the French focus on the former—they and the Swedes were the main protagonists in the Council of Europe's Program for the Evaluation of National Cultural Policies—while most other countries focus on the latter, which is probably the more common understanding of what evaluation entails. Whether or not it is logically possible to evaluate a policy without evaluating the programs and projects intended to implement that policy is an interesting intellectual debate, one that is at the heart of the Council of Europe's program. What is clear is that there are two analytical questions of interest: (1) Is this policy effective?, and (2) Is this program effective? They both should command the researcher's attention.

Advocacy and Research

Introducing the question of advocacy into a discussion of cultural policy research is every bit as problematic as introducing the question of evaluation. Yet, the use of research results for advocacy purposes is often on the minds of those who are calling for (or funding) research. The original design of the Center for Arts and Culture in Washington, D.C., envisioned an organization with two functions: research and advocacy. In no small part, this was a response by the foundations that funded it to the attacks that had been waged against public funding of the arts and culture in the United States. They believed that the arts needed help to fight back.

In commissioning the research project that resulted in the current book, The Pew Charitable Trusts asked me to look explicitly at the extent to which the research infrastructure generates information that is used for advocacy purposes. I expected a clean-hands response to the question of advocacy. What I got was considerably more complex.

Early on in my interviews, Pierre-Michel Menger, the director of a CNRS-supported research center in France and, therefore, somewhat of an outside observer, made an interesting point. He argued that, at the present time in France, there is a strain of research that is intertwined with advocacy. He described this research as "defensive," intended to protect the state funding system that has evolved. He characterized the cultural field as having two parts, a growing private part (e.g. audiovisual, media, and the cultural industries in general) and the part that, in his words, has been "conserved for cultural policy." The argument that there should be more state involvement is essentially spent, in his view. Rather, the state now finds itself playing a more impartial role, albeit somewhat on the left, maintaining equilibrium between the various components of the newly expanded boundary of cultural policy.

In several cases, arts councils have embraced advocacy as they have restructured their arts support infrastructure. Both the Canada Council and the Arts Council of England, in transforming themselves into self-styled strategic policymaking bodies, have come to the conclusion that they need to project a more coherent story about the work that they have done and what they have accomplished and hope to accomplish. In both cases, the reputations of the councils as well as the quality of the information on which they based their work were seen as being at stake. Both councils have come to the conclusion that they need to become more proactive on behalf of the arts and artists, as well as on their own behalf, and, at least for the moment, make no apology for a renewed interest in research that will fuel advocacy. Practicing an increased level of candor, Peter Hewitt sees the Arts Council of England as actively involved in advocacy, speaking to the government on behalf of the arts, while also speaking to, and challenging, the arts community.

Some of my respondents had a very different reaction, however. They did not understand the underlying premise of the question at all. Those who entered the field of cultural policy research as believers in cultural policy see *all* of what they do as advocacy. They believe that their work is in service to that field and do not understand why it would be desirable to articulate any boundary between research and advocacy.

The organization CIRCLE, Cultural Information and Research Centres Liaison in Europe, is a case in point. Though ostensibly a network to promote collaboration and comparative cultural policy research, CIRCLE was conceived with a very strong strain of advocacy. The original proposed statute for the organization that eventually became CIRCLE was quite explicit on this point, stipulating a goal of:

> [S]upporting an improvement of the working conditions and the freedom of expression for artists, writers and other cultural workers,

> while promoting a better use of their talents for the development of society as a whole and for the safeguarding of cultural diversity all over the world.[16]

This is hardly the manifesto of a network of research centers interested in pure social science inquiry.

The melding of advocacy and research has played itself out in a variety of ways among the cases considered here. The roots of the *Boekmanstichting* lie very much on the side of advocacy. It was founded by the Dutch Federation of Artists Associations (with the financial support of the Prince Bernhard Foundation, a private fund). Much of the early work fell into the area of promoting the direct interests of artists, so that by the time support from the Ministry of Education, Culture and Science had replaced its initial support from the Federation of Artists Associations, there was considerable pressure on the *Boekmanstichting* to change its direction toward documentation and away from the more controversial realm of advocacy-inspired research.

Similarly, early in the life of the *Zentrum für Kulturforschung* (ZfKf), its director, Andreas Wiesand, also became Secretary General of the German Arts Council (*Kulturrat*), a consortium of some 220 member organizations in the arts and media that had been created as a platform through which individuals and organizations in the field could meet with the government in Bonn. It operated out of the ZfKf's offices, and many of its activities were clearly forms of advocacy and lobbying. Advocacy and research went hand in hand until 1993, when ZfKf pulled away from the *Kulturrat*, reestablishing to some degree the line of demarcation between advocacy and research.

The relatively recently formed Center for Arts and Culture in Washington, D.C. (not explicitly covered in this book) continues to struggle with the tension posed by the initial expectation that it would combine both advocacy and research under one roof.

The Rise of "Cultural Observatories"

One of the clearest trends to have emerged out of recent changes in the cultural policy information infrastructure is the dramatic proliferation of institutions appearing under the rubric "cultural observatory." Generally speaking, these institutions have come into being to serve as mediators in the process of bringing policy-relevant data and information to the attention of the field. Noticing first only those institutions with the word observatory in their title, a partial list would include the following:

- The *Observatoire des Politiques Culturelles* in Grenoble, France.
- The European Audiovisual Observatory in Strasbourg, France. [http://www.obs.coe.int]
- The *Observatoire du Disque et de l'Industrie Musicale* in Paris, France.
- The *Collectif Observatoire Culturel* in St. Etienne, France. [http://www.asi.fr/~observa/cocpageanglais1.html]
- The *Observatoire de l'Économie Culturelle de Provence-Alpes-Côte d'Azur* in Aix en Provence, France. [http://www.culture.fr/culture/paca/doss/artec/artec2.htm]
- The *Observatoire de l'Emploi Culturel* within the research division of the French Ministry of Culture and Communication in Paris, France. [http://www.culture.fr/culture/dep/fr/cata.htm#typ3]
- The *Osservatorio Europeo sul Turismo Culturale* at the *Centro Universitario Europeo per i Beni Culturali* in Ravello, Italy. [http://www.cuebc.amalficoast.it/osservatorio_europeo_sul_turismo_culturale.htm]
- The *Osservatorio Culturale del Piemonte* under the auspices of the Fitzcarraldo Foundation in Turin, Italy.[17] [http://www.ires.piemonte.it/OCP/]
- The *Osservatorio Culturale e Reti Informative* in Milan, Italy. [http://www.cultura.regione.lombardia.it/dgStruttura.cfm?ID=4]
- INTERARTS Foundation: European Observatory for Cultural Research and International Cultural Co-operation in Barcelona, Spain. [http://www.interarts.net/]
- The *Observatório das Actividades Culturais* in Lisbon, Portugal. [http://www.min-cultura.pt/Organismos/ObservatorioCnt.html]
- The Regional Observatory on Financing Culture in East-Central Europe in Budapest, Hungary (The "Budapest Observatory"). [http://www.budobs.org/about.htm]
- The *Observatorio Cultural* in the Faculty of Economic Sciences, University of Buenos Aires, Argentina. [http://www.econ.uba.ar/www/institutos/observ-cultural/index.html]

- The *Observatório de Politicas Culturais* at the University of São Paulo, Brazil.
- The *Observatorio de Políticas Culturales Municipales* in Montevideo, Uruguay.
- The Canadian Cultural Observatory, in Hull, Canada (currently under development).
- *L'Observatoire de la Culture et des Communications* at the provincial level in Québec, Canada. [http://www.stat.gouv.qc.ca/observatoire/default_an.htm]
- A proposed *Observatoire du Développement Culturel* in Belgium. [http://www.ecolo.be/VIP/Josse/documents/2000_0229_ observatoire_culturel.htm]
- A proposed *Observatoire Culturel* in Corsica. [http://www.cesc-corse.org]
- A proposed African Observatory of Cultural Policies to be developed under the auspices of UNESCO. [http://www.unesco.org/culture/development/observatories/html_eng/news2.shtml]

If one were to add similarly functioning institutions that do not use the word "observatory" in their names—for example, the Southern African Cultural Information System in Maputo, Mozambique—the list would increase substantially. Conversely, it may also be the case that organizations that use the word "observatory" are not actually functioning as an observatory in the sense that that term seems to imply in the cultural policy field.[18]

Nearly all of these observatories have come into existence in the last five to ten years; thus, cultural observatories, whatever they are, are a very recent phenomenon. Even with this proliferation, though, there is evidence that many observatories, particularly local ones, struggle. In Italy, apparently, the high expenses that these observatories entail has led to a collapse of many of them during periods of local government financial constraint.

In a report commissioned by UNESCO, Eduard Delgado, director of INTERARTS in Barcelona, attempted to trace the evolution of the idea of an observatory from its roots in astronomy and meteorology to its more metaphorical use in the field of culture:

> The notion of economic and social "observatories" has taken root in today's political structures. The metaphor, [which] originated in the physical and biological sciences, is applied to the intangible movements of collective behavior in a spirit of empiric[al] analysis along the neo-positivist tradition of contemporary social sciences. The idea of an "observatory" is indebted to astronomy and feeds back on the assumption that regular movements in a complex system can only be appraised by disciplined registry of trends and changes. Conversely, the notion of [an] "observatory" assumes that the analysis of significant data must be fed back to the observing instrument in order to correct its focus. This is of particular interest in [the] . . . social sciences where observation often leads to action and should become, in its turn, the object of further study. The postmodern debate between "cultural studies" and "cultural policy studies" points to the need of a more systematic way of data collecting on arts policies and practices. Social observatories are by nature two-way mirrors, and, like Alice in Wonderland, crossing from one to the other is a metaphor for growth and wisdom.
>
> If there is little in common between observatories in the physical sciences, there is even less homogeneity in the social disciplines. Only a small number of organizations operate with an "observatory" tag and few carry out systematic activities associated to [*sic*] permanently checking socio-cultural change. Existing multilateral monitoring devices in Europe (the Audio-visual Observatory, the Urban and Regional Cultural Policies Observatory, etc.) differ from each other . . . to such an extent that no taxonomy is viable.
>
> It is a paradox that as the cultural sphere contains one of the most dynamic and future-oriented sectors in the world, the instruments for gathering, contextualizing and transferring data or experience remain vastly underdeveloped. Relatively minor aspects of health, education or social behavior are the object of regular monitoring and reporting on the basis of statutory mission. The cultural galaxy has few telescopes pointed at it.[19]

Delgado is quite right in that no taxonomy of cultural observatories is viable. Each of the observatories cited above has its own particular way of operating, its own institutional infrastructure, and its own mandate. Like the Americans and the British, one wonders whether a common language divides them. But he is not quite right when he says, "The cultural galaxy has few telescopes pointed at it." This research has pointed out there are more than a few such telescopes, but they do not cover the entire sky, and they may not be as well focused as one would like.

The use of the word "observatory/*observatoire*" to describe data-gathering, monitoring, and information-disseminating organizations in any number of fields appears to be a French innovation. There are lengthy lists of "*observatoires*" operating in a wide range of societal sectors in France,[20] and the two observatories that are most often cited as the archetypes for cultural observatories—the *Observatoire des Politiques Culturelles* in Grenoble and the European Audiovisual Observatory in Strasbourg—are both in France.

Augustin Girard, former head of the *Département des Études et de la Prospective* of the French Ministry of Culture and Communication, who was instrumental in getting several of the observatories up and running, describes the deliberate choice of the word "*observatoire*" as a "shy" choice. The intended message was quite clear: This new institution was not being created to rule or control; rather, it would observe, monitor, and provide information passively. In his words, "We cannot agree on a Center, but we can have an Observatory. It is a pleasant name. An Observatory is a place of negotiation, of interactivity. It does not deliver judgments."

There is little doubt that the metaphor of an observatory is a powerful one, even if that metaphor does not actually suggest what the content and operation of such an entity should be. Terry Cheney, in his consulting report, had one particular model of a cultural observatory in mind when he recommended that Canadian Heritage

> initiate a feasibility study on creating a cultural industries "observatory" for Canada to provide long term, comprehensive, independent information on the sector, to contribute to the development of consistent survey instruments, to develop a comprehensive analytic framework, to provide expert advice, to develop a critical mass of expertise able to address topical issues, and to serve as a breeding ground for developing careers in culture research. This observatory could carry out short-term surveys of the industry (capital spending and hiring projections); could take over the surveys of the nonprofit culture sector which is not in need of the strict, and restrictive, confidentiality requirements of Statistics Canada; [and] could provide independent estimates and projections of the universe of activity.[21]

This is the model that Canadian Heritage is working to implement at the national level.

But one has to be careful not to conclude that the creation of a cultural policy observatory solves the problem of designing the cultural policy information infrastructure simply by virtue of its existence. An "observatory" can become an ill-defined grab bag into which all types of expectations can be stuffed. The senior observatory in the field, the *Observatoire des Politiques Culturelles* in Grenoble, pays rather little attention to data collection and monitoring, which one might have expected to be at the center of its *raison d'être*. Rather, it focuses on continuing education programs and other venues through which it can communicate research results to the field—a worthy goal, to be sure, but one that most would think secondary to an observatory's main tasks. The temptation to think that one has established the necessary cultural policy information infrastructure when one has cut the ribbon on a new cultural observatory is almost too great.

UNESCO has been tempted to join in the institutional proliferation of observatories. In Stockholm in 1998, the Intergovernmental Conference on Cultural Policies for Development adopted an Action Plan that included the recommendation that the Director-General of UNESCO "encourage the establishment of networks for research and information on cultural policies for development, including study of the establishment of an observatory of cultural policies." But at a meeting in Hannover, Germany,[22] the notion of creating an international observatory of cultural policies was dropped in favor of recognizing the prior existence of many such institutions and the desirability of pulling them together in a network facilitated, if not supported, by UNESCO. Thus the idea of an International Network of Observatories in Cultural Policies was born, but even this initiative now seems to be dormant as UNESCO has restructured and restaffed its Division of Cultural Policies, focusing its attention on other initiatives.

The proliferation of observatories, and of research units specializing in cultural policy more generally, has had another palpable effect. It has dramatically escalated the number of requests for information and the number of surveys (now mostly electronic) circulating among those who have been identified as working in the field. The view seems to be that the information being sought is already sitting on the shelves of one or another research office or documentation center and that all that would be required to obtain it would be to send out a well-constructed survey instrument or to make a well-placed phone call.

During revision of this book, I received just such an e-mail inquiry from the *Observatorio de Políticas Culturales Municipales* in Montevideo, Uruguay. It had launched an international study "to gather information about urban cultural policies in a range of contexts and on different continents . . . to identify the methods and tools used in the design and implementation of sustainable cultural development strategies and to outline a series of best practices in this area."[23] Attached was a questionnaire divided into eight themes and nine sections, which sought a wide variety of detailed information on a city's cultural policies; I was asked to complete the questionnaire for the city of Boston. But what was being asked was impossible. The questions sought such a highly refined level of detail that it was unlikely that any research unit would be able to provide accurate information in response. Yet, the assumption behind launching such a project seems to be that the information is surely out there and easily available.

Thus, the proliferation of observatories has led to a further proliferation of such requests, with a self-referential group of institutions asking one another for information that is simply unavailable at the level of detail demanded or expected. Consequently, the demand for information far outstrips the supply. And seldom is such broad demand linked in any clear way to a set of cultural policy concerns beyond simple curiosity.[24] (This cycle of escalating information demand has been further exacerbated by the entry of private entrepreneurs into the cultural policy research and information infrastructure, a trend that is discussed more fully below.)

The Rise of Networks

Just as observatories have proliferated in the cultural policy field, so too have networks, but the driving forces in this instance are a bit different.[25] To be sure, some networks have been created because of the natural desire to share with and learn from one another; others have been created because of a specific desire to engage in comparative documentation and research. CIRCLE is the clearest example of the latter point; UNESCO's International Network of Observatories in Cultural Policies, if it were ever realized, might become another.

But the formation of networks in the cultural field has also been driven by the new realities of transnational funding, particularly at the European level.[26] Many of the funding programs of the European Union require multiple partners in multiple countries in order for a project to be funded, and this requirement has fueled the creation of networks in anticipation of the need to demonstrate the existence of such partnerships quickly. To some degree, the funding agencies see networks as a way to more efficiently manage demands on their limited resources; they can always insist that one operate through the network, letting the network do some of the sifting and sorting prior to the presentation of a request for funding.

At the next level of aggregation, the European Union's reliance on networks (and the networks' reliance on the Union) can plunge networks into fierce competition for limited funding, allowing the bureaucrats and politicians of the Union to play political divide-and-conquer games. As past treasurer of The European Forum for the Arts and Heritage, Christopher Gordon recalls watching as the European Union played them off against Europa Nostra (a built heritage network) and the European Council of Artists, three organizations that one might have expected to be cooperating with one another because of their natural affinities rather than being forced to work against each other's interests to get funding.

Among those who have worked in the cultural policy research field for a long time, there is quite a bit of frustration with the rise of multiple networks. Augustin Girard's view is that there is no responsibility in a network. Eva Brinkman, who directed the RECAP documentation project on behalf of the *Boekmanstichting* and CIRCLE, echoes this view: "When you are working internationally everyone says 'yes,' but no one has money or time."

Nevertheless, cultural networks do, from time to time, commission research relevant to the needs of their members and, thus, have become important, though occasional, components of the research and information infrastructure. Cultural policy research networks such as CIRCLE make this their primary business.

To the extent that the agencies of cultural policy are relying more and more on networks for cultural policy–relevant research and information, one has to ask a series of serious questions. How do they function? Most networks function on the principle of voluntarily contributed labor. One of the consistent complaints about CIRCLE has been the fact that its most active members have carried the ball, taking on their CIRCLE responsibilities gratis in addition to their "day jobs." This has led to exhaustion, quite a few missed deadlines, and, at various times, the feeling of exploitation. According to an interviewee, "It is becoming quite ridiculous. Somehow, it is quite insidious. If you don't participate you worry you will be left out. You cannot do your research work and run around Europe at the same time. You have to take a stand: I am only doing one type of work now, only going to one type of meeting."

What is the incentive to get involved and to stay involved in yet another network? The early networks in this field—CIRCLE, for example—grew out of the common interest of the participants. They saw a reason to work together and entered into a compact to do so. The later networks are of a somewhat different nature. They are, arguably, being pulled together by another agency more for that agency's purposes than for their members' purposes. This charge has been made, for example, of UNESCO's proposed International Network of Observatories in Cultural Policies and of the Council of Europe's Forum of European Cultural Networks *(Forum des Réseaux Culturels Europeens)*. Similarly, a number of individuals I have spoken with are skeptical about the motivations of Canadian Heritage in actively helping to create the International Network on Cultural Policy and the International Network on Cultural Diversity; they even wonder about the reason for Canada's strong catalytic role in creating the new International Federation of Arts Councils and Culture Agencies.[27] These critics detect the clear fingerprints of a Canadian ministry advancing a Canadian trade policy agenda through the guise of various networks.

Researchers are confronted with the question of whether or not to get involved with evolving networks. What can I reasonably expect if I invest my time in this network? Increasingly, the answer is the possibility of money. To the extent that funding may become more and more linked to networks of individuals working together, one may have to cast one's lot with a network in the hope that it may one day pay off.

This dynamic interacts with another one. The very best people in any field are also those whose skills are in the most demand. As networks proliferate, the best researchers and documentation specialists at some point make the decision that it is no longer interesting for them to remain involved. This has the tendency of leaving the networks in the hands of second-rate researchers who stick it out in the hope that their affiliation with the network will result in project support. One of my interviewees had a particularly cynical view of this process: "While everyone is busy running around creating networks and trans-European organizations, in the end they are used for self-interest."

As networks have proliferated they have become narrower and narrower in their interests. This dynamic has arguably undermined much of the reason for being in a network in the first place; networks were originally places where a disparate and loosely affiliated set of institutions and individuals could make connections that otherwise would be unlikely or impossible. Narrower networks focus on a set of more clearly defined interests that bond like to like. Seen in this way, proliferation has led to overspecialization.

Finally, how are networks to be funded? Through the dues of their members? With budgetary commitments from governmental agencies? Through research grants? Often, networks are not sufficiently funded, and their members find that they have to undertake a variety of short-term projects to keep the network alive, frequently at the cost of goal displacement.

Taken together, these factors help explain why some of the more recently created networks—for example, the Canadian Cultural Research Network or the network initiative of the Center for Arts and Culture in Washington, D.C.—have not taken off as dramatically as their creators might have expected.

The rise of private-sector, profit-making entrepreneurs in the cultural policy field has placed another pressure on networks. To the extent that these entrepreneurs build their businesses on the transmission and sale of information, networks provide them a valuable, low-cost service. These entrepreneurs can mine the meetings, seminars, conferences, and newsletters of the networks to which they belong and then turn around and repackage the information for a broader, subscription-paying audience. More and more entities of this type are coming onto the scene, and, to be fair, they are willing to take up some of the responsibilities that have exhausted the others. The difference is that they bring much less original research to the table; their work tends to be derivative rather than contributory.

How do you create a network? How do you make it stable? Andreas Wiesand, a veteran of a number of network-building efforts as part of the cultural policy information infrastructure, proposes four principles:

1. It has to have its own personality. This is another way of saying that it must have a reason for existence and that it must be identifiably different from other such initiatives.
2. It has to be funded from top to bottom. To be stable it cannot rely on the contributions that individual members may or may not be able to bring to the table.
3. It has to have the right person participating on behalf of each member group.
4. It has to fit into that person's own work (and his or her institution's work).

These are sound principles, but ones that are not often heeded in the excitement of cutting the ribbon on a new network.

The proliferation of networks has become so strong that the field has recently witnessed a new phenomenon: the creation of networks of networks. To take but two examples, UNESCO has funded the Network of Networks for Research and Cooperation in Cultural Development, which operates out of Zagreb, Croatia, under the name Culturelink; and the Council of Europe has formed the Forum of European Cultural Networks (*Forum des Réseaux Culturels Europeens*), which it convenes in Strasbourg on an occasional basis.[28] As one might expect from a network of networks, its goals are unexceptional:

- To allow each network to discover others and understand how they work
- To promote exchange of information
- To reflect on practical programs and philosophical questions related to European cultural development
- To implement concrete cooperation projects

But one wonders what the functionality of this network is for the Council of Europe. At least one of my interviewees suggested that the Forum of European Cultural Networks is the Council of Europe's new invention to serve as its eyes and ears on cultural policy over a wider set of European countries as it gradually withdraws support from its older, more entrenched network, CIRCLE.

The Rise of the Private Sector

The *Zentrum für Kulturforschung* is one of the oldest research centers operating in the field of cultural policy in Europe. It has always had a private corporate structure (though, as Andreas Wiesand points out, having this legal structure and actually realizing a profit are two different things). The fact that cultural policy research services were provided through this sort of structure in West Germany (and now reunified Germany), however, has probably had more to do with the explicitly federal governmental structure and the constitutional prohibition against a central governmental cultural agency—thus, no research division within a national ministry of culture—than with any presumed desirability of providing these services through the private sector.

Still, the recent growth in the cultural policy consulting sector, particularly in Great Britain, heralds a new trend in cultural policy research and information services. Two factors seem to be fueling this growth: (1) privatization as an element in cultural policy, which has led to increasing reliance on consulting services provided by the private sector, and (2) the widespread availability of new information technologies, which facilitates the low-cost communication of information. As a result, private entrepreneurs have made their presence felt in the cultural policy information infrastructure in two ways: (1) through responding to requests for proposal for research services (indeed, the increased presence of for-profit consulting firms, in and of itself, puts pressure on governmental agencies to open up their bidding processes to these firms), and (2) through the packaging and redistribution of information.

Together, these factors and these practices have resulted in a strong impression among those who have worked in the field for a long time that these new entrepreneurs are "stealing" their work and simply repackaging it for a profit. To be sure, there is some validity in these charges, though what the new consultants would say in their defense is that they are simply better able to take advantage of the new information technologies to bring information to the field in a more timely and more creative manner by being nimble.

The rise of profit-making independent entrepreneurs has also affected the functioning of networks and similar organizations. The charge is that these new arrivals are using existing government, quasi-government, and association structures to advance their own private business interests. This, too, is not surprising. The question is the extent to which the quality of the work is being jeopardized, and that is harder to pin down.

The rise of private consulting firms seems to vary from country to country. In France, according to Françoise Benhamou, there has been some increase in private consulting firms working for local authorities and regional authorities. But she argues that there is still very little room for consultants in France because the administration has so much power and because the *Département des Études et de la Prospective* has the advantage of its history and its placement within the Ministry. Even so, DEP commissions a variety of research organizations, some of them profit-making concerns, to conduct its research.

In my interview with Andreas Wiesand, he pointed out that there is a similar trend developing within the university system. Increasingly, university research staff are being asked by government to justify themselves by demonstrating that they are involved in the marketplace (read "real world") by setting up de facto consulting firms as profit centers. This results in a form of convergence: The public university side is moving toward the commercial side by behaving more like a business, while private organizations like Wiesand's *Zentrum für Kulturforschung* are moving toward the public side by getting involved in the administration of programs that had heretofore been public but are now being privatized.

Because the arrival of specialized profit-making firms in the field of cultural policy research and information services is, for the most part, a relatively recent phenomenon, it is too early to assess its impact. What is clear, however, is that it has created consternation, if not raw anger, among those who have dedicated their careers to working in this field in what they believed to be a more public-spirited way. Wiesand describes a generation shift that he sees in the field: the "old folks" believed in the public sector, in volunteering, in the public good; marketing, sponsorship, and profiting from the work were regarded as unseemly. But a problem is created when funders operate as though the old model were still in place. Because they have relied on contributed labor as well as on a publicly supported research infrastructure that has decayed in some places, they are surprised by the costs that are now quoted for research work, even by nonprofit research centers, because they are often quite a bit higher than they used to be.

What is also clear is that profit-making entrepreneurs will not, on their own, create the research and information content that is the ultimate goal of the cultural policy information infrastructure; they might take a speculative risk on generating some content, but, for the most part, their success will rely on the content commissioned and generated by others, most often by the state.

Research Programs versus Research Institutions

In Part III of this document, considerable space is devoted to a discussion of the Council of Europe's Program for the Evaluation of National Cultural Policies. This program is worthy of attention for a number of reasons, but in the current context it is important because it offers a rather different model for how to handle cultural policy research by structuring a research *program* rather than by creating a research *institution*.

Over fifteen years, the Program for the Evaluation of National Cultural Policies has offered a number of European countries the opportunity to document their national cultural policy and to get expert reaction to that policy. The program has created an extensive set of documents on each of the countries whose policies have been evaluated. The key documents are a pair of reports: the National Report prepared by individuals selected by each country and the Examiners' Report prepared by an expert panel selected by the Council of Europe.

Champions of this program would cite a number of positive results: the building of a research sensitivity and, in some cases, a research capacity in the countries considered; the development of quantitative data on which policy decisions can be based and by which policy decisions can be judged; the opportunity to make explicit and to examine policies that often were implicit, if not hidden from view; the encouragement of a healthy and public debate on issues of cultural policy; the development of a comparative mind-set in which countries can begin to learn from one another's experiences; and the identification of examples of good practice and the documentation of patterns of difficulty in cultural policy implementation.

Detractors of this program would point to other outcomes: the fact that the hope for truly comparable data would be generated across countries turned out to be unrealistic; the difficulty of maintaining a high quality of work across the many countries and across the countless individuals who contributed to the various products; the prolonged length of time across which the evaluations spread; the fact that the program changed from evaluating cultural policies to designing cultural policies when the newly emerging democracies of Eastern and Central Europe began to enter the program; and the fact that the process may have had less of an impact on national cultural policies than might have been expected (or hoped for).

Nonetheless, on balance, the program has had much more than a salutary effect on the cultural policy infrastructure. Throughout the countries that have been evaluated, there is, arguably, a new sensitivity to policy-relevant research and information, a sensitivity that would have been difficult to develop in the absence of a good, hard look at each country's policy from an external point of view.

The model of a collaborative research project playing an important role in the development of the research and information infrastructure deserves attention. The Program for the Evaluation of National Cultural Policies suggests that it might be worth considering project models as well as institutional models when setting out to change the infrastructure of cultural policy research. That this Council of Europe model has continued, albeit in an evolving form, for some fifteen years, and that UNESCO has considered adapting it for evaluations in countries outside of the Council of Europe's membership, are testimony to its perceived value. This is a model that may be well suited to adoption at the subnational level, particularly in countries with strong federal governments in which state, regional, or provincial cultural policies make a significant contribution to the overall profile of government cultural policy.[29]

Making Links to the World of Policy

One of the lingering issues in the cultural policy infrastructure has been the perceived gap between researchers, policymakers, and practitioners. During my interviews I heard repeatedly that there was considerable frustration with how poor the links were between research and information, on the one hand, and practice and administration, on the other.

But this is not to suggest that there have not been many attempts to bridge this gap. Generally speaking, most of the cultural observatories have been created with the hope that they will help span this divide, bringing highly selected and processed information to the attention of the field, if not become more proactive through training materials and programs. The *Boekmanstichting* has turned more and more to hosting small expert meetings, expanding its role as an information and documentation center to being a center of informed, independent debate. *Cultural Trends*, the journal that distributes interpreted statistical data to the field in the United Kingdom, is another type of response. The Social and Cultural Planning Office in the Netherlands, which is given a mandate to interpret existing data on cultural life through a variety of lenses, is yet another. And the structured interplay between the National Report and the Examiners' Report and the public hearing at which the two are presented in the Council of Europe's Program for the Evaluation of National Cultural Policies is a highly refined model for bringing the two worlds into contact with one another.

Both the Arts Council of England and the Canada Council, through the process of restructuring themselves into strategic bodies setting out broad policy directions for the arts and culture, hope that they will be able to employ their reinvestment in research to bring that research closer to the day-to-day operating concerns of the agency and the field. The Cultural Policy Directorate of the Dutch Ministry of Education, Culture and Science directly commissions research that it sees as being of strategic importance for policy, while it supports other government agencies (e.g., the Social and Cultural Planning Office) and information and research centers (e.g., the *Boekmanstichting*) to conduct the more basic research that is essential for documenting the evolving profiles of the sectors with which it deals.

These initiatives notwithstanding, there is still a pervasive feeling that not enough is being done in this regard. Simon Mundy, in his short guide to cultural policy, a document prompted, in part, by the reports resulting from the Council of Europe's Program for the Evaluation of National Cultural Policies, calls for a training structure for cultural officials, a structure that in most places is virtually nonexistent.[30]

In describing his career-long commitment to applied research, Augustin Girard has stated that for him, "Coming from the field and going back to the field is more interesting than coming from concepts and going back to research." The trick, of course, is to figure out ways to value that commitment. The role that the cultural policy information infrastructure can play is critical, but that role has to go well beyond generating research results and creating information. It has to extend to the informed communication and use of that information.

But operating in a gray area between the world of politics, with its premium on quick decisions with a minimum of contemplation (in the words of Antoine Hennion, "a political-administrative logic"[31]), and the world of social science research ("a research logic"), with its emphasis on careful, studied social analysis, the world of cultural policy research—and particularly the world of ministry and arts council research divisions—is a world that is caught very much between two different modes of functioning. It is a world that exhibits much of the stress that comes from that type of twin existence.

One way that this tension becomes particularly evident is through research publication policies. Universities and research centers generally take seriously their responsibility to publish their research results in order to contribute to the base of society's accumulated knowledge. But governmental cultural agencies have been noticeably reluctant to expose research results to the light of day, particularly when those research results have evaluative content or are seen as being directly linked to strategic planning. This reticence (if not outright prohibition) is part of the explanation of why states have moved toward private entrepreneurs to provide research services; these entrepreneurs are, generally speaking, less interested in publication and more willing to conduct work constrained with publication moratoria. Having recognized this dilemma, it is rather easy to construct an argument for independent, third-party support of cultural policy research (on the part of private foundations, for example) in which the goals would be knowledge building and knowledge dissemination. There is clearly a role to be played in the cultural policy research ecology by "disinterested" funders, whose actual interest lies in increased understanding rather than in particular forms of advocacy.

The Next Generation of Researchers

Another source of some uneasiness in the cultural policy research field is the uncertainty as to where the next generation of researchers will come from. Will researchers with a specialty in cultural policy be trained and cultivated? Or will the field have to rely on convincing researchers to join on for limited stints? How will fulfilling career paths be developed? Will there be sufficient support for research to allow researchers to develop specialized careers? Within what institutional structure will this happen?

This is a problem that the field has not handled well. One of the main criticisms of the *Département des Études et de la Prospective* registered in Antoine Hennion's evaluative report on the evolution of DEP is the finding that researchers have essentially become research administrators by joining DEP and have found themselves in a self-referential closed system.[32] DEP has trained staff to handle its specialized functions, and only DEP is interested in employing the research staff it has trained. The only way to progress is to stay in place. Of course, in France the existence of the extensive system of university-based research centers funded by the *Centre National de la Recherche Scientifique* offers a parallel career path to researchers who want to take advantage of a clear career ladder while remaining in touch with issues of cultural policy, and those who are inclined toward pure social science research are more likely to choose that path at the outset.

Moreover, a perceptual problem is related to the institutional problem. In his recent book, *Creative Industries: Contracts Between Art & Commerce*, Richard Caves, a distinguished Harvard University economist, admits to a two-decade fascination with the economics of the artistic and creative endeavor, but he also admits that he was worried that other economists would regard this interest as "frivolous." He thought it better to establish his credentials in other, more mainstream areas of economics before turning to this interest late in his career.[33]

Taken together, these two problems may help to explain why, with the apparent increase in demand for cultural policy research and information, the private sector has been staking out its presence so successfully in the field. Until very recently, these consulting firms have not had any particular expertise in the field of cultural policy. Rather, they have provided a wide range of consulting, research, and documentation services to a wide variety of fields. Their flexibility has allowed them easy entrance and exit, though their lack of specialization has led to increasing complaints about the quality and the relevance of the work that they have produced.

In Search of Money

Of course, the cultural policy infrastructure is nothing without the resources necessary to conduct research, compile information, and provide documentation. At the heart of the system there must be a sector that is persuaded of the importance of investing resources in building an information base.

The signs are mixed, though generally positive. Resources are being invested in the creation of cultural observatories, even if it is not yet entirely clear what their ultimate role in the infrastructure will be. Government cultural agencies, particularly the Arts Council of England and the Canada Council, seem to be turning back toward an investment in research, albeit research that is seen as being in the strategic best interest of the agency.

More and more research is happening at a multinational level, partly because researchers and the agencies commissioning research are interested in multinational questions (particularly with respect to trade, the protection of intellectual property, and the cultural industries), but partly because that is where the money is. Research is rising to the level of transnational organizations—the European Union, the Council of Europe, and UNESCO—because they have become funders of cultural policy research.

With the increased use of the Internet, there is a lot of sorting out that will have to happen. A few sources of reliable information and many sources of less reliable information are made to appear even more extensive through repetitive cross-linking of Web sites. Information developed by one agency ends up on the Web site of another, sometimes attributed, sometimes not, but rarely accompanied by the caveats and conditions applicable to the original work or by an understanding of the methodology that was used to collect or develop that information. Repackaging of information will continue to proliferate, but a true contribution to the research and information infrastructure can be made only with investment in the development of the information on which it relies. Without a commitment to the basic research necessary to develop the underlying foundation of data and a commitment to the interpretation of those data once they are available, the cultural policy information infrastructure will stagnate.

It is probably fair to say that there is more demand for policy-relevant data and information than there has ever been before. What remains to be seen is the extent to which governments and governmental agencies will prove willing to make the necessary investment to ensure that that information will be sought out, collected, analyzed, and disseminated.

The Absence of the United States from the Policy Debate

There is one last theme that emerged a number of times during my interviews. Time and time again, my interviewees expressed their dissatisfaction with the fact that the United States has not been participating in the cultural policy discourse.

With increased privatization and decentralization in cultural policy in Europe, there is a sense that there is a lot to be learned from the United States, beginning with tax incentives and matching grants and extending to the encouragement of a healthy civil society. At a time when trade in cultural goods, the protection of intellectual property, and the role of the cultural industries are all under consideration, it is particularly timely for there to be an American involvement within the research community as well as within the foreign policy and diplomatic community. But structures for the participation of Americans in cross-national research have not evolved. To take one small example, the National Endowment for the Arts has not provided the staff of its research division with any funds for travel outside of North America, so research staff members are able to participate in opportunities with their international colleagues only if they take time off and pay for the travel themselves, or if another organization is willing to pay to have them participate.

Canada has made a different choice. It continues, of course, to be a working member of UNESCO, but it has also chosen to become a hands-on observer at the Council of Europe, which has led to active participation in both CIRCLE and ERICArts.[34] For Canada, comparative work is of sufficient importance to justify maintaining the only explicitly comparative research office in the cultural policy field: the International Comparative Research Group of the Strategic Research and Analysis Directorate of Canadian Heritage.

As a cultural policy information infrastructure is built (or evolves) in the United States, it can only benefit from interaction with the already well-established efforts in other countries. The point of reference that can be provided by strong, reliable comparative data can make a clear contribution to cultural policy design and implementation. But, at the moment, it is not clear who the logical institutional partner would be in the United States. The European and Canadian interviewees argue that the field of cultural policy, in general, and the field of cultural policy in the United States, in particular, are both being hampered by the fact that there is none.

Part I. Notes

1. Andreas Wiesand has looked at the question of how cultural policy research in Europe is distributed among various institutional types. While quite preliminary and subject to many caveats, his results, presented here in tabular form, do suggest how the research function is typically parceled out. His primary sources of data are the institutions currently listed in the *Handbook of Cultural Affairs in Europe*, a catalog of agencies, organizations, and institutions in the field of cultural policy, and the individual researchers who are currently fellows of the ERICArts Institute. His conclusions from this exercise:

> What first seemed as a clear dominance of state institutions including universities, is less obvious if one takes the actual research output into account and also the somewhat more elaborate (or better funded) activities in larger . . . countries. Nongovernmental organizations and [other] third sector institutions, as well as some private institutes, would play a much larger role if such a perspective [were] used.
>
> If one tests these results by looking at the largest institution in this domain, the European Research Institute for Comparative Cultural Policy and the Arts (ERICArts) with . . . seventy fellows and board members in twenty-five countries, a similar picture emerges. The institutional background of the members seems to indicate again a comfortable 70 percent margin in favour of the state-sponsored

sector, with universities playing the major role. A closer look [at] the . . . main funding sources of their research shifts the focus, on the one hand, to state or European bodies and, on the other, to the third sector, e.g., foundations; the latter seems to play an increasing role in facilitating large research projects.

Andreas J. Wiesand, "Cultural Governance as a Learning System? Synthesizing Cultural Policy Reports and Ideas: How to Improve European Research Efforts," unpublished paper presented at the *Creative Europe* workshop, Norrköping, Sweden, December 1, 2001; and private e-mail correspondence with J. Mark Schuster.

Institutional and Financial Background of Cultural (Policy) Research in Europe

		State or European Union Institutions, e.g., Ministries (%)	Public Universities and University-Based Institutes (%)	Nongovernmental Organizations and Other Nonprofit Institutions, e.g., Foundations (%)	Private Bodies (%)
Institutions	Unweighted figures[a]	35.0	35.0	21.0	9.0
	Weighted figures[b]	30.0	21.0	33.0	17.0
Individual Researchers	Institutional background	29.0	41.0	21.0	9.0
	Main origin of funds[c]	42.0[d]	19.5	27.0[e]	11.5

Notes:

a. Unweighted figures are based on 71 institutions in 48 European countries including statistical offices, academies of science, and other similar institutions whose cultural research activities are not generally known.

b. Weighted figures are based on a point system that awarded a total of 483 points to 53 institutions in 30 countries for which sufficient data were available. The points were roughly weighted according to known research output and size of the country. Institutions with unknown research activities were excluded.

c. The analysis of main origin of research funds for the fellows of ERICArts is based on 110 known sources.

d. Including funding from the European Union and from intergovernmental organizations such as the Council of Europe.

e. Including funding from international nongovernmental organizations, networks, and research bodies.

Source:

Andreas J. Wiesand, ed., *Handbook of Cultural Affairs in Europe* (Baden-Baden, Germany: Nomos-Verlag, 2000); and membership lists of Fellows and board members of the ERICArts Institute.

2. INTERARTS has also been known as the European Observatory for Urban and Regional Cultural Policies and as the European Observatory of Area-Based Arts and Cultural Policies.

3. As this book goes to publication, it appears that this initiative is dormant. Some information is available at: http://www.unesco.org/culture/development/observatories/index.shtml

4. This new interest on the part of UNESCO has been described variously as "cultur*al* development," "culture *for* development," "culture *in* development," and "culture *and* development." The differences among these descriptions are not merely semantic. It remains to see which of these directions, if any, UNESCO will pursue and what the implications will be for its programmatic initiatives.

5. I am grateful to Julia Lowell of the Rand Corporation for suggesting this interesting hypothesis.

6. This program has alternatively been known as the European Program of National Cultural Policy Reviews, substituting the more neutral word "review" for the more politically perilous word "evaluation."

7. Among other documents, the organizers of this meeting collected a wide variety of course syllabi for current cultural policy courses, materials that amply illustrate the wide diversity (or, the lack of consensus) in conceptions of cultural policy.

8. This story is discussed at some length in Part II.

9. Professor Sir Alan Peacock, "Introduction: Calling the Tune," in Professor Sir Alan Peacock et al., *Calling the Tune: A Critique of Arts Funding in Scotland* (Edinburgh, Scotland: The Policy Institute, February 2001), p. 15.

10. Terry Cheney, "Summing Up . . . Better Data in an e-Culture Age: DGCI Needs for Better Data—A Review and Recommendations," report prepared for Research, Analysis and Compliance; Publishing Policy and Programs; Canadian Heritage, February 2000.

11. For further discussion of European cultural statistics, see "Cultural Statistics in the European Union," *Circular: Research and Documentation on Cultural Policies*, No. 1, 1995, pp. 8–10; "European Cultural Statistics: In Search of a Common Language," *Circular: Research and Documentation on Cultural Policies*, No. 9, 1998, pp. 12–14; and *Cultural Statistics in the E.U.: Final Report of the LEG*, Eurostat Working Papers, Population and Social Conditions 3/2000/E/N° 1 (Luxembourg: Eurostat, 2000).

12. Chris Smith, *Creative Britain* (London, England: Faber and Faber, 1998).

13. Creative New Zealand is a restructuring of the Queen Elizabeth II Arts Council of New Zealand and its semi-independent component, the Maori and South Pacific Arts Council. Creative New Zealand comprises the Arts Council of New Zealand plus two "arts boards": the Arts

Board, which provides general funding, and Te Waka Toi, the Maori arts board. The Pacific Island Arts Committee is a committee of the Arts Board.

14. Creative Industries Task Force, *Creative Industries Mapping Document* (London, England: Department of Culture, Media and Sport, 1998). A second such document has since been issued: Ministerial Creative Industries Strategy Group, *Creative Industries Mapping Document, 2001* (London, England: Department for Media, Culture and Sport, 2001).

15. The change in the title of the head of the Arts Council of England, from Secretary General to Chief Executive Officer, is itself significant here. Presumably, a more corporate approach is likely to emphasize data, information, and evidence more heavily.

16. Zentrum für Kulturforschung, "Proposal for a Statute of the Association for Cultural Research and Documentation (ACREDO)," Bonn, Germany, 1980.

17. For a brief discussion of cultural observatories in Italy, see: http://www.culturelink.org/culpol/italy.html. Some of these appear to be little more than local information centers on cultural events.

18. The list of those organizations announced as founding members of UNESCO's International Network of Observatories in Cultural Policies suggests a marked lack of consensus on just what a cultural observatory is. The list includes "true" observatories but also includes a wide variety of university research units, cultural policy networks, consulting firms, and others: http://www.unesco.org/culture/development/observatories/html_eng/members.shtml

19. Eduard Delgado, draft paper commissioned by UNESCO, "UNESCO World Observatory of Cultural Policies: SCANARTS", 1999(?).

20. For one such list, see: http://www.admi.net/obs/

21. Terry Cheney, "Summing Up," p. 24.

22. UNESCO, "Workshop: Towards an International Network of Observatories on Cultural Policies," Hannover, Germany, 19–20 September 2000.

23. E-mail correspondence with attached questionnaire to the author from Silvia Vetrale and Cynthia Paes de Carvalho, *Observatorio de Políticas Culturales Municipales*, Montevideo, Uruguay, 23 July 2001.

24. In a way, this experience replicates the experience of CIRCLE, which found time and time again that the one individual who had become each country's representative to CIRCLE did not necessarily have easy access to appropriate and accurate national answers to the wide range of inquiries in which the organization engaged.

25. There are undoubtedly many more networks beyond those I have identified in the current report. To mention just two, while I was interviewing the staff of Canadian Heritage I discovered that Canadian Heritage has been instrumental in creating at least two other networks: the

International Network on Cultural Policy and the International Network on Cultural Diversity.

26. This works both ways, of course: The funding system provides an incentive to form networks, and then the networks make demands on the funding system. As a result of this dynamic, the Dutch Council for Culture *(Raad voor Cultuur)* commissioned a report on the rise of cultural networks with an eye toward formulating future Dutch policy with respect to them and their work: Simon Mundy, *The Context and Structure of European Cultural Networks* (The Hague, Raad voor Cultuur, July 1999). The questionnaire on which this study was based was sent to some 213 networks that had been identified by the Council of Europe; ninety-nine responded.

27. For a description of the federation, see its Web site: http://www.ifacca.org

28. For further details on the Forum, see its Web site: http://www.interarts.net/web_forum/01/01.htm

29. Recently, The Pew Charitable Trusts made a grant to The Cultural Policy Center at the University of Chicago to adapt the Council of Europe's Program and apply it to one pilot state in the United States.

30. Simon Mundy, *Cultural Policy: A Short Guide* (Strasbourg, France: Council of Europe Publishing, May 2000), pp. 35–56.

31. Antoine Hennion, "Le Grand Écart entre la Recherche et l'Administration: Rapport sur le Enjeux, les Atouts et les Difficultés de la Recherche au DEP en Socio-économie de la Culture," Centre de Sociologie de l'Innovation, École des Mines de Paris, Paris, France, 12 June 1996, p. 2.

32. Hennion, "Le Grand Écart," p. 10.

33. Richard Caves, *Creative Industries: Contracts Between Art & Commerce* (Cambridge, Massachusetts: Harvard University Press, 2000).

34. The United States also has observer status but has not made effective use of it.

II

Research and Documentation Centers

INTRODUCTION

The key components of the research and information infrastructure for cultural policy are the many research and documentation centers that have come into being. Some are located within arts councils and ministries of culture; others are affiliated with universities; still others are independent nonprofit research centers; and a growing number are private firms. Within a single country the work is often shared across a variety of institutions, so much so that it is impossible to appreciate fully how the research and information function operates without getting a sense of the institutional ecology within which each research and documentation center operates.

This section of the book contains a detailed discussion of twenty different organizations that are active participants in the research and information infrastructure. These cases represent a small but important sample of the existing cultural policy research and documentation centers in Europe and Canada. Most of the better-known centers with substantial research or documentation agendas are included.[1] Although they are discussed individually, these cases are grouped by country, so that one can more fully appreciate the interrelationships that characterize each country's cultural policy research ecology. France, the Netherlands, Great Britain,[2] and Canada are explored in some detail. Finally, two other important centers are discussed, one a well-established research center in Germany and the other a new cultural observatory in Hungary.

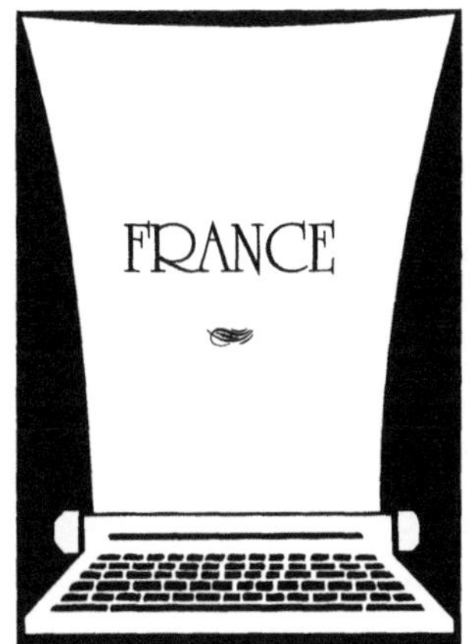
FRANCE

Ministry of Culture and Communication
Département des Études et de la Prospective
Paris

Coming from the field and going back to the field are more interesting than coming from concepts and going back to research.

AUGUSTIN GIRARD

Significance

What makes the *Département des Études et de la Prospective* (DEP) unique in this field are its long track record and the fact that it combines many of the functions that in other countries are divided among a number of different institutional entities. The roots of DEP lie deeply in the social indicators and social planning movement, which is premised on a strong monitoring function on the part of the state. Even so, the network of institutions engaged in cultural policy research in France extends well beyond the Ministry of Culture and Communication and its research division.

DEP is also unique in that it is arguably the best-documented research center working in cultural policy, especially because of the attention that it attracted around the retirement of Augustin Girard, its longtime director.

Description

The *Département des Études et de la Prospective* arose out of the social and economic planning movement of the 1960s. At a time when French society was enjoying new economic growth, there was a desire to figure out how to situate culture among the other sectors of the economy and social life. Planning could not be done without data, and no data were available: nothing about the institutional structure of the arts, nothing about facilities, nothing about attendance, and nothing about expenditures. The emphasis was on cultural development (a concept that has only recently begun to show up in the research of other countries), and the first task was to do the research necessary to establish the concepts according to which data would then be collected. In the words of Augustin Girard, "We were not intellectuals, we were practitioners, and we worked with those considered 'bad' social scientists." This continues, in a sense, today. The staff are still not identified as "researchers," and they do not belong to the *Centre National de la Recherche Scientifique*; rather, they are considered "*ingénieurs*" or administrative technicians. Girard, himself, makes no apologies for his applied approach: "After forty years I am not a great appreciator of research or of researchers." Yet, he founded what is arguably the preeminent research center dealing with cultural policy.

At first, the new research was supported with private money channeled through private associations because the Ministry of Culture saw this new research unit as marginal if not unwelcome. Girard and his staff relied on person-to-person influence, instituted an ambitious publication program to gain attention, and worked through university programs that were training managers who would then become clients for their research, assuring a long-term demand for DEP's work. They also worked closely with journalists who would use the results of their research and thereby promote it.

Today, DEP is specifically responsible for social and economic studies of the arts and culture and the provision of cultural statistics along six main research themes:

- Employment
- The Economics of Culture
- Artistic Education
- The Audience, Participation, and Cultural Practices
- Local and Regional Planning and Public Financing of Culture
- The International Dimension of Cultural Activities and Cultural Policies

DEP focuses on four types of projects:

- *Transversal projects that are of interest across the offices of the ministry* (e.g., *pratiques culturelles*, *dépenses des collectivités locales*, the structure of artistic education, international aspects of culture). These projects get a lot of support and publicity and are generally seen as the most successful of the work undertaken by DEP.
- *Work within a particular artistic domain.* Such work is allocated to a team of three responsible individuals, one from DEP with relative expertise in that field, one from the relevant

direction of the ministry, and one consultant who conducts the actual research. Thus, although there are three people responsible for the research project, only one is responsible for carrying it out.

- *Economic and social studies that DEP would like to finance but for which it does not have the means.* DEP may well serve as an advocate for these studies, hoping that they can be financed through the envelope of research funds available to the ministry and overseen by other offices within the ministry.
- *Research projects that require expertise outside of the social science disciplines.* These projects are not considered by DEP, although other offices within the ministry may do them.

Since 1982 the mandate of DEP has been increasingly shaped by the growing importance of local and regional government in cultural financing. In recent years there has been a major shift in the cultural policy of the ministry as decentralization has finally taken hold. According to DEP's data, 51 percent of government support for the arts and culture in France now comes from local and regional government; of the 49 percent that comes from the ministries of the central government, only 30 percent comes from the Ministry of Culture and Communication. A reflection of this change in policy is that the ministry now makes extensive use of partnerships and contractual agreements with local governments to initiate and carry out programs and projects. A considerable amount of authority and responsibility has been turned over to the ministry's regional cultural affairs offices, *Directions Régionales des Affaires Culturelles* (DRACs). Traditionally, the ministry laid out the grand direction for policy and evaluation, with the staffs of the *directions régionales* acting more as managers than as policymakers because their training was such that they were naturally inclined to operate within administrative rules. Increasingly, under decentralization those rules are being relaxed, and substantial policy leeway is being accorded to the DRACs. The *directions* do not have access to the information that they need to promulgate informed policies and programs on the regional and local levels, however, so they often feel that they are flying blind.

This change has resulted in a debate between the regional offices and the central administration of the ministry, a debate that has had substantial research implications. The regional directorates, exercising their newfound independence and authority, refuse to respond to the information demands of the art discipline–specific offices at the ministry on matters concerning, for example, the visual arts, dance, or music. But the DRACs have neither sufficient information to make policy decisions at the regional and local levels nor the means to analyze that information. The result is that the regional offices demand a lot of information from DEP (rather than from the discipline-specific offices), but DEP does not have the staff or resources to undertake data-collection exercises that would be more easily dealt with by other offices in the ministry as part of their routine operations. Moreover, it does not have the means to undertake, for example, twenty-seven studies of regional employment in the arts and culture (one of the most pressing issues for the regional offices). In a sense, every actor in the system wants someone else to use their resources to collect and disseminate the information that is needed to do their jobs. At best, DEP can provide advice at the level of methodology; it has coordinated a collaborative effort between the Decentralization Mission of the Department for Regional Development and the regional offices of the ministry. One hope is to put in place a battery of indicators that would provide a kernel of information that could be used by both the regional offices and the central administration of the ministry. It is too early to know how this effort will pan out.

A further complication is that the DRACs are very different from one another, so their experiences cannot be generalized to the ministerial level. Some of the DRACs believe that they need only some numbers in a statistical table. A lot of education will be required to sensitize the DRACs to the appropriate interpretation and understanding of data.

Moreover, the decentralization of responsibility to local governments and the resulting deconcentration of decision making have meant that all of the offices within the central ministry find their role now focused more on defining a direction for policy and programs (*pilotage*) and on evaluating those policies and programs than on the actual operation and supervision of programs. As a consequence, many offices within the ministry have now been given more resources to do research themselves; still others use exterior agencies and firms with expertise in a particular field rather than trying to undertake the research themselves. Because of this change in national cultural policy, which renders centralized policy and centralized research less attractive, the field of cultural policy research in France has become much more diverse, with many more actors.

In the words of DEP *ingénieur* François Rouet, "Twenty years ago we had a monopoly on numbers and statistics. Now you find expertise in all parts. We are no longer the sole place. Therefore, it is necessary for us to have a new role: to organize more transversal reflection across sectors." DEP has adopted a new mode of operation through organizing working group seminars around themes. One example is the *Seminaire sur la Publique*, which incorporates those who are concerned about and are attempting to study audiences for the arts and culture. This group meets to discuss the problems it has with respect to studying and understanding audiences, to share experiences, and to shape the research that is done on this theme. DEP organizes a monthly meeting of the contractors who are doing this work so that they can coordinate their efforts, particularly with respect to questionnaire design. Another example is in the area of admission prices: A similar committee pulls together all of the offices of the ministry that are concerned with admissions prices and designs studies to help inform its decisions.

The movement toward making the DRACs more important in cultural policy has had another research impact as well. It is what has fueled much of the expansion of *observatoires culturelles* in France. They are being cofinanced by the DRACs, the elected regional councils, and other regional organizations, but there is some question about the research leverage that they have been able to provide. As DEP *ingénieur* Jeannine Cardona observed, the sentiment seems to be "I have put in place an observatory, so I know what is going on." So far, though the slogan *observatoire culturelle* has been quite popular, the experience has been quite mixed. (The ministry itself has created an internal *Observatoire de l'Emploi* with representatives from different interest groups who discuss issues of employment, conduct research, and publish the results.)

All of these new directions notwithstanding, much of the work of DEP and much of its impact continue to revolve around two major keystone studies, or *enquêtes-phares*:

- *Pratiques Culturelles des Français*. This study of cultural participation and the cultural behavior of the French adult population was conducted in 1973, 1981, 1989, and 1997.
- *Dépenses Culturelles des Collectivités Territoriales*. This series of studies documents the cultural expenditures of regional and local authorities on a longitudinal basis.

The results of these studies have been published regularly in numerous reports and documents. Both are quoted often, enjoying considerable attention in the field and among the media. The regularly published data on local expenditures even fueled a bit of local competition when they revealed that Strasbourg led the pack by spending 25 percent of its town budget on cultural activities!

For the most part, DEP's studies are carried out in collaboration with, and under contract to, researchers, laboratories and consulting firms. Thus, it is more a financier and manager of research than a doer of research. Certain firms and institutions are used often because of their track record. For example, CREDOC (*Centre de Recherche pour l'Étude et l'Observation des Conditions de Vie*), a semipublic, semiprivate firm, does the cultural expenditure reports; it also analyzes the cultural data in the household expenditure surveys done by the national statistics office, *Institut National de la Statistique et des Études Économiques* (INSEE). Research on the art market is generally done by a university research center. A recent research contract on designers has been given to a private firm. The typical study is based on a survey of one sort or another and backed up with a variety of other research including the use of established statistical data files and the documentary work carried out by DEP's documentation center. DEP staff does the preliminary work leading up to the contract and the work that is necessary after the completion of the actual research project. Typically, someone at DEP writes the final report (which is based on the consultant's report) for more general distribution. But almost no research of any magnitude is done in-house.

In general, DEP conducts or oversees three types of research projects:

1. Low-cost projects for which DEP can simply choose a research team and bargain directly (≤ 300,000 francs)
2. Larger projects that are subject to a request for proposal process (*appel d'offre*), in which researchers are asked to submit bids and qualifications on a competitive basis
3. Small applied-research projects that can be done quickly in-house

There is, additionally, the possibility for researchers to approach DEP directly with a research idea and ask if it is interested. If the budget is available, DEP can support such projects, but budgetary restrictions have meant that DEP is becoming less and less open to such proposals.

Finally, DEP works with other agencies and research centers to try to get them to focus on cultural topics as a way of developing fresh contributions to the accumulated research in the arts and culture.

Conseil Ministériel des Études

A ministerial studies council, *Conseil Ministériel des Études*, oversees the work of the various offices of the ministry that are engaged in research, most particularly DEP. It ratifies the research plan on an annual basis and works to assure the diffusion and exploitation of research results. The council both provides scientific advice and serves as a committee of engagement with the field and with the various offices of the ministry. It acts as a filter, separating out demands for short-term, politically based work. It is very difficult (and, from DEP's perspective, undesirable) to do this kind of work within DEP, so the council provides a welcome layer of protection.

In the council's experience, requests for research from the cabinet level of the ministry are rarely clear. This is partly because the ministry's policies and programs change very quickly and partly because the cabinet is not particularly attuned to the uses of research. Now, however, the council is expecting greater involvement with work that might be done at the behest of the regional offices of the ministry (the DRACs).

Each *direction* in the ministry now has a line of credit for doing research, but that budget line is managed by DEP. The different *directions* express their need for research to the *Conseil des Études*, which then determines research priorities. On occasion, certain *directions* are asked to submit research projects; thus, the *Conseil des Études* may become proactive in promoting a research agenda.

DEP itself never really felt a need for this type of council; DEP's modus operandi was to sell ideas for research to the various offices of the ministry rather than the other way around. Still, it was Girard who proposed the creation of the council in 1986 in order to give DEP a more formal relation with the *directions*. Its creation encouraged those offices to come to DEP with research problems, but they generally have brought relatively minor managerial problems that do not require the kind of socioeconomic data that DEP was created to deliver. The most expensive research proposals, however, are always sent to DEP rather than retained at the *direction* level, the logic being that DEP will pick up the full cost so that the expense will not be drawn from the *direction*'s line of credit. Thus, even though the *directions* use their research credits, the system has fueled a bit of a tension between them and DEP. The requests that are received tend to be either disappointing to DEP because of their limited interest and applicability, or ambitious undertakings that DEP regards as exceeding the policy and management concerns of the individual *directions*.

Although it may have played a role in rationalizing research and in communicating with the other offices of the ministry, the council's biggest role may have been in protecting DEP. In 1986, DEP, with the council's approval, relaunched *Pratiques Culturelles*. The study was conducted for the third time in 1989, asking about participation in the arts, culture, leisure, and sports during the previous year (1988). Although the ministry had not requested the report, the council convinced the ministry that it was a horizontal/transversal research project that was essential. In 1989 Jack Lang returned for his second term as minister of culture. He was hoping that the results of *Pratiques*

Culturelles des Français 1988 would validate the success of the cultural policies he had implemented during his prior term as minister (1981–86) and was unhappy that it contained some bad news. While the participation rates in many domains had increased, some had decreased. Lang focused particularly on the reading statistics for respondents who indicated that they were "strong readers," reading at least twenty-five books in the previous year. The percentage of strong readers had declined from 22 percent in 1973 to 19 percent in 1981 to 17 percent in 1988. Lang saw this result, among others, as an indictment of his democratization policies, and, to make things worse, an indictment that was coming *from within his own ministry*. Lang's inclination was to kill the messenger that had been the bearer of the bad news, in this case DEP itself. Claude Seibel, the vice chairman of the *Conseil des Études* and an individual with a considerable research reputation throughout the French government, fought successfully to save DEP.

Seibel would like to move to improve the planning of the budget for research within the ministry and give this role over to the council, but the minister has not wanted the council to assume this role. The ministry's budget currently includes research credits for DEP and research credits for the *directions*. A rationalized system would, in Seibel's view, move the entire research budget under the influence of DEP with the research planning function delegated to the *Conseil des Études*.

THE QUESTION OF EVALUATION: *COMITÉ MINISTÉRIEL D'ÉVALUATION*

The National Evaluation Council has asked each ministry to establish an evaluation effort. Within the Ministry of Culture, DEP serves as the secretary general of the *Comité Ministériel d'Évaluation*. In theory, the various *directions* propose evaluations to the committee. Generally, the resources for evaluation come through the budget of DEP, ensuring some distance from the field. However, carrying out evaluations of ministerial programs and policies has proven problematic. The central administration is not really equipped to do evaluation, and the evaluation committee is in decline. In reality, the committee is engaged more in evaluations of organizations that are clients of the ministry in the form of audits of those organizations than it is in evaluation of the ministry's programs. Still, some evaluations that are more along the lines of "conscious reflections" have been carried out.

Tension between evaluation and research is something that one finds throughout the research divisions of arts councils and ministries. There is a strong feeling, at least among the members of the *Conseil des Études*, that to do evaluation well would be much more demanding of time, resources, and political capital than is possible within DEP. Given this view, the *Conseil* works to make sure that evaluation does not affect the work of DEP. Yet it recognizes that an appropriate role for DEP would be the development of a protocol for evaluation that could be adopted throughout the ministry.

With respect to the question of evaluation, Augustin Girard draws a distinction between what he terms an "American approach," which focuses on evaluating programs, and a "French approach," in which it is believed that one can evaluate policies. He argues that the concept of evaluation in the American sense of evaluation of programs is a concept that is quite foreign to the French. Yet, through DEP, he points out, the French have been in the forefront of the move to evaluate national cultural policies as a whole. (If pressed, he would probably agree that there is a role for ex ante evaluation through which the suitability of a particular organization receiving state funds is assessed. It is ex post evaluation, whether of individual clients or of ministry programs, that is problematic.)

Whether or not it is possible to evaluate a policy without evaluating individual programs is an interesting debate, one that has run throughout the Council of Europe's Program of Evaluations of National Cultural Policies. Clearly, the French believe that it is possible to evaluate how the entire policy that underlies a range of programmatic initiatives is working. Others continue to wonder how that is possible without evaluating individual programs.[3] It is clear that there are two analytical questions of interest: Is this policy effective? Is this program effective? Both questions should command the researcher's attention.

Budget and Personnel

DEP makes an annual budget proposal to the *Direction de l'Administration* of the Ministry of Culture and Communication. The amount that it is allocated is decided by the minister, presumably taking into account current policy concerns and the coherence and relevance of each of the proposed research projects. In assembling its research/budget proposal, DEP tries to consider the current preoccupations of the minister, the needs of the various offices of the ministry, the current work and themes of the European Union, and the ideas of the researchers themselves.

As of mid-2000, the staff included about thirty-five people: eight in the administrative secretariat; nine to ten *chargées d'études* who supervise research projects; two in charge of publications; eight in the statistics section (three detached from INSEE—the national statistics office—

and five ministry staff); six full-time and three part-time in documentation; and three working for the Committee of the History of the Ministry.[4] DEP oversees twenty-five to thirty research contracts per year with each *chargée d'études* responsible for four to five. The staff is hired to represent different disciplines: economics, sociology, statistics, and, occasionally, political science. Part of the original design of DEP was to provide for an interaction of these disciplines through multidisciplinary research groups of two to three *chargée d'études* who would work together across disciplines, though in practice this multidisciplinarity is not often evident.

Beyond personnel and material, the annual budget for research is 5.5 million francs—3.8 million francs for grants to the external institutions undertaking the research projects and 1.5 million francs for publications. This budget is relatively stable, with more or less predictable growth; thus, in years when larger studies are undertaken, fewer small studies are possible. The problem is more in human resources. Three or four positions have been cut, so fewer and fewer individuals are supervising the research volume.

Statistics

The way in which cultural statistics are handled in France is a bit unusual. Each ministry has the possibility of hosting a statistics department that is officially designated by and operated under the authority of the national statistics office, INSEE. When Augustin Girard created DEP, there was a strong emphasis on numbers, but he chose to operate outside of the INSEE system, wanting to retain more control over the work.

Over the years the relationship with INSEE waxed and waned until DEP was finally designated as a "Ministerial Statistical Office" with INSEE coordinating its statistical work. In the older, more traditional ministries, the statistics bureau has functioned directly with INSEE personnel. In the newer ministries, INSEE was not implanted from the outset. In the case of the Ministry of Culture and Communication, Jeannine Cardona now has three people working for her who are "detached" from INSEE but paid through the budget of the ministry, despite considerable resistance from the ministry. The ministry wanted people who it was sure were sensitive to the field and its issues, and the cabinet of the ministry did not want a research function that was controlled from the outside, preferring, instead, to maintain its autonomy. (Some ministries have completely reorganized their statistical services, believing that INSEE was not able to provide analysis that was useful to the ministry.)

Yet, because DEP is an outpost of INSEE, it can benefit from the competence of INSEE's statisticians and maintain contact with, and some influence over, the major surveys that the government undertakes. DEP has an advantage here because the *directions* in the ministry do not have statisticians and are not able to generate their own reliable statistics.

DEP has been assigned by INSEE to produce and disseminate statistical data in the cultural field that are closely linked to the six research themes of its study program: (1) economics, (2) employment, (3) education and training, (4) audiences and cultural behavior, (5) government policies and funding, and (6) regional development and the international cultural context. The regular surveys conducted by this statistics unit include an annual survey of entertainment venues and arts-training establishments, a triennial survey of cultural expenditures of local and regional authorities, and the survey of participation and cultural practices, which is conducted every eight years. The unit also conducts other surveys from time to time. DEP's statistical work also depends on the exploitation of data from the management systems for health, unemployment, and holiday-pay rights in the entertainment field; surveys carried out by INSEE and other government services; and data gathered from producer organizations and institutions such as the National Publisher's Association or the *Société des Auteurs, Compositeurs et Editeurs de Musique* (SACEM), the French music copyright protection organization.

The data that are gathered and produced by DEP are assembled into a cultural statistics database that currently contains more than 30,000 data series. The database is used in the department's work as well as to generate its statistics publications. Statistical data are provided to professional organizations, researchers, and business establishments.

The statistical documents and reports produced by DEP on a regular basis include the following:

- *Chiffres-clés*, a comprehensive directory of cultural statistics
- *Mini Chiffres-clés*, a shortened version of the statistical directory
- *Atlas des Activités Culturelles*, a cartographic presentation of cultural activities
- *Notes de l'Observatoire de l'Emploi Culturel, The Cultural Employment Observatory Review,* which presents findings on cultural employment

A number of these reports are available on DEP's Web site. In 1999, DEP published, for the first time, a CD-ROM containing the raw data obtained from the survey on cultural behavior and made it available to researchers.

DEP has also been involved in the statistical projects of the European Union. Brussels requested the development of comparable statistics on culture, and an initial study was undertaken on book publishing, a sector within which all the member countries produce statistics. Even so, there have been many problems because of cross-national differences in definitions and institutional structure. Moreover, there is tremendous variation in how the cultural agencies and the statistical agencies collaborate on a national level. For example, in Sweden the ministry commissions studies from the statistical agency; in Spain, on the other hand, "the two do not know one another." Eurostat, the enormous European statistical service, is overwhelmed with managing relationships with the fifteen national agencies with which it has to interact and, until recently, has not believed that it had a mandate in culture. The cultural ministers have been asked to vote a resolution that would allow Eurostat to get involved in the development of cultural statistics, and a "leadership group" was formed in 1997 to provide mutual moral support to those countries wishing to develop a program of coordinated cultural statistics. DEP has been very active in the working groups formed under the coordinating umbrella of the leadership group.[5]

Publications

Statistical publications comprise only a portion of the documents, reports, and books that are published by DEP. Over the years it has evolved a multilayered publishing program:

- A collection of books, *Questions de Culture*, is available through *Documentation Française*, the government printing office. These publications are for sale.
- A series of reports, *Les Travaux du DEP*, is available directly from the department. These reports are available free of charge.
- DEP publishes two general reviews, *Notes de l'Observatoire de l'Emploi Culturel* and *Documents de Travail*, as well as a regular newsletter, *Développement Culturel*, all available online.
- DEP also publishes *Circular*, the newsletter of CIRCLE.

A full catalog of publications is available on the Internet. Some publications can be downloaded from this site; others must be ordered using the instructions listed there.[6]

Documentation

Established in 1965 and computerized in 1990, DEP's documentation center gathers, organizes, and circulates information and documentation on the political and socioeconomic aspects of the department's research themes. Unfortunately, access to the documentation center is limited to ministry personnel, cultural professionals, journalists, outside researchers, teachers, and graduate students. Access is restricted because of limited space and personnel as well as security concerns. Individuals who seek information from the center are asked to begin with an Internet search of the catalog, which is publicly available. Once it is established that there is something in the collection that is of interest, an individual sets up a meeting with a documentation specialist who is knowledgeable in the field of the request.

The center offers the following materials:

- More than 30,000 documents including books, conference proceedings, surveys, reports, reference works, directories, and indexed listings
- A full collection of the approximately 400 studies that have been completed under the auspices of DEP
- Approximately 250 journals and periodicals, mainly in French
- Approximately 5,000 documentary dossiers on a wide range of topics

The dossiers are perhaps the most interesting service provided by the documentation center. They are maintained by a team of documentation specialists who continually scan the field for material of interest on each of the topics. Staff make a particular effort to collect and categorize the "gray literature" (conference proceedings, technical documents, unpublished reports, privately published works, and the like), which is often extremely difficult to obtain. They also prepare bibliographies by topic, a review with brief summaries of reports and documents in the field, and a daily press review. These are disseminated to government departments but can be consulted by others in the documentation center.

The center has also developed a bibliographic database on the socioeconomic aspects of culture. Called "MNEMO," this computerized database comprises a catalog of some 42,000 entries providing references to a wide variety of documents including publications of the ministry, various forms of the gray literature, periodicals, and dossiers of press clippings. The documents are not accessible online, but they can be consulted if the individual interested in them qualifies for access to the center.[7]

A monthly listing of the center's most recent acquisitions can be downloaded from the Web. A list of the most important books and articles in the bibliographic database, *Repères Bibliographiques: Institutions et Vie Culturelle*, can be downloaded from the same site.[8]

Beyond the salaries of its nine staff members (six full-time and three part-time), the budget of the documentation center is very small—only 110,000 francs per year: 50,000 francs for the purchase of books and reports, 50,000 francs for journal subscriptions, and 10,000 francs for subscriptions to daily and weekly publications. Many of the publications received by the center are donated; others are offered in exchange for newsletters, reports, and documents published by DEP.

Assessment

The overall impression one receives is that the *Département des Études et de la Prospective* continues to function smoothly doing essentially what it has always done. Some argue that the department has aged and has become less motivated. Both the ministry and the minister are, arguably, less important than they were previously, and that is mirrored in the importance and reputation of DEP. For years, DEP received many requests for its services; now, with the exception of requests from the DRACs, there are fewer. There is quite a bit of repetition and not much innovation.

In many ways these changes are due to the fact that the field has moved away from the concerns of the ministry and the concerns of DEP. Cultural policy in France is changing and experiencing something of an identity crisis: Centralization is being replaced by decentralization, and decentralization is gradually leading to the introduction of private management of cultural institutions and initiatives. As a result, the cultural field is now becoming populated with hybrid organizations and private organizations that are very political. The cultural policy research field is mirroring this change.

To the extent that cultural policy is percolating up to the European level, there are those who think that the English and the Germans, in particular, will become the cultural policy leaders because they are more dynamic and speak English. These same individuals predict that the French will not become leaders in cultural policy at the European level and that DEP is not particularly well equipped to engage in these discussions at that higher level.

To the extent that cultural policy is sifting down to the local level through decentralization and devolution policies that are finally taking hold, the demand for research at the central government level has changed. DEP cannot satisfy all of the demands for cultural policy research that now emanate from the field; it must struggle and innovate to participate in, and help shape, that research.

But the field of cultural policy has also moved from fields that were close to the state and state intervention toward more of a relationship with, and dependence upon, industry. As a result, the center of gravity in research is moving away from general units such as DEP to more specialized research groups familiar with the terrain of various segments of the cultural industries. For example, drawing upon his experience serving on the *Conseil des Études*, Claude Seibel took the ways of working that were developed at DEP and used them to create a research unit within the Ministry of Labor in 1993, but with one major difference: At the Ministry of Labor, he linked the research effort more to the interests of the field (rather than to the interests of the ministry per se) by developing formal links with three associations of corporate leaders and five union organizations.

In the final analysis, the quality of the leadership that is in place and the will of the minister predominantly determine the fortunes of a research unit in a ministry of culture. A research division such as DEP is in need of a good administrator who can bargain, make proposals, and launch projects; it does not necessarily require a good researcher. But, most of all, it requires a minister who respects and understands the need for research; and, for better or worse, ministers come and ministers go.

Interviews and Contacts

Augustin Girard
Président du Comité d'Histoire du Ministère de la Culture
Ministère de la Culture et de la Communication
former Director, Département des Études et de la Prospective
2, rue Jean-Lantier
75001 Paris
France

Phone: 011-33-(0)1-40-15-79-16
Fax: 011-33-(0)1-40-15-79-99

Paul Tolila [*not interviewed*]
Director, Département des Études et de la Prospective
Ministère de la Culture et de la Communication
2, rue Jean-Lantier
75001 Paris
France

Phone: 011-33-(0)1-40-15-79-17
Fax: 011-33-(0)1-40-15-79-99
e-mail: paul.tolila@culture.gouv.fr

Also Interviewed

Claude Seibel, Vice-Président, Conseil Ministériel des Études
François Rouet, Ingénieur de Recherche
Jeannine Cardona, Ingénieur de Recherche, Responsable Statistique
Frédérique Patureau, Chargée d'Études
Anna-Michèle Schneider, Responsable de la Documentation
Dominique Jamet, Chargée d'Études

Web Site

http://www.culture.gouv.fr/culture/dep/eng/anglais.htm

Documents and Publications Consulted

Département des Études et de la Prospective, Ministére de la Culture, *Les Études Réalisées par le Département des Études et de la Prospective 1983-1992* (Paris, France: Ministére de la Culture, no date).

Département des Études et de la Prospective. Various internal documents:

"Programme d'Études et Recherches 1999–2000"

"Programme d'Études et Recherches 2000–2001"

"Publications 1992–1998"

"Publications du Département des Études et de la Prospective 1998–1999"

"Rapport d'Activité, 1989–1992"

Développement Culturel, bulletin of the Département des Études et de la Prospective, various issues.

Donnat, Olivier, and Denis Cogneau, *Les Pratiques Culturelles des Français: 1973-1989* (Paris, France: La Découverte/La Documentation Française: 1990).

Girard, Augustin, "Cultural Indicators for More Rational Cultural Policy," in Stephen A. Greyser, ed., *Cultural Policy and Arts Administration* (Cambridge, Massachusetts: Harvard Summer School Institute in Arts Administration, 1973).

Girard, Augustin, "Un Cas de Partenariat entre Administration et Recherche Scientifique: La Socio-économie de la Culture," in P.-M. Menger and J.-C. Passeron, eds., *L'Art de la Recherche: Essais en L'Honneur de Raymonde Moulin* (Paris, France: La Documentation Française, 1994).

Girard, Augustin, in collaboration with Genviève Gentil, *Cultural Development: Experiences and Policies*, 2nd ed. (Paris, France: UNESCO, 1983).

Hennion, Antoine, "Le Grand Écart entre la Recherche et L'Administration: Rapport sur le Enjeux, les Atouts et les Difficultés de la Recherche au DEP en Socio-économie de la Culture," Centre de Sociologie de l'Innovation, École des Mines de Paris, Paris, France, 12 June 1996.

Maresca, Bruno, and Laurent Pouquet, *Les Dépenses Culturelles des Français au Milieu des Années 1990: Les Charactéristiques des Dépenses en 1995 et leur Évolution depuis 1979* (Paris, France: Ministère de la Culture et de la Communication, January 2000).

"Sciences Sociales et Politiques Culturelles: Entretiens avec Joffre Dumazedier et Augustin Girard," *Politix*, No. 24, 1993, pp. 57–77.

Service des Études et Recherches, Ministére de la Culture, *Études Réalisées de 1964 à 1983* (Paris, France: Ministére de la Culture, 1984).

Trente Ans d'Études au Service de la Vie Culturelle, Round table organized on the occasion of the retirement of Augustin Girard, Director of the Département des Études et de la Prospective from 1963 to 1993 (Paris, France: Ministère de la Culture et de la Francophonie, 8 March 1993).

Observatoire des Politiques Culturelles Grenoble

What we are trying to do (with many reservations) is to create a convergence between what researchers know and what politicians can, and should, do.

RENÉ RIZZARDO

Significance

The *Observatoire des Politiques Culturelles* (often referred to simply as the *Observatoire Culturelle*) of Grenoble has become an important reference point for the creation of many research and information centers in cultural policy, particularly in Europe and North America. This is partly due to the noninterventionist cast of its name: One is observing, not shaping, the cultural field and cultural policy. The model of the *Observatoire des Politiques Culturelles*, however, turns out to be a very particular one, one that is not necessarily copied when other observatories with the same or similar names are created.

Background

According to Augustin Girard, during the first ten years or so of the French Ministry of Culture the ministry did not interact with the country's municipalities and did not think that they had an important role to play in cultural policy. Yet, the data collected by DEP showed that there was considerable local activity. Indeed, contrary to the tradition of new ideas coming from Paris and trickling out to the rest of the country, most of the money and innovation was no longer coming from Paris but was originating in the provinces, particularly at the local level. It became clear that to talk about cultural policy one needed to have a coherent and comprehensive view of the many levels at which cultural policy was being designed and implemented.

It was about 1987, with the first push of Jack Lang, that the ministry became more aware of local authorities, particularly as the dossier of local activities reflected an increasing professionalism at the regional and local levels. It became possible for local authorities to enter into areas of culture that had previously been difficult for them to enter. Even so, at that time there was no one either at the ministry or at the local level who was able to pull together and synthesize the information necessary to discuss and understand this emerging area in cultural policy.

It was at this point that an *Observatoire des Politiques Culturelles Territoriales* was proposed as an initiative coming out of, and largely funded by, the ministry's research division (DEP). The observatory was formed around three central ideas:

1. Decentralization as a major element in cultural policy
2. Promoting networking among local authorities
3. Promoting networking among local institutions

It was the hope that these local efforts would assume greater influence if a way were found to bring them to the attention of one another, to draw lessons, and to work together. In a sense, the proposal for an *Observatoire des Politiques Culturelles Territoriales* was an admission on the part of the administration of the ministry that it was no longer able to be aware of all of the local activity in the field (and that it, too, needed information back).

The original title of the observatory was chosen quite deliberately. Girard describes the choice of the word *observatoire* as a "shy" choice. The message was quite clear: This new institution was not being created to rule or control; rather, it was intended to document and record, to show what was going on. In other words, it was not intended as a research institute (even though it later acquired something of this reputation, rightly or wrongly). The word *territoriales* was also important, intended to signal a focus on *local and regional* cultural policy, but René Rizzardo, the founding director of the observatory, dropped *territoriales* almost immediately. He wanted to assure the observatory a larger mandate from the outset, even though this had the effect of putting the observatory into direct competition with its parent, the *Service des Études et de la Recherche* (now DEP).

René Rizzardo was a city councilor and assistant to the mayor in Grenoble. His portfolio included sport and culture. At the time, Grenoble was engaged in a number of innovative local cultural policy initiatives, and Rizzardo proudly wanted to spread the word to other local authorities as to how they could become involved in cultural policy. Rizzardo continues as the director of the observatory, which many say operates extensively on the force of his personality and commitment. As an institution, the observatory has relied substantially on the charisma of its main staff members, Rizzardo and Jean-Pierre Saez, for its visibility and its support.

With decentralization came an enormous pressure on local governments to define and evaluate their cultural actions. Françoise Benhamou points out, though not in particular reference to the *Observatoire des Politiques Culturelles*, that local authorities have become very active funders in France. As a rough rule of thumb, the Ministry of Culture and Communication spends 15 billion francs; other ministries, particularly the Ministry of Foreign Affairs, another 15 billion francs; and local authorities, 30 billion francs. From time to time the local authorities are called upon to explain and justify these expenditures. Consequently, they ask for two kinds of studies: studies concerning administrative problems (e.g. problems of budgetary deficits among the cultural institutions of Avignon) and economic impact studies.[9] At the local level, there has been a shift in funding priorities, as well. During the 1980s it was fashionable for mayors to invest in cultural facilities—museums, libraries, arts centers, and the like. Now the focus is much more on small projects with small budgets and a quick timeline. All of this cries out for research.

Moreover, these changes in cultural policy in France have been accompanied by an important change in how the ministry itself operates. Today, it would not be too difficult to argue that the real ministries of culture are the *Directions Régionales des Affaires Culturelles* (DRACs), which operate at the regional level. Because they are the ones who give money to the arts, they want to decide how it is spent, and they want to evaluate it. In other words, the DRACs want to have their own independent responsibility and want to create little ministries, each with its own research capability, but they recognize that they lose professionalism and coordination as they move in this direction. As a result, some of the DRACs have turned to the observatory (and other similar bodies in other regions) to supply information and research rather than to DEP, which, in any event, would be hard-pressed to add this volume of research to its agenda. This has resulted in some pressure on the observatory to move more explicitly in a research direction.

Today, the observatory describes itself as "a national organization whose mission is to accompany the decentralization of public cultural policies through the organization of research, meetings, continuing education and the release of information." In particular, the observatory:

- Provides advice to local and regional groups concerning the design of studies and evaluations of their cultural policy
- Directs studies of general interest to accompany the decisions and actions of regional and local public authorities
- Promotes meetings, discussions, and debates

- Publishes a newsletter that presents dossiers of information on various themes of interest
- Publishes books and reports
- Provides information through its documentation center
- Organizes continuing education courses, in particular the course "Administration of Cultural Projects," designed for employees of municipal cultural services
- Makes educational experiences available to elected officials and professionals in the field through internships or study tours

Thus, the activities of the observatory focus less on research than one might expect. The research that is done in-house tends to be secondary, desk research, and the focus of much of the work of the observatory is qualitative rather than quantitative; there are no statisticians on staff. Very little primary research is conducted, or even commissioned, by the observatory. The observatory has been engaged in some research at the demand of the ministry, working with DEP on research projects whose destination was the local level. One research project that is cited involved the region of Rhônes-Alpes, which created a voucher program (*chèque culture*) and asked the observatory to initiate an evaluation project, to find a group to do the work, and to evaluate the results.

What is important to note with respect to research, however, is that the observatory does not operate on its own at the regional level. Rather, it benefits from the presence at the University of Grenoble of CERAT, the *Centre de Recherche sur le Politique, l'Administration, la Ville et le Territoire*, a university-based research center supported by the *Centre National de la Recherche Scientifique*. The observatory and CERAT work closely together in a symbiotic research relationship, with CERAT providing much of the research horsepower and the observatory providing the public interface. It is only together that they provide what one might expect from a fully operational observatory.

Much of the work of the observatory is focused on its training programs for personnel working in cultural posts in local administration. These students, who are typically thirty to forty years old, come to Grenoble a week at a time, eight different times a year. They bring practical problems from their jobs and discuss them with one another; the model is described as "living case studies." A variety of guest lectures are arranged. The students produce a 100-page thesis on an actual program whose administration they are concerned with. The University of Grenoble contributes some of its staff to help in the teaching and grants continuing education diplomas to the students, but there is little direct financial participation, only in-kind participation.

The observatory also provides valuable documentation and library services. The documentation service develops bibliographies on topics of concern to the field. The library collection includes some 5,000 documents, eighty periodicals, and one hundred thematic dossiers. Because of its role in continuing education at the university level, the coverage of the observatory's collection tends to be broader than the one at the documentation center at DEP. The observatory publishes an extensive newsletter, *L'Observatoire*, twice a year; a yearly subscription costs 160 francs.

Budget and Personnel

It was difficult to gauge the budget of the observatory. Girard estimates the annual budget of the observatory at some 5 million francs, 3.5 million francs from the government in subsidy through DEP and the *Délégation au Développement et à l'Action Territoriale*, and 1.5 million francs in its own resources (its work with the city of Lyon brings in some 500,000 francs per year).

According to *Directeur de la Formation* Jean-Pierre Saez, the base operating budget is made up of approximately 2 million francs from the Ministry of Culture and Communication; another 300,000 francs from the Regional Council of Rhône-Alpes; and 300,000 to 400,000 francs in-kind from the Université Pierre Mendès France (Grenoble II), including offices and positions for documentation specialists; as well as money from the city of Grenoble and the *Centre National de la Fonction Publique Territoriale*. Individual funded projects provide further income. The continuing education activities of the observatory are partially funded through the ministry, partially through other activities of the observatory, and partially through tuition paid by individuals or associations.

The core staff of the observatory includes eight people: a director, one person in charge of continuing education and the newsletter, one person in charge of research studies, one person in charge of documentation, one secretary general who is in charge of administration, and three secretaries.

Assessment

It is likely that the international reputation of the *Observatoire des Politiques Culturelles* is greater than it merits. Much of that reputation derives from the choice of the word *observatoire* as the name of the organization. In the words of Augustin Girard, "We could not agree on a 'center,' but we could have an 'observatory.' It is a pleasant name. An observatory is a place of negotiation, of interactivity. It does not deliver judgments. It is more structured than a network; in a network there is no responsibility." (Indeed, DEP now runs an in-house observatory of its own—the *Observatoire de l'Emploi Culturel*, and former DEP staff have gone on to run observatories in other fields, e.g., an observatory within the Ministry of Justice.) Today there are many different observatories in the cultural field, each different from the next, but most modeled, if only vaguely, on their ancestor in Grenoble.

In the words of René Rizzardo, at the local level of cultural policy there is "too much attention to funding and not enough to advice. There is a lot of effort (and money) being expended foolishly by public authorities." This is undoubtedly true, and here is where the observatory finds its true vocation. Most cultural policy researchers do not regard the observatory as an important contributor to research in the field. What they do acknowledge, though, is a not inconsiderable contribution in the areas of service, advice, training, and consulting.

Interviews and Contacts

René Rizzardo
Director
Observatoire des Politiques Culturelles
1, rue du Vieux Temple
38000 Grenoble
France

Phone: 011-33-(0)4-76-44-33-26
Fax: 011-33-(0)4-76-44-95-00
e-mail: opc.culture@wanadoo.fr

Also Interviewed

Jean-Pierre Saez, Directeur de la Formation

Cécile Martin, Responsable des Études

Documents and Publications Consulted

L'Observatoire, various issues of the newsletter of the *Observatoire des Politiques Culturelles*.

L'Observatoire des Politiques Culturelles, information sheet describing the Observatory, no date.

CERAT: Centre de Recherche sur le Politique, l'Administration, la Ville et le Territoire Université Pierre Mendès France (Grenoble II) Grenoble

Significance

To understand the *Observatoire des Politiques Culturelles de Grenoble*, one must also understand the *Centre de Recherche sur le Politique, l'Administration, la Ville et le Territoire* (CERAT) at the Université Pierre Mendès France (Grenoble II). These two institutions work side by side on issues of cultural policy, particularly local and regional cultural policy, and, generally speaking, it is CERAT that provides the research capability. CERAT is one example of the university-based research centers funded by the *Centre National de la Recherche Scientifique* (CNRS), a number of which contribute to the research base in the cultural policy field.

Background

The French *Centre National de la Recherche Scientifique* is a cross between a research-funding agency like the National Science Foundation in the United States and a network of state-supported research centers operating in parallel with the academic departments at various French universities. The research centers are funded and, for the most part, staffed by CNRS, which operates its own equivalent of the university tenure system, providing a ladder of research positions through which researchers selected by CNRS can be promoted. The reward structure for CNRS researchers functions much as the tenure structure in many American universities. There is a high value placed on research reputation built through publication and participation in all types of conferences, seminars, and colloquia. The main difference is that CNRS-sponsored researchers are not as responsible for day-to-day university teaching, though they might also have appointments as faculty members. Thus, the focus is even more on research productivity than in the United States.

A number of the research centers supported by CNRS play a role in the field of cultural policy, some explicitly so, others as part of their disciplinary or sector-specific interests. The *Centre de Recherche sur le Politique, l'Administration, la Ville et le Territoire* (CERAT) at the Université Pierre Mendès France (Grenoble II) is probably the center that deals most directly with issues of cultural policy, though its broad mandate to conduct research on local and regional policy and governmental administration takes it well beyond the fields of the arts and culture. Other CNRS research centers deal more explicitly with various aspects of the arts, though their focus often moves somewhat away from policy (see the next section of this book).

CERAT is a large research center with a total staff, as of January 2000, of 101 people. Seventeen are CNRS researchers, of whom nine are certified to be research directors; twenty-two others are professor/researchers, of whom eleven are certified to be research directors; another seventeen have various other research positions; and thirty-four are doctoral students. There are eleven administrative staff members. The research program is broad, touching on many areas of local and regional policy, but approximately six of the researchers focus their work on issues of cultural policy.

The focus on cultural policy was particularly evident in the recent years during which Guy Saez, one of the researchers most interested in cultural policy, served as the director of CERAT. The dossiers summarizing the publications of various CERAT researchers show lengthy lists of articles, book chapters, books, and reports, indicating an active and productive research agenda. The annual reports of CERAT also indicate considerable interchange with other research centers, both nationally and internationally, and a heavy involvement in the supervision of doctoral and master's theses, many of which also touch upon matters of cultural policy. Many of the publications of CERAT are available through a variety of online bibliographic services.

Assessment

CERAT and the other CNRS research centers are important because they bear witness to what can be accomplished in terms of research in any field with a substantial and ongoing commitment. Because of its financial stability, the work of CERAT concentrates much more on basic research in the field than does the work of university-based research centers in other countries, which are forced to rely more on one-off contracts for applied, short-term research, functioning, in essence, as university-based consulting firms. This is not to suggest that CNRS research centers do not do contract research; they certainly do. But even when they undertake contract research they tend to bring a much more theoretical, social-scientific framework to bear because the reward system has much more to do with building a knowledge base than with solving practical administrative problems.

For this reason, the relationship between CERAT and the *Observatoire des Politiques Culturelles* is particularly interesting. The two function together in a symbiotic relationship. CERAT concentrates on research, while the observatory concentrates on communicating the research done by CERAT and by other researchers and research centers to the field through continuing education, seminars, conferences, and publications. From the standpoint of affecting cultural policy at the regional and local levels, each would be much less effective without the other.

Interviews and Contacts

Guy Saez
Directeur de Recherche au CNRS (former director of CERAT)
Centre de Recherche sur le Politique, l'Administration, la Ville et le Territoire
Institut d'Études Politiques
Université Pierre Mendès France
B.P. 48
38040 Grenoble Cedex 9
France

Phone: 011-33-(0)4-76-82-60-41
Fax: 011-33-(0)4-76-82-60-99

e-mail: Guy.Saez@iep.upmf-grenoble.fr

Also Interviewed

Mireille Pongy, Chargée de Recherche au CNRS, CERAT

Web Site

http://www.upmf-grenoble.fr/cerat/

Documents and Publications Consulted

Centre de Recherche sur le Politique, l'Administration, la Ville et le Territoire, dossier summarizing the structure and activities of CERAT, March 1999.

Centre de Recherche sur le Politique, l'Administration, la Ville et le Territoire, dossier summarizing the structure and activities of CERAT, January 2000.

Centre de Recherche sur le Politique, l'Administration, la Ville et le Territoire, dossiers summarizing the cultural publications of various CERAT researchers, various dates.

Centre de Recherche sur le Politique, l'Administration, la Ville et le Territoire, list of theses supervised in the field of culture, July 2000.

Centre de Recherche sur le Politique, l'Administration, la Ville et le Territoire, *Rapport Scientifique: June 1994-June 1998* (Grenoble, France: CERAT, no date).

Saez, Guy, "Deux Controverses dans la Politique Culturelle Française," *Society and Leisure*, Vol. 22, No. 2, Autumn 1999, pp. 423–451.

Other CNRS Research Centers

Centre de Sociologie du Travail et des Arts
École des Hautes Études en Sciences Sociales

Significance

The *Centre de Sociologie du Travail et des Arts* is, arguably, one of the best-known CNRS research centers working in the field of the arts. Directed for many years by Raymonde Moulin, a well-known sociologist of the arts and culture, it is now directed by one of her former students, Pierre-Michel Menger, who has also developed a considerable reputation, particularly with respect to the sociology of artists. Though not primarily concerned with cultural policy per se, this center does find itself contributing to many cultural policy debates.

Background

The *Centre de Sociologie du Travail et des Arts* conducts its own research on artistic production (artistic professions, arts organizations, and labor markets); the "career" of works of art (transactions, collections, entry into museums); national cultural identities, art markets, and cultural policy; new forms of artistic employment; and heritage and architecture. The center is probably best known for its work on the conditions and careers of artists, and it often undertakes subcontracts for DEP, particularly in the areas of employment and labor markets, in which it serves as a sort of mini-INSEE. As part of this work, the center has, for example, built yearly employment indicators working with data from secondary sources. It may be more expensive to do such work in this manner than to do it inside DEP, but DEP is not equipped with a sufficient number of personnel who have the necessary skills. Therefore, DEP subcontracts with research centers when there is considerable external accumulated experience and when there is a need for repetitive, recurrent work such as in the case of regular surveys of employment.

The center is very much integrated into the *École des Hautes Études en Sciences Sociales*. The research staff also hold positions as faculty members. As with other CNRS research centers attached to universities, an ongoing problem is how to achieve an appropriate balance between consulting and more fundamental research. The "consulting" work tends to be projects resulting from a short-term, immediate demand from the government or the repetitive work that is not particularly interesting to researchers who are building research careers and reputations. These researchers want to move on to new questions and to develop new methodologies, not do the same project yet again. Nevertheless, the funding reality is that the center must seek to cross-subsidize its "real" research through consulting work.

Despite its inclination toward more theoretical, fundamental research, Pierre-Michel Menger points out that the center's reputation is such that each time there is a reflection on cultural policy, particularly when it involves individual artists in the performing arts, it is consulted. As such, Menger plays a role that is a mix of expert and advisor. When launching work, researchers discuss the project with the field before beginning, with the hope that the resultant product will ultimately have some relevance for the field. Still, the researchers do not work solely on projects that will be "usable," because they have their own research questions that they wish to, and are encouraged to, pursue. Because much of the center's emphasis has been on the live performing arts and because the live performing arts are much more decentralized than other art forms, researchers find themselves playing an important role with respect to policy in this field.

One example is of particular interest. In France, various artist unions contract out for research from time to time. The center has been engaged with them in a project examining the taxonomy of employment in the cultural sphere. The goal was to rename and reclassify the whole array of jobs in the performing arts to capture better the evolving employment situation in the field. Because the center has worked cooperatively with DEP's internal *Observatoire de l'Emploi Culturel* as well as with the unions, it expects that it will be successful in implementing the new classification scheme. Most importantly, INSEE has indicated that it will adopt and use this typology.

Budget and Personnel

It is difficult to completely untangle the budget and personnel situation of any of the CNRS centers because they are generally linked with universities and because the personnel portion of the budget, which is the largest portion, is basically hidden from view. The *Centre de Sociologie du Travail et des Arts* is affiliated with the *École des Hautes Études en*

Sciences Sociales (EHESS). The Center has a staff of twenty-seven: six CNRS-supported researchers (five sociologists, one with a Ph.D. in literature); three non-CNRS researchers (professors at EHESS who are affiliated with the Center); eight technical staff with the title *Ingénieur Technicien Administratif* (four CNRS and four non-CNRS); and ten nonpermanent staff (primarily graduate students who are pursuing Ph.D. degrees in the sociology of the arts). Some staff members have appointments as both university professors and CNRS researchers.

The basic operating budget of the center is fairly small: 140,000 francs over and above the cost of personnel. The remainder of the operating budget comes mainly from contracts and projects from DEP, the Ministry of Culture and Communication, and other ministries, and by responding to requests for proposals from other groups. The center does not currently receive any private foundation money or money from the European Union, though it is beginning to think about going after European money in the future. It is considering this reluctantly because the center does not want its research agenda to be pressured further by external demand.

Assessment

What is notable about the *Centre de Sociologie du Travail et des Arts* (as well as the other CNRS-supported research centers) is the fact that the government is making a substantial investment in basic research on the arts and culture. One would be hard-pressed to find a similar investment in other countries. As a result, a number of French researchers, particularly those in sociology, have developed an international reputation in the field. The fact that the work of the center is valued is reflected in the number of external demands it receives for its work. There is a continual stream of requests for the center to undertake research on actors, dancers, musicians, and other cultural workers. The volume of desired research could easily overwhelm the staff.

Interviews and Contacts

Pierre-Michel Menger
Directeur d'Études a l'École des Hautes Études en Sciences Sociales
Centre de Sociologie du Travail et des Arts
E.H.E.S.S. – C.N.R.S. – E.S.A. 8082
105, boulevard Raspail
75006 Paris
France

Phone: 011-33-(0)1-45-49-76-38
Fax: 011-33-(0)1-45-49-76-01

e-mail: menger@ehess.fr

Web Site

http://www.ehess.fr/centres/csa/

Documents and Publications Consulted

Menger, Pierre-Michel, *La Profession de Comédien: Formations, Activités, et Carrières dan la Démultiplication de Soi* (Paris, France: La Documentation Française, 1997).

Other CNRS Research Centers

MATISSE: Modélisations Appliquées, Trajectoires Institutionnelles, et Stratégies Socio-Economiques Laboratoire d'Economie Sociale Université Panthéon-Sorbonne (Paris I)

MATISSE is another CNRS research center that focuses on applied economics. This center has a staff of approximately one hundred people. As is the case with CERAT, only a small portion of MATISSE is devoted to the economics of the arts and culture. Three staff members of the *Laboratoire d'Economie Sociale*—Joëlle Farchy, Dominique Sagot-Duvauroux, and Françoise Benhamou—make up that team. Since cultural policy has gradually shifted away from fields that were close to the state and state intervention toward the private sector and the cultural industries, its research focus has had to shift accordingly.[10]

These three researchers are also university professors and are paid by the university. They receive a small amount from CNRS for travel grants, computers, and the like. Contracts come through MATISSE (in which case a 10 percent overhead fee is charged), the only exception being money from the European Union. Because Benhamou has been designated as an expert advisor to the European Commission, E.U. money comes directly to her without overhead.

This research center is also involved in educational programs. Benhamou is currently involved in creating a new university program that will offer a diploma in the management of public institutions with an option of specializing in cultural institutions.

Interviews and Contacts

Françoise Benhamou
Université Panthéon-Sorbonne (Paris I)
Maison des Sciences Economiques
MATISSE
106-112, boulevard de l'Hôpital
75647 Paris Cedex 13
France
Phone: 011-33-(0)1-43-26-14-78
Fax: 011-33-(0)1-43-26-14-78
e-mail: fbenhamo@univ-paris1.fr

Web Site

http://matisse.univ-paris1.fr/recherches/recherches.htm

Documents and Publications Consulted

Benhamou, Françoise, *L'Economie de la Culture*, new edition (Paris, France: Éditions La Découverte, 2000).

Farchy, Joëlle, *La Fin de l'Exception Culturelle?* CNRS Communication (Paris, France: CNRS Éditions, 1999).

Related CNRS Research Centers

It would be nearly impossible to compile a complete list of CNRS research centers that deal with the arts and culture in one way or another, but in addition to CERAT, the *Centre de Sociologie du Travail et des Arts*, and the *Laboratoire d'Economie Sociale* (MATISSE), there are at least three others that were mentioned in interviews:

- *Centre de Recherche en Gestion, École Polytechnique*, particularly the work of Pierre Jean Benghozi
- *Centre de Sociologie de l'Education et de la Culture, École des Hautes Études en Sciences Sociales*, the research center created by Pierre Bourdieu
- *Sociologie, Histoire, Anthropologie des Dynamiques Culturelles, École des Hautes Études en Sciences Sociales* (Marseille), particularly the work of Jean-Louis Fabiani

It is evident that CNRS supports a rich and complex research system, one that is probably much more pervasive than in any other country. While the publications of the CNRS research system likely find their natural audience among academics and other social scientists, there is also considerable evidence that the research of these centers is taken into account in policymaking. Indeed, particularly in its early years, DEP employed or worked in collaboration with a number of social scientists who went on to establish important CNRS research centers.

THE
NETHERLANDS

The Boekmanstichting/The Boekman Foundation Amsterdam

Significance

The *Boekmanstichting* in Amsterdam is probably the best model of a stand-alone library and documentation center in the field of cultural policy. It functions at the interstices between research and policy. Here is how it describes itself:

> The Boekman Foundation is an expert centre for policy regarding the arts, culture and related areas. The Foundation collects, digests and disseminates information with regard to the cultural sector and cultural policy. It favours the active application of information within the cycle of cultural policy, and it serves an ever-growing clientele from professional areas, including politicians, policy implementers, advisors, students, researchers and teachers in higher education. Equally important are the staff of art and cultural bodies and all others with an interest in questions concerning the arts, culture and their relation to policy and management.
>
> The Boekman Foundation addresses the question of the relation between public administration and culture. The available research material is made public, collated and analyzed, whereby the Foundation aims to clarify the trajectory of the management processes as they are related to the arts and culture.[11]

Description

The Dutch Federation of Artists Associations founded the *Boekmanstichting* in 1963, with the financial support of the Prince Bernhard Foundation, a private fund.[12] The Federation believed that there was a need for an independent institution that could carry out research on the relationship between the arts and government and on the role of art in society. In the 1960s and 1970s there was little arts policy research going on in the Netherlands, and the *Boekmanstichting* became an important venue for such research. Some research was commissioned by the Dutch Ministry of Education, Culture and Science, which made grants to the *Boekmanstichting* since, at the same time, only a small group of organizations were able to do this type of work. Eventually the ministry began to support the *Boekmanstichting* through a regular grant in support of its work.

After 1978, however, the subsidy of the *Boekmanstichting* was cut by 50 percent. This has been described as a political attack, the motive of which was to get the *Boekmanstichting* to change its direction toward documentation and away from research, which had become too intertwined, it was thought, with advocacy. Apparently, there had been considerable difficulty in communicating with the ministry and, one would expect, considerable disagreement.

Most of the staff of the *Boekmanstichting* left and went to universities where they could continue in research positions. This split contributed to the growth of university-based research centers in the Netherlands; there are now seven or eight such research centers including ones at the universities of Amsterdam, Utrecht, and Gröningen and at Erasmus University in Rotterdam. At the same time, the government's Social and Cultural Planning Office, the Central Bureau of Statistics, and the Ministry of Education, Culture and Science have all become involved in research related to cultural policy.

Despite having been divorced from its activist research roots, the *Boekmanstichting* is still closely connected to the subfields that it serves. (Indeed, of the centers considered in the current study, it is probably the one that is best linked to the field of practice.) The board includes representatives from management and policy, education and research, and the arts and culture. Members are appointed through a highly collaborative process following discussions with the Association of Dutch Local Municipalities, the Inter-Provincial Consultation on Welfare, the Council for Culture, the Association of Collaborating Dutch Universities, the Federation of Dutch Trade Unions, the Federation of Artists' Associations, the Dutch Museum Society, and the National Coordinating Committee for the Protection of Monuments and Historic Buildings.

Today, the Boekman Foundation focuses on government policies concerning the arts and culture (including fine art, music, architecture, theatre, design, photography, film, literature, libraries, dance, museums, and popular culture); socioeconomic and legal issues relevant to this field; marketing and sponsorship in the cultural sector; cultural organizations and events; art in relation to the new media; the cultural heritage; art education; amateur arts; and professional arts education.

Information, documentation, and publication have become the main activities of the *Boekmanstichting*. These functions are actually managed by two different foundations operating in the same facility: the *Boekmanstichting*, which maintains the library and documentation center, arranges conferences, seminars, and expert meetings, and publishes *Boekmancahier*; and *Boekmanstudies*, which produces books, some written by staff and based on desk research and some written by outsiders. *Boekmanstudies* works only through commissions. The books that result are published either by the *Boekmanstichting* or by private publishers. In a sense, this is the reverse of the situation with the *Zentrum für Kulturforschung* in Bonn (discussed below). Here the publishing arm is, in theory, for profit, while the *Boekmanstichting* itself is nonprofit; whereas at ZfKf, the publishing arm is nonprofit while the basic institution is (at least in legal form) profit making.

The *Boekmanstichting* maintains an ambitious publishing agenda, with many of the publications coming from the *Boekmanstudies* side of the house. Since 1994, *Boekmanstudies* has published some thirty to forty books, including its best-selling handbook on the theory and practice of audience research, which is very popular with students and has sold about 2,000 copies in two editions. Recently, a number of books have been published in English, including:

- Ineke van Hamersveld and Niki van der Wielen, eds., *Cultural Research In Europe 1996* (Amsterdam, The Netherlands: *Boekmanstichting*, 1996)
- Annemoon van Hemel, Hans Mommaas, and Cas Smithuijsen, eds., *Trading Culture: GATT, European Cultural Policies and the Transatlantic Market* (Amsterdam, The Netherlands: *Boekmanstichting*, 1996)
- Peter B. Boorsma, Annemoon van Hemel, and Niki van der Wielen, eds., *Privatization and Culture: Experiences in the Arts, Heritage and Cultural Industries in Europe* (Boston, Massachusetts: Kluwer Academic Publishers, 1998)
- Diane Dodd and Annemoon van Hemel, eds., *Planning Cultural Tourism in Europe: A Presentation of Theories and Cases* (Amsterdam, The Netherlands: *Boekmanstichting*, 1999)
- Dorota Ilczuk, *Cultural Citizenship: Civil Society and Cultural Policy in Europe* (Amsterdam, The Netherlands: *Boekmanstichting*, 2001)

As part of its work plan for 2001, the *Boekmanstichting* planned to move forward on a number of publications including a "Future Studies in Culture" series in collaboration with the Social and Cultural Planning Office, a cultural policy reader targeted for arts administration courses, a new report as part of its copyright series, and a report on the amateur arts.

Another growing part of the work plan is to organize "Study Days" to assess the needs of the field and then to ramp up publishing and the distribution of information related to the issue under consideration. Director Cas Smithuijsen's intent is to provide a product that is not already there: "Every day in the Netherlands we have a conference in the arts, but we do not have many expert meetings." The intent is clearly to be more proactive and to have such expert meetings become an important component of the *Boekmanstichting*'s activities. Smithuijsen cites as one example a meeting convened to discuss the "State Collection." (In the Netherlands, objects that are in state museums do not belong to that museum, but rather belong to the State Collection, which raises a number of interesting collection management questions.) The occasion for this meeting was the fact that the Rijksmuseum stood to benefit from a substantial amount of money for restoration, and it wanted to be sure that it could justify this expenditure. It was interested in a series of four or five meetings on the role of museums in society. The *Boekmanstichting* argues that it is uniquely suited to bringing together interested parties because it is seen as an independent voice working between the public administration, the cultural field, and the world of social science.

The *Boekmanstichting* is now developing plans for additional expert meetings including: (1) the private market for the visual arts/the evolving role of galleries, (2) the representation of Dutch history in art museums (at the request of the Council for Culture), and (3) current topics on the cultural policy agenda. In a similar vein, the *Boekmanstichting* holds occasional Boekman debates, which are open to the public.

Though it can no longer be accurately characterized, first and foremost, as a research center, the *Boekmanstichting* does get involved with research in the following ways:

- The preparation of background literature reviews to summarize the existing research literature on various topics ("desk research"). These reviews are most often done to compile readers and background papers for the various conferences, seminars, and courses of the *Boekmanstichting*. The *Boekmanstichting* is known for the high quality of the background readers that it prepares; they are often in as much demand as the final reports or books that emerge from its conferences.[13]
- The preparation of inventories of ongoing research, typically completed as part of the *Boekmanstichting*'s documentation function.

- On rare occasions, the commissioning of original academic research with the intent that this research will be published as part of the *Boekmanstudies* series.

Budget and Personnel

The current annual budget of the *Boekmanstichting* is approximately 2 million guilders. Nearly all this amount, 1.9 million guilders, comes as an annual subsidy from the Ministry of Education, Culture and Science. The basic subsidy comprises 1.8 million guilders, and 100,000 guilders is designated for projects negotiated on top of the basic subsidy. Just like other Dutch arts institutions, this subsidy is part of a four-year planning system, and each institution is separately assessed to retain its subsidy. Thus, in a legal sense, the government subsidizes the activities of the *Boekmanstichting* in the same way that the government might subsidize the activities of an orchestra or a theater company or any independent foundation operating in the public interest with a private board. A very small portion of the annual income of the *Boekmanstichting*, approximately 130,000 guilders, comes from direct operations—sale of publications and nominal fees for borrowing from its library.

The *Boekmanstichting* maintains twelve full-time personnel slots, but eighteen people currently occupy these. Only three are full time. The eighteen individuals include one director, seven scientific staff (the so-called "small" or central staff), six library staff, three administrative staff, and a computer systems manager.

Library and Documentation

The crown jewel of the *Boekmanstichting* is its library, which collects documents and publications dealing with the production, distribution, and consumption of art and culture, and art policy. There are approximately 50,000 titles in the library, three-quarters of which are in Dutch. Many of these, of course, deal with Dutch issues. Documents enter the collection at a very rapid rate; in 1999 some sixteen meters of shelf space were needed for new acquisitions.

In addition to books and journals, the collection includes government policy papers, parliamentary reports, general reports, statistical reports, electronic databases, newspaper clippings, public research studies, and articles from magazines and journals. It serves as a national repository for student research in the field, and it systematically collects and catalogs Ph.D. theses and short dissertations written for the Dutch Doctorandus degree (the equivalent of a master's degree). As an incentive to deposit theses in the *Boekmanstichting*'s collection, an annual De Groene–Boekman Prize is offered for the best thesis completed each year.

Unlike other documentation centers in the field, the *Boekmanstichting*'s library is open to everyone. The catalogue for documents and publications acquired since 1983 is computerized; the catalogue for items acquired between 1963 and 1983 is not yet computerized. The most recent acquisitions are presented on the Web site. A small sum is charged when books are reserved or borrowed from the library. Documents and publications may be ordered by telephone or in writing. If requested, the staff will make a literature review on a particular topic for a small fee. Also, the staff will photocopy and fax documents and publications on a fee-for-service basis.

Boekmancahier

The *Boekmancahier* (*Boekman Notebook*) is a quarterly publication presenting articles that focus, for the most part, on Dutch and Flemish issues in the arts, culture, and related policy areas. This journal closely monitors the current cultural–political debate and strives to bring together the academic world, the government, and the various cultural sectors. It includes a column, *Tegendraads* ("In Opposition"), which is intended to address controversial issues. The editorial policy is to edit articles so that they are accessible for a wide readership—researchers, students, policymakers, and the staff of cultural bodies. Thus, it is not considered an academic journal. Occasionally, articles are published in English, and each issue includes English summaries of the articles and the *Tegendraads* contributions.

RECAP

RECAP is a project funded initially by the *Boekmanstichting* to improve the quality and flow of documentation in all forms on the theme of cultural policy in Europe. The objective is to foster cooperation among documentation centers, making their collections available to a wider audience. Many documentation centers in the field have limited time, staff, and funds and are therefore constrained in their ability to make their collections accessible to a wider audience. In a number of cases these resources are badly neglected and woefully underdocumented. By pooling information on methods of documentation and developing common protocols, RECAP hopes to change this situation.

The first step in this process is to develop a thesaurus of terminology related to culture and cultural policy. The thesaurus is being produced in Dutch, but it is anticipated that it will be translated into other languages by partner documentation centers. This is not a trivial task, as cultural policy terms in one language are not easily translated into another; indeed, the concept may not even exist. (Note that the Canadian Cultural Research Network has also announced the development of a thesaurus as one of its collective projects.) After testing the thesaurus and translating it, the next step will be to get documentation centers to use it as a basis for their indexing and cataloging; once that begins to happen, the information technology portion can then be outsourced.

Because the implementation of this project depends, for the foreseeable future, on the voluntary participation of other centers, the project has had difficulty in gaining momentum. At the moment, two other partners have joined the *Boekmanstichting* in the RECAP project: the *Fondazione Fitzcarraldo* in Turin[14] and *Kulturdokumentation* in Vienna.[15]

One impetus for this project is the perceived necessity for increased sharing of information at the European level. Because European Union funding requires multiple national partners for sponsored projects, there is an even more important emphasis on knowing what is happening elsewhere in Europe. Ironically, the RECAP project itself is unlikely to qualify for European funding (even though there is a European Framework Program for Technological Development) because it is not really innovative, relying on relatively standard technologies and library and documentation techniques.

The *Boekmanstichting* has also been maintaining an online database, Cultural Research in Europe (CRIE), which summarizes research that is under way or recently completed. (Early editions have also been made available in printed form and on disk.) This database is being incorporated into the RECAP project.

The Boekman Chair for Research into the Sociology of Art

The Boekman Foundation maintains a chair in the Sociology of Art at the University of Amsterdam for a visiting professor. This chair is intended to stimulate the study of the sociology of the arts in the Netherlands. The chair has been held by Jan Vaessen (director of the *Openluchtmuseum*, Arnhem), Vera Zolberg (New School for Social Research, New York), Bram Kempers (University of Amsterdam), and Nathalie Heinich (a CNRS researcher at the *École des Hautes Études en Sciences Sociales* in Paris). The cost of this program is approximately €10,000 per year.

Assessment

The trajectory of the *Boekmanstichting* has been from activism to intentional passivity. During the 1990s this trend was reversed slightly with a move toward being an active, though independent, intermediary. It has been trying to get ahead of the curve on a number of topics in cultural policy and to assist in shaping the emerging debate on those topics. Accordingly, the *Boekmanstichting* is more and more conscious of the need to transform the raw materials delivered by large research organizations (both governmental and nongovernmental) into information and knowledge that will actually be useful in policymaking. To adopt a conceptual division popular in the field of public policy analysis, the *Boekmanstichting* might characterize its role as translating data into information. Others then complete the process of turning that information into the evidence that figures in the ongoing policy debate.

Many of the things the *Boekmanstichting* does are done very well. Staff have refined the process of developing readers in preparation for conferences, seminars, and meetings, and these readers are in as much demand as the final publications of the various events. *Boekmanstichting* documents are thoughtful, all the more so because it now insists on partnering with university faculty, who bring a stricter social science sensibility to bear on each project, for each of its undertakings. A respected university professor becomes the scientific chair of each endeavor; still, the importance of voices from the field being heard as well is acknowledged.

On the other hand, the *Boekmanstichting* is probably not the first place to which one would turn to commission research beyond "desk research" that relies on existing data sources and materials, the form of research that is most closely allied to its vocation as an information and documentation center.

Interviews and Contacts

Cas Smithuijsen
Director
Boekmanstichting
Herengracht 415
1017 BP Amsterdam
The Netherlands

Phone: 011-31-(0)20-624-3736
Fax: 011-31-(0)20-638-5239

e-mail: c.smithuijsen@boekman.nl

Also Interviewed

EVA BRINKMAN, former director of the RECAP Project (Resources for Cultural Policy in Europe)

INEKE VAN HAMERSVELD, Editor, *Boekmancahier*

WEB SITE

http://www.boekman.nl

DOCUMENTS AND PUBLICATIONS CONSULTED:

Boekmanstichting, *Jaarverslag 1998 [Annual Report 1998]* (Amsterdam, The Netherlands: Boekmanstichting, 1999).

Boekmanstichting, *Jaarverslag 1999 [Annual Report 1999]/Beleidsplan 2001–2004 [Policy Plan 2001–2004]* (Amsterdam, The Netherlands: Boekmanstichting, 2000).

Boekmanstichting, *RECAP: Resources for Cultural Policy in Europe* (Amsterdam Boekmanstichting, 1999). See particularly Cas Smithuijsen, "The Need for a European Liaison for Cultural Policy Resources," pp. 13–19.

Boekmanstichting, "Werkplan 2001," photocopy of internal document, 2000.

Boorsma, Peter B.; Annemoon van Hemel; and Niki van der Wielen, eds., *Privatization and Culture: Experiences in the Arts, Heritage and Cultural Industries in Europe* (Boston, Massachusetts: Kluwer Academic Publishers, 1998).

Dodd, Diane, and Annemoon van Hemel, eds., *Planning Cultural Tourism in Europe: A Presentation of Theories and Cases* (Amsterdam, The Netherlands: Boekmanstichting, 1999).

van Hamersveld, Ineke, and Niki van der Wielen, eds., *Cultural Research in Europe 1996* (Amsterdam, The Netherlands: Boekmanstichting, 1996).

van Hemel, Annemoon; Hans Mommaas; and Cas Smithuijsen, eds., *Trading Culture: GATT, European Cultural Policies and the Transatlantic Market* (Amsterdam, The Netherlands: Boekmanstichting, 1996).

Ministry of Education, Culture and Science
Cultural Policy Directorate
Zoetermeer

Knowledge for policy making. Knowledge about policy making.
To be able to reflect you need a mirror.

THEODOOR H. ADAMS

Significance

In the case of the Dutch Ministry of Education, Culture and Science, the cultural policy research function is actually situated within a Cultural Policy Directorate, establishing an unusually close link between research and policy. While not functioning as a research center on its own, it commissions research that has direct policy relevance, works closely with the Social and Cultural Planning Office and the Central Bureau of Statistics, and supports the basic library and documentation activities of the *Boekmanstichting*.

Description

Over the years the structure of cultural policy at the national level in the Netherlands has changed as more and more implementation has been outsourced to a variety of organizations and funding bodies, as state agencies have been restructured to be more autonomous from government, and as privatization of national institutions has been emphasized. Within the ministry itself one of the implications of these trends has been that the ministry can now concentrate on what is seen as its "true role," the development of the main outlines of policy within which all of its initiatives take place. Accordingly, this has meant that the research function within the ministry has focused on research that is seen as having direct policy relevance. More general work developing ongoing indicators of the nature of cultural life in the Netherlands happens outside of the Ministry at the Social and Cultural Planning Office (see the next case below).

Two people in the Cultural Policy Directorate oversee the research function, and they have a budget of approximately 1.5 million guilders per year to commission research to develop specific information of policy relevance. Small research projects with budgets up to 25,000 guilders (usually "desk research" as opposed to field research) can be commissioned quite easily. Larger projects are subject to bidding requirements. Generally, a judgment is made as to the two or three firms or centers best equipped to do the research, and they are invited to bid. Projects on the order of 500,000 guilders and higher would typically necessitate a partnership with some other source of money.

To give a flavor of the type of research that is commissioned, some examples of recent projects include:

- *A project to study foreign visitors to Dutch museums.* What are their motives for visiting the museums? What priorities do they take into consideration in making attendance choices? This work is being done in conjunction with the Central Bureau of Statistics.
- *A project assessing how and to what extent immigrants use the special television programming that is intended for them.* This is driven by the question of whether these groups actually need special programs and is directly related to the ministry's policymaking in the area of broadcasting.
- *A project to ascertain how visual artists earn their living.* There is an interest in what job combinations artists use and how they fit together.
- *Research on the backlog of heritage restoration activities* with an eye to redesigning the system to do small projects quickly and avoid higher restoration and conservation costs later.

When asked about evaluation, the director of the Cultural Policy Directorate, Theodoor Adams, distinguished between two types of evaluation. The first is the evaluation (assessment) of grantee institutions to establish that they deserve support and to ascertain what they have accomplished with any prior support. This assessment is divided into two portions: The Cultural Policy Directorate is asked to handle the financial and technical side of the assessment, and the Council for Culture, an independent body that distributes funding on behalf of the state, handles the artistic quality assessment. These two forms of information are then combined and taken into account in funding decisions.

The other form of evaluation addresses the question of how policymaking is working with respect to the government's broader goals and objectives. One such project is focused on the fixed-price policy for books. Does it work? Another looks at the art collections that are in the possession of the university sector rather than the state museum sector. Are the universities taking care of these collections well? What issues are raised by the fact that the State Collection is split in this way?

The Cultural Policy Directorate uses both university research centers and private firms to conduct research. When a university is contracted with, the contract is passed to a special foundation attached to the university that is designed to administer this type of research grant, but care is taken to specify the researcher in the contract. Thus, the skills of a particular individual are being sought, more than the reputation of a particular center. University research centers can also apply for research grants to the Royal Academy, a rough equivalent of the National Science Foundation in the United States or CNRS in France.

The annual grant for the *Boekmanstichting* comes through, and is administered by, the Cultural Policy Directorate. This grant leads to the recurring question of exactly why the Directorate believes it is important to maintain a separate, specialized library. No other such specialized library is maintained in the system of Dutch ministries. As a consequence of this scrutiny, the Directorate is constantly concerned about whether the *Boekmanstichting* is open and accessible enough and whether people actually find their way to their documentation resources.

The Cultural Policy Directorate is also involved in what might be called a second level of cultural policy research at the European level. In the Dutch case, it was the Directorate that was responsible for preparing the National Report as input into the Council of Europe's Evaluation of Dutch Cultural Policy. Theodoor Adams, who was in charge of writing that report, was so positive about the experience and his involvement in other countries' evaluations—he was a member of the team of examiners for Italy and chair of the team of examiners for Slovenia—that he decided to write a second such report some years later, *Cultural Policy in the Netherlands*, as a useful exercise for the Dutch ministry (even without the accompanying promise of a response from a group of expert examiners).

In addition to working with the Council of Europe in its initiatives, the Cultural Policy Directorate is participating with Eurostat in the European Union's program for the development of cultural statistics across Europe.

When asked to cite an example of the work of the Cultural Policy Directorate that had directly influenced policy, Adams cited work in the field of orchestras. The relationship between the ministry and many of its grantee institutions is structured as a four-year contract; such a contract must be precise enough so that the institution knows what it is expected to deliver and so that the ministry can evaluate how successful the contract has been, but it also has to be sufficiently flexible so as not to be deadening. The directorate urged that the functions of orchestras be disaggregated into their main components, e.g., performing, traveling, educational programs, and the like. Once this was done, they asked whether it was necessary to contract with all orchestras to deliver all functions or whether it would be preferable to allow for some specialization of function.

When asked about the current agenda of the ministry and how it might impact the work of the Cultural Policy Directorate, the director mentioned two themes. As in many other places around the world, the current Secretary of State for Culture is very interested in broadening the public's interest in the arts and culture and would like to see more attention focused on education and youth programs. The policy questions are, What makes sense? And what are the practical limits to such policies? Also on the agenda is cultural entrepreneurship: To what extent can cultural institutions generate their own income? What would be reasonable targets for earned income?[16]

Assessment

The Dutch Cultural Policy Directorate provides a clear example of research in the service of policymaking. The focus is very much on applied research with policy relevance. This is not to say that other forms of research have been neglected. Rather, they have been vested in other institutions, both governmental (e.g., the Social and Cultural Planning Office conducting basic research) and nongovernmental (e.g., the *Boekmanstichting* conducting secondary desk research as part of its documentation function). University research centers work for a wide variety of clients, most importantly artist organizations and arts service organizations, providing research on themes that are of concern to those sectors of the field. As a result, an unusually clear division of labor has evolved.

Interviews and Contacts

Theodoor H. Adams
Director, Cultural Policy Directorate
Ministry of Education, Culture and Science
Europaweg 4
P.O. Box 25000
2700 LZ Zoetermeer
The Netherlands
Phone: 011-31-(0)79-323-4521
Fax: 011-31-(0)79-323-4989
e-mail: th.h.adams@minocw.nl

Dr. Vladimír Bína [*not interviewed*]
Research Coordinator
Cultural Policy Directorate
Ministry of Education, Culture and Science
Europaweg 4
P.O. Box 25000
2700 LZ Zoetermeer
The Netherlands
Phone: 011-31-(0)79-323-4526
Fax: 011-31-(0)79-323-4989
e-mail: v.bina@minocw.nl

Web Site

http://www.minocw.nl/english/

Documents and Publications Consulted

Ministry of Education, Culture and Science, *Cultural Policy in the Netherlands* (Zoetermeer, The Netherlands: Ministry of Education, Culture and Science, 1998).

van der Ploeg, Frederik, *Making Way for Diversity* (Zoetermeer, The Netherlands: Ministry of Education, Culture and Science, no date).

van der Ploeg, Frederik, *Principles on Cultural Policy 2001–2004: Culture as Confrontation* (Zoetermeer, The Netherlands: Ministry of Education, Culture and Science, November 1999[?]).

Note: Publications of the Ministry of Education, Culture and Science are available online.

Social and Cultural Planning Office
The Hague

Significance

The Social and Cultural Planning Office (SCP) is quite unlike any of the other institutions considered in this study. It is a government data-collection and data-analysis agency that documents the statistical and information backdrop against which policy decisions are made in the social and cultural spheres of government. The key ideas here are *monitoring* and *interpreting* social and policy changes and trends.

Description

The Social and Cultural Planning Office is one component of the Dutch government's commitment to evidence-based planning as a key element in formulating and implementing policy. It is very much an outgrowth of the social indicator and social report movement of the 1960s and is based in large part on the work of the Organisation for Economic Cooperation and Development (OECD) in that era.

The Dutch government has four such planning offices: the *Central Planning Office*, which deals with economic matters; the *National Physical Planning Agency*, which deals with the physical aspects of policy and development; the *National Institute of Public Health and the Environment*, which focuses on environmental planning; and the *Social and Cultural Planning Office*, which studies the social and cultural aspects of Dutch life and informs policy in these areas. These four planning offices are at the disposal of the various agencies of the Dutch government when they need information, but they also provide an ongoing service to analyze and publish available data on a regular basis. All four planning offices draw heavily on the statistical information that is collected by the Central Bureau for Statistics (Statistics Netherlands).

The Social and Cultural Planning Office was established by Royal Decree in 1973. In theory, the SCP considers all areas of government policy to the extent that social aspects are involved in those policies, but the emphasis is on health, welfare, social security, the labor market, education, and culture. Its tasks are threefold:

- To describe the social and cultural situation in the Netherlands and to identify expected developments
- To broaden the choices available to policymakers by developing alternatives and by identifying the resources necessary to implement those alternatives
- To evaluate government policy, especially interministerial policies

The focus is on the medium term and the long term. Issues of current interest are generally addressed through other mechanisms.

The Social and Cultural Planning Office sees its audience as fourfold: the staff of the national government (ministers, the Parliament, and civil servants); the staff of regional and local authorities; professionals in the service sectors subsidized by the government; and the public, through its information communication functions.

The primary product of the Social and Cultural Planning Office is the biennial *Social and Cultural Report*. This report provides a voluminous snapshot of the nature and quality of Dutch life. Drawing heavily on government statistics, the report is arranged with one subsector per chapter. The *Social and Cultural Report* is published in Dutch and English and is available on SCP's Web site. SCP also publishes a wide variety of regular and occasional publications. One part of the work of the Social and Cultural Planning Office that is not very visible outside the government is the policy recommendations that are made in memorandum form and addressed to ministers, their staffs, and various government committees.

In the area of culture, a rhythm and structure of working has evolved over the past five years or so. The Ministry of Education, Culture and Science has contracted with the Social and Cultural Planning Office, which has specialists in the field of culture on its staff, to produce a rotating series of documents on a cyclical basis with one appearing every other year. This sequence of documents is referred to as the "Cultural Base." The cycle includes the arts, the media, and the cultural heritage. This structure mirrors the tripartite structure of the ministry's cultural section. This cyclical rotation was established in part to regularize employment for the SCP's cultural staff. (Prior to instituting this rotation, the work beyond the preparation of the Social and Cultural Report was sporadic, responding more to unpredictable demands from various cultural offices in the ministry.)

The Cultural Base documents draw from two large-scale national surveys that contain information on cultural participation and that are conducted regularly on behalf of the Social and Cultural Planning Office. The Time–Budget Survey (TBO) asks a random sample of approximately 3,000 individuals twelve years of age or older to keep a diary and to report on how they spend their time during the week. The TBO, which was first conducted in 1975, has been repeated once every five years. The Amenities and Services Utilization Survey (AVO) is designed to ascertain to what extent and in what ways the Dutch population is accessing the services and amenities supported by the Dutch government. It was begun with the idea that it would help answer the question of who gets what from government and government-supported services. This study, a random national sample of households that surveys all members of the sampled households six years of age or older, was first conducted in 1979 and has been repeated every four years. This survey results in detailed data on many different forms of cultural participation as well as data on the use of a broad package of public services in the social and cultural sectors.

These surveys are used for several purposes: to describe the breadth and level of participation in various cultural activities; to describe ancillary yet related activities of the participants; to describe the demographic characteristics of the participants; to describe changes in participation and in the composition of groups of participants; and to attempt to explain the pattern of participation and changes in that pattern. Because the data are collected in two forms—as participation data and as time–budget data—the data resource is particularly rich, and the fact that the data have been collected consistently over time makes it possible to map and analyze trends.

The staff of the Social and Cultural Planning Office mine these two data sources and any others that are appropriate and available to write their Cultural Base reports. An interesting aspect to this work is that while staff members are expected to give a complete overview of the available data, they are also encouraged to explore the data through a theme of current interest. In other words, instead of producing a rather neutral compilation of statistical tables, they are encouraged to develop a topic for each report, focusing, for example, on youth and their cultural practices or on city culture. In other words, the staff has some freedom to explore themes and issues and to push the analysis in particular directions. About these reports the staff say, "In the end, if we want to publish something we do." (The exception to this is the biennial *Social and Cultural Report*; this is overseen by the ministry, which has much more at stake in this official view of the quality of Dutch life and, by implication, what it has done about it.)

Four studies in this series have been published: *Performing Arts in an Age of Remote Control* on attendance at theaters and concert halls (Knulst, 1995); *Reading Habits* (Knulst and Kraaykamp, 1996); *The Shared Cultural Heritage* (de Haan, 1997); and *The Reach of the*

Arts on the performing and visual arts (de Haan and Knulst, 2000). These documents are published in Dutch, but extended summaries are prepared in English as well. These reports and summaries are also available on the Web site.

Taken together, all of this work represents something of a shift in the cultural work of the Social and Cultural Planning Office, from focusing on data that depict the supply side of cultural afffairs (number and location of various cultural facilities, size of budget, and the like) to data that depict the demand side through participation, attendance, and actual cultural practices.

The cultural work of the Social and Cultural Planning Office is supported by a grant from the Ministry of Education, Culture and Science. That relationship is reevaluated on a six-year basis. Thus, its relationship to the ministry is similar to the *Boekmanstichting*'s relationship. The Social and Cultural Planning Office has fifty to sixty full-time-equivalent staff in research and some eighty-five people in total, including secretaries, statisticians, and public relations. Out of this total, only 1.5 researchers focus on cultural material. The grant from the ministry to support this work is on the order of 200,000 guilders per year. ("But we do more than they pay for!") Because of the modest size of this budget as well as the normal mode of operation of the Social and Cultural Planning Office, the staff primarily analyzes and interprets government data and does not conduct field research.

The Social and Cultural Planning Office is one of the few agencies studied that had a specific policy with respect to the wider distribution of its data. The data it collects are made available gratis but with a three-year delay. This gives the SCP the chance to be the first out of the box with publications. The SCP then delivers the data to a data bank run by the Dutch Academy of Sciences, which subsequently accepts the responsibility of responding to other demands for the data. Anyone who wishes to make data available in this way can do so, and one can specify who can have access to the data according to four or five broad categories. On occasion, the three-year limit is relaxed for requests for data relevant to specific questions.

Assessment

The work of the Social and Cultural Planning Office is guided by a faith in planning and policymaking as rational activities. Moreover, its work is based on the belief that at the highly aggregated level of SCP data, it is still possible to see the effects of policy. This attitude is refreshing in an era in which there is considerable cynicism about government policy and intervention. The SCP fulfills an important function—the analysis and interpretation, through a cultural policy lens, of the data that are being generated on a regular basis by the government. One might criticize the lack of engagement in direct short-term issues of concern to the ministry, but for that sort of engagement one simply has to look elsewhere in the Dutch system. Whether it actually influences policy in the ways it claims is difficult to say. Perhaps it offers only the illusion of rationality in policymaking. Yet, the role of the SCP is clear and precise, and its work appears to be valued.

The desire here is to produce, on a regular basis, a picture of the state of the arts and the cultural life of the nation and its citizens. In this way it is similar to such efforts elsewhere—the *Kulturstatistik* reports in Sweden, Statistics Canada's *Focus on Culture* bulletins, or the attempts to provide statistical backup to the semiregular *State of the Arts* reports in the United States[17]—but few such efforts achieve the level of integration between data and policy that the Social and Cultural Planning Office, through its intentional independence, can achieve; even fewer such efforts turn out to be both informed and opinionated.

Interviews and Contacts

Dr. Andries van den Broek
Ondersoekscoördinator
Cultuur, media en vrije tijd
Social and Cultural Planning Office
Parnassusplein 5
2511 VX The Hague
The Netherlands

Phone: 011-31-(0)70-340-7833
Fax: 011-31-(0)70-340-7044

e-mail: andries.van.den.broek@scp.nl

Postal Address:

Social and Cultural Planning Office
Postbus 16164
2500 BD The Hague
The Netherlands

Dr. Jos de Haan
Projectleider Het Culturele Draagvlak
Social and Cultural Planning Office
Parnassusplein 5
2511 VX The Hague
The Netherlands

Phone: 011-31-(0)70-340-7832
Fax: 011-31-(0)70-340-7044

e-mail: j.de.haan@scp.nl

Postal Address:

Social and Cultural Planning Office
Postbus 16164
2500 BD The Hague
The Netherlands

Web Site

http://www.scp.nl/defaultuk.htm

Documents and Publications Consulted

de Haan, Jos, *The Shared Cultural Heritage* (The Hague, The Netherlands: Social and Cultural Planning Office, 1997), English summary.

de Haan, Jos, and Wim Knulst, *The Reach of the Arts* (The Hague, The Netherlands: Social and Cultural Planning Office, 2000), English summary.

Knulst, W. P., *Performing Arts in an Age of Remote Control* (The Hague, The Netherlands: Social and Cultural Planning Office, 1995), English summary.

Knulst, W. P., and G. Kraaykamp, *Reading Habits* (The Hague, The Netherlands: Social and Cultural Planning Office, 1996), English summary.

Note: Publications of the Social and Cultural Planning Office are available online.

GREAT
BRITAIN

The Arts Council of England
Research and Development Directorate
Research Department
London

If we are going to have the authority to speak with confidence and be listened to, we have to put resources into research.

PETER HEWITT

Significance

Until relatively recently, arm's-length arts councils arguably have been less subject to central government's expectations for explicit policy and planning than have ministries of culture, so it is perhaps not surprising that arts councils' attitudes toward, and their relationship to, research has fluctuated considerably over time. Recently, however, as central governments have applied increased pressure on arm's-length arts councils in an attempt to assure that they are operating within the general direction of government policy, there has been a marked rise in the call for *evidence-based* policy and planning, a call that arts councils are finding difficult to resist: At the end of the day, they are, after all, reliant on government for their budgets and their continued institutional existence. Like any number of other arts councils, the Arts Council of England has come to the decision that it must pursue a much more aggressive research strategy. This has been encouraged, in part, by the most recent reorganization of the arts council, which has the intent of transforming it into a strategic body that will be more concerned with advocacy and laying out broad policy directions for the arts than with day-to-day funding of a set of clients. The research department of the Research and Development Directorate of the arts council is one of several recent initiatives around the world that symbolize a new investment in cultural policy research, albeit one with a rather particular point of view.

Background

The history of research and information services at the Arts Council of England (and its predecessor agency, the Arts Council of Great Britain) has been a mixed one.[18] Over the years the council's interest in, and commitment to, research has waxed and waned depending on the policy questions that were perceived to be on the table, the budget that was available for staff, and the degree of pressure exerted by central government on producing evidence for program design and funding decisions. As the arts council has traditionally functioned primarily as a funding agency, there have been the usual pressures from within the council itself as well as from the fields that it funds to grant money directly to arts organizations, artists, and projects rather than investing it in research. Nevertheless, there have been occasional demands to document more fully, from a statistical point of view, one or another aspect of the field or of the council's operations. This ambivalence toward research has undoubtedly also derived from a feeling that the government ought to fulfill this function through one of its more central government agencies rather than relying on an arm's-length agency to do the job. Nevertheless, for many years a partial research role has been played by the arts council, joined by the culture program at the Policy Studies Institute, an independent think tank, and, more recently, by staff of the Department for Culture, Media and Sport.

Several years ago, the Arts Council of England was dramatically restructured (with yet another restructuring announced during the summer of 2001). Except for a few national cultural institutions, it would no longer be in the business of giving away money directly to arts organizations. Most of that work was delegated to other funding bodies, particularly the Regional Arts Boards. And the arts council was reconceived as a strategic body, planning and developing policy for the sectors of the arts and culture that fall under the council's umbrella.[19] When interviewed in the fall of 2000, Peter Hewitt, the chief executive officer of the arts council, characterized the council's new role as being actively involved in advocacy, speaking to the government on behalf of the arts, while also speaking to, and challenging, the arts community. The government reaffirmed the "independence" of the arts council from government and made a commitment to building the arts council's budget so that over three years it would increase to £100 million more per year. Among other things, these dramatic changes seem to have resulted in a new emphasis on research, particularly the building of a strong evidence base for strategic planning and strategic initiatives.[20]

The council is now organized into four directorates: Arts, Communications, Planning and Resources, and Research and Development. The Research and Development Directorate is responsible for taking the lead within the council on research, arts education and training, employment in the arts, and the social and economic impact of arts practices. Most importantly, it is charged with setting a national agenda for the arts, and it foresees that much of the research that it will commission (or undertake itself) will be in the service of developing this agenda.[21] Quoting from an internal arts council document, "The creation of this Directorate, and the allocation of considerable additional resources to it, demonstrates the Arts Council's commitment to ensuring that our cultural agendas are underpinned by sound research and that we are engaged at senior level to maximise our influence in the fields of lifelong learning, education, social inclusion and economic regeneration, and that our advocacy is based on solid foundations."

Accordingly, this department is responsible for developing a national framework for arts research in England. While it will commission and manage research, it will also work with a variety of partners to implement research programs of a broader interest. It is expected that research will particularly address five themes that are in line with the council's current strategic priorities: (1) arts practice (including measuring performance), (2) arts policy and education, (3) employment in the arts, (4) the arts economy, and (5) audiences for the arts.

The research department will be involved in a number of research-related activities. These include commissioning and undertaking research; evaluating arts council initiatives and interventions; statistical monitoring to develop a foundation of data on the condition of the arts; mapping and auditing of the provision of the arts; preparing briefing papers for speeches, policy documents, and press coverage of the council's activities; providing advice, support, technical expertise, and quality assurance to colleagues in the art-form departments of the council and in the Regional Arts Boards when they undertake research; disseminating research findings through conferences, seminars, publications, and online resources; and advising on public opinion research.

A number of research projects have been carried over from previous commitments, and a number of new ones have been launched. As of late 2000, approximately sixteen were under way, three or four had just been contracted out, and another seven were being developed for eventual tender. Considerable attention was being focused on developing an omnibus survey of attendance, participation, and attitudes toward the arts. The department hoped to run a pilot with 1,500 to 2,000 respondents by early January 2001 with a full sample of 7,000 to 9,000 respondents later in the year. It is expected that various departments in the arts council will, over time, develop the habit of proposing research projects and providing money from their budgets to pay for it.

The data sets generated from the research of the arts council will eventually be deposited in a data archive maintained by Essex University, but they will not be deposited there until the first government publication has been released. At that point the data sets will be available free to researchers and for a fee to the private sector.

The fact that evaluation has been included in the mandate of the research department is an optimistic move. Because research divisions have found it hard to protect the research side of their work when they have also undertaken the evaluation function, which, inevitably, steps on someone's toes, evaluation has often quickly disappeared. There is optimism, at least for the moment, that evaluation can be taken on responsibly if only to document what is happening in the field with the implementation of the projects and initiatives of the arts council and its clients. Peter Hewitt seems to be determined to use council research to put a lot of questions on the table for debate and wants the council to be much more courageous in putting out material that might be seen as critical in one way or another.

One specific task that the research department has taken on is called the "Research Round Up." It will ask all of the arts-funding agencies to indicate what research they have commissioned. These research projects will be documented electronically and made available on a Web site, so that current research can be more readily accessed by the arts-funding system. This information will also be passed along to *Arts Research Digest*, an independent periodical produced under the auspices of the University of Northumbria, which publishes regular summaries of research in the field.[22]

Budget and Personnel

As recently as 1999, the research staff at the arts council had shrunk to one staff member. Since May of 2000, however, a research department has begun to be rebuilt within the Research and Development Directorate. Ann Bridgwood was recruited from the Office for National Statistics to become research director, and she was given authority to recruit 3.7 researchers to staff her office (plus one administrator already in place). This level of staffing will allow the implementation of an ambitious research agenda for the first time at the arts council. Ms. Bridgwood currently has a budget of £250,000 to commission research and hopes to augment this through agreements with other agencies and with resources provided from other departments within the council.

Assessment

At the time I conducted my interviews (late 2000), everyone involved was hopeful that a new commitment to research was at hand within the Arts Council of England. Ann Bridgwood was quite optimistic. She believed that the current staff of the council was very supportive of research, particularly given the government's emphasis on "value for money." She was also optimistic about the possible working relationships between the council and the Department for Culture, Media and Sport, as well as with the Scottish Arts Council, the Arts Council of Wales, and the Regional Arts Boards.

But, as I worked on revising this book for publication, the policy ground shifted yet again. In July of 2001 the council proposed a self-styled "radical plan" to reorganize the arts-funding system in England by creating a new national arts-funding and development organization.[23] The proposed organization would recombine the arts council and the ten Regional Arts Boards, claiming the following benefits:

- Greater leadership and authority regionally and nationally
- Greater financial flexibility and capacity to respond to artistic ambition regionally and nationally
- Less red tape and greater simplicity for artists
- Substantial savings, which will be redirected to the arts
- A strengthened voice in making the case [presumably to government] for the arts

The proposed organization would have nine regional offices with increased decision-making powers (but under more control of the central organization than the ten more highly independent Regional Arts Boards). The national strategic office would provide coordination, overview, and national leadership in the arts. Thus, one organization would be created out of the current eleven in the hope that the voice for the arts in government would be stronger, that efficiencies in administration could be achieved, and that a new opportunity for national initiatives would be created.

This plan has been widely criticized by the Regional Arts Boards as well as by local authorities who see in it, in Christopher Gordon's words, the signs of a "neo-Blairite institution that claims to be decentralizing, but first has to take all power unto itself."[24] Some interpret the proposal as a reassertion of the influence of the centralized art-form departments that are trying to reclaim agendas that had been devolved. Either way, vested self-interests are being challenged, and one would expect a negative response.

The implications that this proposed reorganization would have for the recently rejuvenated commitment to research and on the research agenda itself are difficult to predict. On the one hand, with an even stronger role for a national strategic office for arts funding, one might expect research to play a stronger role; on the other, to the extent that this reorganization represents a restrengthening of the hegemony of the disciplinary art-form offices, one might expect a move away from research as an unnecessary expense.

Historically, it has been particularly difficult for arts councils to develop and sustain a research commitment. When a coherent research policy has evolved, it has typically been within ministries of culture, which are less reluctant to be seen as exercising central control and monitoring over the field. While it is too early to tell if this new research initiative will stabilize over time, particularly in light of the current proposals for further reorganization, the fact is that it accompanies a reorientation of the central arts agency and that, in and of itself, necessitates a renewed emphasis on research. In the end, the support of the field will prove critical. If it finds the research results to be useful and compelling, then it will be less likely to see the investment in research as "taking money away from the arts," as has often been the perception in the past. On the other hand, if the current reorganization is being driven by the discipline-based art forms reasserting their influence, the shift toward research is likely to be framed as an unacceptable trade-off of resources.

This last point suggests an intriguing possibility: To the extent that the reorganization of arts councils leads to an internal structure that focuses on transversal issues that have a close link to perceived public interests—a direction that many arts councils are taking—the relevance and utility of research might become more clearly perceptible, and one might expect additional resources to be invested in research. To the extent that the reorganization of arts councils leads to a restrengthening of discipline-based structures, one might expect considerable resistance to an investment in research that is not clearly linked to the health of one or another of the artistic disciplines.[25] Indeed, it would probably be quite easy to construct an account of the waxing and waning fortunes of the various research divisions in arts councils as a direct function of such shifts in internal organization and in relative power and influence.

Interviews and Contacts

Peter Hewitt
Chief Executive
The Arts Council of England
14 Great Peter Street
London SW1P 3NQ
United Kingdom

Phone: 011-44-(0)20-7973-6575
Fax: 011-44 (0)20-7973-6584

e-mail: peter.hewitt@artscouncil.org.uk

Pauline Tambling [*not interviewed*]
Executive Director, Research and Development
The Arts Council of England
14 Great Peter Street
London SW1P 3NQ
United Kingdom

Phone: 011-44-(0)20-7973-6842
Fax: 011-44 (0)20-7973-6449

e-mail: pauline.tambling@artscouncil.org.uk

Ann Bridgwood
Director of Research
The Arts Council of England
14 Great Peter Street
London SW1P 3NQ
United Kingdom

Phone: 011-44-(0)20-7973-6837
Fax: 011-44 (0)20-7973-6449

e-mail: ann.bridgwood@artscouncil.org.uk

Also Interviewed

Christopher Gordon, former Chief Executive, English Regional Arts Boards

Web Site

http://www.artscouncil.org.uk/

Documents and Publications Consulted

Arts Council of England, *Publications*, April 2000.

Arts Council of England, "The Research and Development Directorate," "The Research Department," and "List of Current and Proposed Research Projects." Internal documents, 2000.

Arts Council of England, *Working Together for the Arts: The Arts Council's Detailed Plan for Future Support of the Arts in England* (London, England: Arts Council of England, 18 July 2001). [http://www.artscouncil.org.uk/towards/index.html]

Hackett, Keith; Peter Ramsden; Danyal Sattar; and Christophe Guene, *Banking on Culture: New Financial Instruments for Expanding the Cultural Sector in Europe*, Final Report, The European Commission, September 2000.

Robinson, Gerry, "The Creativity Imperative: Investing in the Arts in the 21st Century," New Statesman Arts Lecture 2000, London, England, 27 June 2000.

Department for Culture, Media and Sport Statistics and Social Policy Unit and Economics Branch London

It was a marriage in search of a dowry.
Statisticians, policy makers and arts managers converged on
the Royal Statistical Society on the edge of London's Square Mile,
to examine the progress each is making towards the production
of useful cultural statistics. . . .
[They] were invited to consider how they might produce more trustworthy
cultural statistics and then employ them in support of the cultural sector.

PHYLLIDA SHAW
[Describing "Crunching Numbers,"
a seminar held on June 25, 1998]

Significance

One would expect that a government's central cultural agency would have a research capability to monitor the field and to advise in the formulation of policy. But, at least in the English context, it has been difficult to establish that capability within the Department for Culture, Media and Sport.[26] Indeed, other organizations, both public and private, have been forced to fill in many of the gaps. The research activities of the department are interesting to note because they illustrate how a policy imperative seems to be leading, in the end, to the development of such a research capability.

Background

The Department of National Heritage was created in April 1992. It gathered together all of the cultural agencies of the English government under one umbrella at the Cabinet level. Renamed the Department for Culture, Media and Sport (DCMS) in 1997, it is one of the youngest departments in the English government. More than fifty public bodies receive funding from DCMS to deliver government support directly to the fields of sport and culture. The department was the lead agency in creating the National Lottery in 1994, and its funding bodies became the main redistribution channels for lottery funding to so-called "good causes."

The role of DCMS in all of its domains has been to serve as a coordinating and funding agency, supporting the fields of culture, the media, heritage, and sport both for their own sake and to the extent that they further the goals of the government of the day. For New Labour, these goals include social inclusion, regeneration, and urban neighborhoods. Five areas have been particularly targeted: improving education results, lowering crime rates, improving the standard of social housing, increasing employment, and increasing the quality of health care. While these targets are a bit outside the mandate of DCMS, they do have the effect, in Paul Allin's words, of "morphing cultural policy towards them." Together they suggest a research agenda based on how much the arts and culture can be demonstrated to further these goals and achieve these targets.

Another theme that has become important is "modernizing government" or "better government," or improving the way the government listens to its citizens. One strand of this effort has been described as the development of "evidence-based policy." As Allin, former head of the Statistics and Social Policy Unit (the department's chief statistician), and Stephen Creigh-Tyte, the department's chief economist, have both pointed out, government should have been doing this all along, but the fact that it is coming to the foreground once again has led to something of a resurgence in research. They have found a renewed interest in the so-called "ROAMEF" framework—Rationale, Objectives, Appraisal, Monitoring, Evaluation, and Feedback—as a basis for policy modeling and development. Both Allin and Creigh-Tyte argue that the Department for Culture, Media and Sport has been better at the first three steps, particularly the ex ante appraisal of proposed projects, than it has been at monitoring, evaluation, and feedback. (We have seen that this characteristic is shared by many governmental cultural agencies, as they mostly shy away from ex post monitoring and evaluation.) They argue, further, that the largest gap is at the level of policy evaluation, as compared to program or project evaluation.

Two offices within DCMS collaborate to provide the research function. The chief statistician heads the Statistics and Social Policy Unit and reports to the director of Strategy and Communications; the chief economist, on the other hand, reports to the director of Finance.

The Statistics and Social Policy Unit is comprised of nine individuals: its head, three statisticians, plus one additional statistical support person (in addition to four people in the social policy area, who are also assigned to the unit). The Statistics and Social Policy Unit buys in data from the outside, sharing the cost with other government partners, e.g. the National Time Use Survey, but its primary role is to look at secondary data that have been collected by others and to interpret them for the benefit of DCMS. Thus, its audience is, at the moment, almost exclusively internal. Only recently have there begun to be some moves to make its data and analyses more widely available to the fields that the department serves. The research budget of the unit (over and above salaries) is approximately £250,000 per year, roughly split between the unit's share of the cost of ongoing data efforts and money available for the commissioning of one-off research. At present, the primary data sources include the time-use survey, various tourism surveys, participation surveys, employment surveys, surveys of the funding of cultural activities, and surveys investigating the perceived benefits to society of culture, media, and sport.

The chief economist is served by a staff of three additional economists plus one support person. The role of this office is to provide economic research and support to the various policy divisions of DCMS. They find themselves working with, and relying on, the data of any number of outside bodies. They often work with the Department of Trade and Industry and the Department of Finance and Economics on projects. Recently, they have been called upon to participate in debates around the economics of broadcasting. They have also recently been involved in the Labour government's policy of removing entry charges to the core national collections. They are responsible for an annual report that documents how proceeds from the National Lottery have been distributed. This office has a modest budget of £50,000–£60,000 per year for commissioning research. Consequently, most of the work is done internally through the development of a series of technical papers.

Both offices generally rely on a limited invitation to tender as the primary means of commissioning research. Bidders typically include market research companies and university research centers. In the early days, contracts were generally awarded to the big five market research companies, who had the ability to deliver but who did not necessarily have the best understanding of the field in which they were being asked to operate. They often had to buy in additional expertise. A few actually put in place specialized cultural policy research units, but the specialized units seem to have disappeared. The use of university research centers, on the other hand, often comes with the problem of determining appropriate publication policies, which is particularly problematic given the penchant of DCMS for keeping this work internal and the desire of universities to build a knowledge base. More recently, there has been a rise in what might be termed university-based consulting groups, which function more as private consultants than as university research centers. These consulting groups are a response to the desire of the British government to have its universities become more entrepreneurial and to develop new revenue sources. DCMS has had limited interaction with these groups, often viewing them as nothing more than an alliance of two or three faculty who happen to have a set of more or less common interests but without the infrastructure a true center would need to deliver high-quality work on time. Generally, DCMS has also steered clear of private arts-management consulting firms when commissioning research because it believes that they do not have the requisite level of social science methodology.[27]

Unlike the research products of the cultural policy research units in other countries, these offices of DCMS publish very little material externally. Their work has been primarily internal, and they have paid very little attention to dissemination. No annual report or annual list of publications is available. With the advent of the Internet, however, this is beginning to change, and they are starting to make technical papers and the National Lottery Database available online.

Both offices interact with a wide variety of researchers at the Tourist Board, the British Film Institute, the various bodies funded through DCMS, and a growing variety of university-based research centers. In the past, this interaction has been limited to the sharing of information, but more recently there has been an effort to build a coordinated common information base. Both Allin and Creigh-Tyte were involved in an effort to review the current status of research and information gathering within the department and to make recommendations along these lines. A recent step in this direction has been the compilation and publication of two *Creative Industries Mapping Documents*,[28] which have resulted from a cross-departmental effort to compile all of the currently available data on the shape, size, and profile of all of the sectors within the creative industries in the United Kingdom. Finally, these efforts are happening in the context of a National Statistics Program that is intended to tidy up the government's collection, analysis, and dissemination of statistical material by creating an independent, national statistical service.

Assessment

By most measures, the level of research undertaken by the Department for Media, Culture and Sport seems surprisingly low. To be fair, it is a relatively young government department, and, therefore, it may not be too surprising that the research function has yet to be well developed. Also, the work has been primarily internal, so it may be unfair to judge it by its lack of visibility. In a way, the department finds itself in a chicken-and-egg situation with respect to research. In order to demonstrate the usefulness of the work these research offices would be able to provide with better resources, they need a couple of visible successes, but in order to be successful they need increased resources from the department to do the work in the first place. Perhaps the increased emphasis on research at the Arts Council of England, which has the promise of dramatically improving the statistical base of information for at least part of the field with which the department interacts, will provide some pressure back on the department to get its own research efforts better established.

In the words of Paul Allin,

> There has undoubtedly been a view that we can do arts policy without the data. I think that view has long since passed, but it means that we are starting from a low base. It may be a complex field in some ways, but it is not intrinsically difficult to ask questions about it, until you get into the area of appreciation and the non-quantifiable benefits of the arts.[29]

Interviews and Contacts

Paul Allin
former Chief Statistician, Statistics and Social Policy Unit,
Department for Culture, Media and Sport
Director of Integration and Harmonisation Division
Social Statistics Directorate
Office for National Statistics
Room B2/06
1 Drummond Gate
London SW1V 2QQ
United Kingdom

Phone: 011-44-(0)20-7533-6151
Fax: 011-44-(0)20-7533-6154

e-mail: paul.allin@ons.gov.uk

Stephen Creigh-Tyte
Chief Economist
Department for Culture, Media and Sport
Economics Branch, Finance Division
2-4 Cockspur Street
London SW1Y 5DH
United Kingdom

Phone: 011-44-(0)20-7211-2181
Fax: 011-44-(0)20-7211-2170

e-mail: stephen.creigh-tyte@culture.gov.uk

Web Site

http://www.culture.gov.uk/index_flash.html

Documents and Publications Consulted

Creative Industries Task Force, *Creative Industries Mapping Document, 1998* (London, England: Department for Media, Culture and Sport, 1998).
[http://www.culture.gov.uk/creative/creative_industries.html]

Ministerial Creative Industries Strategy Group, *Creative Industries Mapping Document, 2001* (London, England: Department for Media, Culture and Sport, 2001).
[http://www.culture.gov.uk/creative/creative_industries.html]

Shaw, Phyllida, "Crunching Numbers: Seminar Report," *Arts Research Digest*, Issue 14 (Autumn 1998).

Shaw, Phyllida, "Sources of Cultural Statistics: The UK and the Republic of Ireland—Statistics: A Matter of Trust," *Arts Research Digest*, Issue 13 (Summer 1998).

International Intelligence on Culture London

Significance

International Intelligence on Culture (IIC) is the successor to the International Arts Bureau (IAB), itself a private-sector spin-off from the former Arts Council of Great Britain and a successor to the arts council's in-house International Affairs Unit. IIC is particularly interesting in that it is an example of privatization of what has heretofore been thought of (and funded) as a public function—the provision of information and the communication of research results, especially concerning the international activities of the Arts Council of England, various European governmental organizations, and British arts organizations and artists. By its own description, International Intelligence on Culture is a multifaceted company "designed to meet the developing needs of organisations and individuals for accessible, relevant information and advice on the international cultural sector through: research; consultancy; training; information services; and publications." Although its roots are in providing information on culture and cultural programs in other countries to a British constituency, in its latest incarnation International Intelligence on Culture serves an international client base with an even wider range of information-based and consulting services.

Background

For several decades, the Arts Council of England and, earlier, the Arts Council of Great Britain have maintained an in-house information and research capacity, though the staffing commitment has waxed and waned depending on the financial situation of the council. Perhaps the era in which there was the most commitment to maintaining the research and information function—excepting the quite recent effort to rebuild substantially the council's research capacity—was in the mid- to late-1970s, when Robert Hutchison served as senior research and information officer, George Darroch as the unit's statistician, and Rod Fisher as information officer. The original focus of this unit was on regional issues, and, accordingly, it was located in the regional department of the council, though this later changed.[30]

Rod Fisher's official role as information officer included publishing council reports and documents, maintaining the council's library, and press monitoring. But he broadened his role to include filling gaps in the information that was available to the council's staff and to the field as a whole. In the late 1970s, for example, he became involved in the emerging field of the arts and disability, an involvement that eventually led to an explicit arts council policy in 1983–84.

One of the most significant gaps in information was in the area of international relations and the arts. Fisher found himself monitoring European and international developments in the arts and culture on behalf of the arts council, paying particular attention to the Council of Europe and the European Union. Significantly, the then Department of Education and Science selected him to be the British representative to the meeting at the Council of Europe at which the creation of CIRCLE (discussed further in Part III) was proposed; Fisher became a cofounder. Consequently, the arts council gradually developed a reputation for having good information on these issues, and artists and arts organizations sought out Fisher with their inquiries in these areas.

Over time, Fisher wrote a variety of papers and documents on cultural funding in various European countries and on the operation of European agencies and organizations. The most successful of these were *More Bread and Circuses: Who Does What for the Arts in Europe?* and *Arts Networking in Europe*. Gradually, an International Affairs Unit emerged with a mandate that included developing an international policy for the arts council. Fisher was named international affairs manager, and gradually his responsibilities expanded to include a number of research and documentation functions. Note that it was the quasi-autonomous arts council that took on this role. In effect, the council decided that it would have to fill a documentation and research void that might have been more appropriately filled by a central government agency if there had been one at the time.

In the meantime, the research and information staff had been reduced during several rounds of government cutbacks. In 1991 a major reorganization of the arts council occurred, prompted by a nationally touted participatory process that led to the development of the "National Arts and Media Strategy." But the various arts departments fought the transversal nature of this new strategy, putting activities such as the International Affairs Unit in jeopardy.

In 1992 the government created the Department of National Heritage, with the explicit goal of saving money that was being spent on public funding bodies, including the arts council. The arts council was then forced by the department to bring in Price Waterhouse for a round of management consulting with an eye to streamlining its operation. At that point, in Fisher's view, the writing was on the wall. Price Waterhouse had a reputation for looking first at travel and conference expenditures, seeing them as a quick way to achieve budget savings; much of the work of the International Affairs Unit relied on travel and active participation in conferences and European working groups. Moreover, Price Waterhouse thought (and Fisher agreed) that the International Affairs Unit was more properly a function of a government agency than of an autonomous funding body.

Fisher thus made a preemptive strike, proposing to the Secretary General of the arts council that he take the International Affairs Unit out-of-house, with a guarantee of funding for a transition period of three years. Overnight, three staff positions would be removed from the council. Beginning in March 1994, Fisher was given six months to set up what became the International Arts Bureau, all while finishing his arts council work, managing the production of the report *In From the Margins* for the Council of Europe, and chairing the Council of Europe's evaluation of national cultural policy in Finland.

The arts council contract with IAB called for the provision of two services: (1) policy intelligence, particularly at the European level, and (2) the provision of a free information service to the arts sector on international matters. (Eventually, IAB signed separate contracts with the Scottish, Welsh, and Irish Arts Councils; the British Film Institute; the Crafts Council; and, later, the Museums and Galleries Commission to provide similar services.) Direct services to the field included a dedicated enquiry service operated free of charge on behalf of the arts council; monthly one-on-one "surgeries" (consultations) to provide arts organizations and arts practitioners with more detailed guidance on their funding needs for projects that have an international dimension (first priority was given to clients of the Arts Council of England or the Regional Arts Boards); the organization of European funding seminars; and participation in university and postgraduate training programs.

IAB also took on an applied research function, contracting to conduct research and information projects on a one-off basis. Each year the arts council would ask IAB to assess the information gaps in the field and indicate what IAB might be able to produce. It would then perhaps sign a supplemental contract with IAB to provide those services. For the Irish Arts Council, IAB completed a research project on comparative arts spending in various countries and has been developing an International Policy to assist in the Irish Arts Council's attempt to reposition itself as a development agency working through cultural policy. More recently, it worked for the Tokyo metropolitan government documenting and comparing concert admission prices in four world cities—London, Paris, Berlin, and New York. For the Arts Council of England, it completed a worldwide survey of travel grants available to artists and published *On the Road: The Start-up Guide to Touring the Arts in Europe* and *To Travel, Hopefully! A Guide to Travel Grant Opportunities*; and it has prepared a series of International Arts Briefing booklets, which summarize the policies, organizational structures, key contacts, and sources of information on the arts in different countries (Canada, France, Japan, the Netherlands, South Africa, Sweden and Finland [in one volume], and the United States).

But its contractual relationship with the arts council did not entirely guarantee the long-term stability of IAB. At the end of the original three-year period, the arts council felt obliged to change the nature of this contractual relationship and to open the provision of services to competitive tender. The contract was split into two separate parts—policy intelligence and international information. IAB won both contracts for a two-year extension, although substantive competition emerged during the bidding process. Around the same time, the European Union (E.U.) announced the creation of a system of Culture Contact Points, which would provide information services on the cultural programs of the E.U. in each member country. The system was designed to ask each country to name its own Culture Contact Point through a competitive process and to provide money to match the E.U. grant. In the first year of this program, IAB was also selected to be the official U.K. Culture Contact Point (though the government match never materialized). After one year, the Department for Media, Culture and Sport decided to award the Culture Contact Point to EUCLID International (discussed below) instead of to IAB. The arts council has been reevaluating its information services as well, though it is not yet clear in what direction it will move.

Over the years, the International Arts Bureau's purview gradually expanded well beyond Europe. Its traditional clients wanted more and more information on cultural policy and cultural opportunities in a wide variety of countries, and its client base grew to include clients from all over the world. Because IAB had been so closely identified with European concerns and because Fisher wanted to further distinguish his organization from the emerging private-sector competition, he decided to restructure the organization once again as International Intelligence on Culture.

International Intelligence on Culture provides many of the same services that were provided by IAB, including responding free of charge to inquiries and offering free surgeries to provide project-funding advice (both still supported under contract to the Arts Council of England), but it has broadened its purview considerably.

The International Arts Bureau published two periodicals. *International Arts Navigator* was a bimonthly newsletter that summarized activities in Europe with respect to funding, legislation, policy, and the like. This newsletter, one of the most complete then available in the field, was marketed to local governments, libraries, training institutions, networks and umbrella bodies, consultants, and agencies interested in international arts in the U.K. and elsewhere. The *International Arts Quarterly Digest* provided a summary of international issues related to the cultural sector and was produced on behalf of the Arts Council of England. It contained information on funding programs, cultural policies, publications, conferences, and other international news. The arts council distributed it free of charge on a quarterly basis along with copies of its *Arts Council News*.

These publications have now been replaced by *International Cultural Compass*. This service is designed to take fuller advantage of the newly available information technologies. Various versions of this service are available in hard copy, by e-mail, and through a Web site. While there is still a strong focus on prospective European Union legislation, policy developments, and programs emanating from the European Commission, the Council of Ministers, and the European Parliament, it is not simply focused on E.U. matters. Coverage now includes the programs of the Council of Europe and UNESCO, the activities of the many nonprofit cultural organizations and networks that have developed in the field, and the activities of a wide variety of governments and their cultural agencies. It attempts to provide complete documentation on new reports, publications, conferences, and training opportunities. Most importantly, the intent is not simply to repackage information that is otherwise available but to analyze and interpret that information.

Budget and Personnel

International Intelligence on Culture employs 3.5 full-time-equivalent staff in London—a director, an office manager, an information officer, and a part-time marketing person—and an additional staff member in Brussels to monitor E.U. programs. The annual budget has been approximately £175,000–£200,000, more than 60 percent of which has come from its contracts with the Arts Council of England (though this percentage is likely to decrease). Apart from the tendering process with the arts council and with the Department for Media, Culture and Sport, IIC generally does not bid for work. Rather, potential clients seek it out based on its reputation and past performance.

Assessment

Though a private corporation, International Intelligence on Culture continues to operate as though it has one foot in the public sector (it does not charge for many of its information-giving activities, it draws its staff from the public sector, and that staff is involved in a number of quasi-governmental and trans-European activities that are not reimbursed) and one foot in the nonprofit sector (all "profits" are reinvested in its work). Accustomed to operating in certain ways, IIC has found it difficult to operate in the newly competitive environment fueled by the provision of information services available on the Internet. It may be that the change in the environment for IIC is part of a more general sea change in which "old school" principles and ways of working are being replaced by "new school" principles. While the IIC has no peer when it comes to its depth of knowledge of the field, it is increasingly constrained in its ability to deliver that knowledge in a timely manner, and it has made itself vulnerable to services that deliver more quickly, albeit at a more superficial level. IIC illustrates nicely the questions that one has to address when deciding whether to locate the information function for cultural policy in the public, private, or nonprofit sectors.

It is also possible that with a renewed emphasis on research in the reorganized Arts Council of England, the need for particular types of information services will change in ways that will affect the work of the International Intelligence on Culture and its competition.

Interviews and Contacts

Rod Fisher
Director
International Intelligence on Culture
4 Baden Place
Crosby Row
London SE1 1YW
United Kingdom

Phone: 011-44-(0)20-7403-7001
Fax: 011-44-(0)20-7403-2009

e-mail: rod.fisher@intelCULTURE.org

Web Site

http://www.intelCULTURE.org

Documents and Publications Consulted

International Arts Bureau, "Empowering the Cultural Sector," brochure, no date.

International Arts Bureau, *The International Arts Country Briefings* (London, England: Arts Council of England, various dates). [Briefing books on the policies, organizational structures, key contacts, and sources of information on the arts in Canada, France, Japan, the Netherlands, South Africa, Sweden and Finland (one volume), and the United States.]

International Arts Bureau, "Publications List 2000," brochure.

International Arts Navigator, bimonthly newsletter of the International Arts Bureau, various issues.

International Cultural Compass, monthly publication of International Intelligence on Culture, various issues.

EUCLID International
Liverpool

Significance

EUCLID represents a new generation of actors in the cultural policy and research field: profit-making consulting groups. With an emphasis on information delivery through the new information technologies, EUCLID has emerged as a competitor to the more traditional research and information groups, many of which grew out of the public sector and still retain more of a public-service ethos. EUCLID and other organizations like it have entered the field, creating a much more complicated institutional ecology than had previously been the case.

Background

The roots of EUCLID date back to 1987 when Geoffrey Brown and two other partners founded an arts consulting firm, Positive Solutions. When the two other partners left the U.K. to set up a similar firm in Brisbane, Australia, Brown created EUCLID. EUCLID started with work that was very similar to Positive Solutions' work, particularly in education and training.

The event that led to restructuring EUCLID into a consulting organization more concerned with the arts and culture at the European level was the designation of Merseyside (where EUCLID was located) to receive special structural funds from the European Union. EUCLID saw an opportunity to pitch the arts as an economic regeneration tool and worked to get criteria to this effect into the E.U. funding guidelines. Brown realized that only a small percentage of the money that the European Commission spent on cultural projects actually came from budgets that were designated as "cultural."[31] He saw the chance both to tap that money and to help others tap that money at a European scale. The fact that European Union programs often required multiple partners in multiple countries before money would be granted also opened a window for individuals who could broker partnerships across countries.

At the time, there were very few continental consulting groups operating at the European level. There were many more British groups, but those groups tended to be large-scale, generic management/accounting firms. Brown attributes this to the gradual privatization that had occurred in the field during the Thatcher years. This privatization often required the services of consulting firms that could help design and manage the transition as well as assist the wide variety of private and nonprofit organizations in fulfilling the new documentation required by the public authorities to qualify for, and gain access to, public funding programs. Unlike the Council of Europe, which had been friendly to culture and had become accustomed to working with a wide variety of individuals and firms, the European Union was less accustomed to working with the field. Its standard procedure was to identify preferred vendors for possible consulting services, and the big accounting and consulting firms were the ones who managed to get themselves on the list. Very few had any relative expertise in the arts or culture, so here too was an opportunity.[32]

Recognizing this new set of needs and opportunities and also recognizing that clients for consulting services usually expected to contract for the time of the principal rather than the time of unknown staff, Brown restructured EUCLID once again, moving it away from doing applied research and toward providing information services. The idea was to create a much more flexible business that would take advantage of the widespread availability of the new information technology and would provide information services to the arts and culture at the European level. Brown's diagnosis of competing services that were available at the time, most notably the services of the then International Arts Bureau, was that they left a lot to be desired. He saw them as thorough and comprehensive but not adapting to the times. Information dissemination still relied, for the most part, on quarterly newsletters and the like, printed and distributed at great expense. This meant that information was often distributed too late to be useful. Moreover, these services were marketed to arts councils and arts-funding agencies that would pay for information to be provided to their clients. Brown thought he saw an opportunity for the electronic distribution of information directly to artists and arts organizations, who would pay for subscriptions if they were low cost and timely.

The European Union provides two types of funding programs: (1) structural funds, distributed to deprived areas, with decisions made at the local level with approval from Brussels; and (2) transnational funds, provided to transnational projects to bring people together and fuel trans-European cooperation. Each of the transnational programs has a small budget for the creation of a "Contact Point" in each country. This Contact Point is to provide information on the programs of the

European Commission and tell potential users how to access these funds. In part, the intention is that the official designation of Contact Points will actually stimulate interesting proposals.

The culture program of the E.U. has established Cultural Contact Points, and grants of between €30,000 and €80,000 per year have been distributed to support each of them. In each case, the national government designates the Cultural Contact Point for its country and is expected to match the E.U. funding. In fourteen countries, the Ministry of Culture (or its equivalent) opted to become the Cultural Contact Point itself; these tended to be the countries in which significant research departments still function within the ministry. In three countries—France, Germany, and Italy—the contract was given to independent agencies that are funded by government. In the case of the United Kingdom, it was decided to give the contract to a private, profit-making firm.[33] In the first round, the International Arts Bureau was invited to serve as the official Cultural Contact Point for the United Kingdom. EUCLID then inquired as to whether the Department for Media, Culture and Sport would be changing this designation in future years, and EUCLID was chosen for a trial year in late 1999.

This designation has provided a wedge for EUCLID, which now wishes to expand to the provision of other information services. For example, it would like to take over the arts council's contracts with International Intelligence on Culture; similarly, it would like to expand its work for the European Union to providing information on all funding with cultural content, not just the designated programs of the culture program. It has created an online subscription service, DICE (Direct International Cultural Exchange). This e-mail service provides regularly updated information to its list of subscribers. A key element of this service is the expectation that individual subscribers will also be the sources of much of the information that the service will contain. In other words, DICE is designed, in part, to provide automatic, no-cost publication for whatever news and information one wants to put out to individuals interested in the arts and culture. EUCLID hopes that the volume of this information will be sufficient to warrant a major compilation and codification effort so that the information can be easily stored in, and retrieved from, an electronic database on the DICE Web site. EUCLID is promising to produce DICE in at least six European languages.

Today, EUCLID describes itself as "an independent cultural research agency with a commitment to European and international information exchange." Its services revolve around the production and circulation of "Alert," its e-mail newsletter with roughly 3,000 recipients; the development of the subscription-based DICE system (which it is marketing to an e-mail list with some 12,000 addresses); the maintenance of a Web site; and, occasionally, the undertaking of a range of research and evaluation projects for U.K. and European agencies.

Personnel

EUCLID has three permanent staff members, two in Liverpool and one who staffs both the Cardiff and Brussels offices. In addition, several part-time people are employed for various tasks, and freelancers are hired to assist with specific projects.

Assessment

In its reorganized form, EUCLID represents a new type of actor in the field of cultural policy research and information. Taking advantage of the widespread availability of information technology, EUCLID is working to outdistance its competition in the delivery of information services. The catch is that EUCLID is generating very little *new* information and documentation on its own. Rather, it functions as a repackager, taking the information generated by others and distributing it by new mechanisms. Thus, in terms of content, it is hardly different from the newsletters already generated by International Intelligence on Culture, Culturelink, and CIRCLE, among others. For its new DICE initiative, it is relying on the willingness of actors in the field to submit much of the content, which it will then simply redistribute (much as is currently the case with Culturelink). It is hoping to create a relative advantage with respect to speed, with respect to publishing in multiple languages, and, eventually, with respect to whatever indexing it may be able to accomplish that will allow subscribers to access the database to answer individually crafted inquiries.

EUCLID also departs from earlier such firms in that it has focused its attention much more on the European Union than on the Council of Europe and, at least for the moment, seems to have a relative advantage in this regard.

The arrival of EUCLID on the scene has forced other research centers to rethink their strategies for delivering timely information, documentation, and advice. The risk is that content and quality will be sacrificed in a rush for fancier electronic distribution of information, and this has been the most common criticism of the information services that EUCLID provides.

Interviews and Contacts

Geoffrey Brown
Director
EUCLID International
46-48 Mount Pleasant
Liverpool L3 5SD
United Kingdom

Phone: 011-44-(0)151-709-2564
Fax: 011-44-(0)151-709-8647

e-mail: euclid@cwcom.net

Web Site

http://www.euclid.co.uk

Documents and Publications Consulted

EUCLID International, "DICE: Direct International Cultural Exchange," brochure describing Web-based subscription service, 2000.

EUCLID International, "Working for Culture," brochure describing the services of EUCLID, no date.

Cultural Trends
Policy Studies Institute
University of Westminster
London

Significance

Cultural Trends is an exception in the field of cultural policy research. It is a British journal whose mission is to provide, summarize, and interpret the statistical information that is available on the arts and culture. It quite consciously occupies a middle ground between the world of pure statistical information and the world of commentary and debate.

Background

Cultural Trends grew out of the work of the culture program of the Policy Studies Institute (PSI). PSI was originally created by the Rowntree Trust to provide an objective think tank to do research and comment upon a wide variety of public policy issues. Eventually, PSI became the largest independent research think tank in Europe. Outside of *Cultural Trends*, the culture program of PSI has probably been best known for its publication of two volumes of *Facts About the Arts*, a compendium of all of the available statistics on the arts and culture in the United Kingdom, and its series of widely cited studies directed by John Myerscough on the economic importance of the arts in Britain. A recent volume, *The U.K. Cultural Sector: Profile and Policy Issues*, is very much in the tradition of *Facts About the Arts*, but it goes well beyond these earlier efforts by including some twenty-five commissioned papers interpreting the available data subfield by subfield. This volume has received considerable attention in the British press.[34]

When the Rowntree Trust finally withdrew its core funding of the Policy Studies Institute, PSI was forced to subsist entirely on commissioned research, which was not sufficient to pay for overhead and maintain its core services. PSI was then purchased by the University of Westminster as a way of establishing research credibility for the university, even though PSI's work was reduced in scope. The university decided to keep PSI's employment and social welfare programs, which brought in the most research money, and to build them up as research specialties. Two other areas, ethnic minorities and culture, despite their small size, had developed high public profiles and were also kept functioning. At this point Sara Selwood, who was the remaining head of the culture program, was named a research fellow in the School of Communication, Design and Media of the university and was given the mandate of relaunching *Cultural Trends*, which happened in 1998.

Originally, *Cultural Trends* had been little more than a compendium of available statistics. Issues were prepared along broad themes, and whatever data were available were summarized and presented with little commentary. *Cultural Trends* was supported with approximately £90,000 per year from the various arts-funding agencies including the arts councils, the Crafts Council, and the British Film Institute. At this time, *Cultural Trends* did little more than add a column to the previous year's tables and publish more or less the same material once again. When funding for PSI collapsed, it appeared that the arts council was gearing up to take over this function when it launched its own ARTStat project. This project used up much of the money that had previously been available for *Cultural Trends*, forcing the journal to reevaluate its mission.

Today, *Cultural Trends* is a peer-reviewed journal with substantially wider coverage. Sara Selwood has worked to make it more readable and more interesting by inviting authors who are a bit outside of the field to contribute, and by publishing commentary. The journal now publishes new research as well as collating and interpreting existing data. It is published quarterly, and each issue has a theme focused on one of four broad sectors: visual material culture (museums, galleries, crafts, and the art trade); media; the performing arts; and the built environment. Each issue of the journal typically includes three articles: two on the theme of the issue and a third "cross currents" article, which examines more general themes such as the impact of the Internet; poverty and access to the arts; local government support for the arts; and so on. The journal currently has 400 to 500 subscribers. Costs are covered by subscription fees ($195 [£115] for individuals and $275 [£175] for institutions) and by Selwood's research fellowship, which supports her as the editor. The main subscriber base includes libraries, local authorities, arts-funding bodies, and consultants. Although the focus remains on the United Kingdom, recent issues have included a summary of the results of the 1997 Survey of Public Participation in the Arts in the

United States and a comparison of British, German, and American performing-arts data. Authors are generally not paid for their contributions.

Assessment

Cultural Trends represents a very different take on the interpretation and distribution of cultural policy–relevant data. Because it consciously attempts to combine solid statistical evidence with commentary and interpretation, it is unique in the field. When government research offices publish empirical results, they tend to shy away from much interpretation, preferring to leave interpretation to the predilections of the reader. On the other hand, when research results are reported by publications firmly rooted in the field of practice, rigor is often sacrificed. *Cultural Trends* is a model of how to occupy the middle ground, and it is worth monitoring to see how stable it can become in its new form. In the end, it does rely, of course, on the assumption that others will commission or support the basic research that it will then report and comment upon; it cannot function outside of a collaborative ecology of research on cultural policy. Because of the high cost of subscriptions, access is effectively limited to library and reference collections rather than facilitated through wide distribution to individuals in the field.

Interviews and Contacts

Sara Selwood
Quintin Hogg Research Fellow
University of Westminster
Editor, *Cultural Trends*
Policy Studies Institute
100 Park Village East
London NW1 3SR
England

Phone: 011-44-(0)20-7468-2288
011-44-(0)20-7468-0468
Fax: 011-44-(0)20-7388-0914

e-mail: selwoos@wmin.ac.uk
pubs@psi.org.uk

Web Site

http://www.culturaltrends.org.uk

Documents and Publications Consulted

Cultural Trends, Carfax Publishing for the Policy Studies Institute, various issues.

Myerscough, John, *Facts About the Arts* 2, 1986 ed., number 656 (London, England: Policy Studies Institute, September 1986).

Myerscough, John, ed., *Funding the Arts in Europe*, Studies in European Politics 8 (London, England: Policy Studies Institute, October 1984).

Myerscough, John, et al., *Economic Importance of the Arts in Britain* (London, England: Policy Studies Institute, 1988).

Myerscough, John, et al., *Economic Importance of the Arts in Glasgow*, (London, England: Policy Studies Institute, 1988). [Similar reports on Merseyside and Ipswich are also available.]

Nissel, Muriel, *Facts About the Arts: A Summary of Available Statistics*, number 615 (London, England: Policy Studies Institute, September 1983).

Selwood, Sara, ed., *The U.K. Cultural Sector: Profile and Policy Issues* (London, England: Policy Studies Institute, 2001).

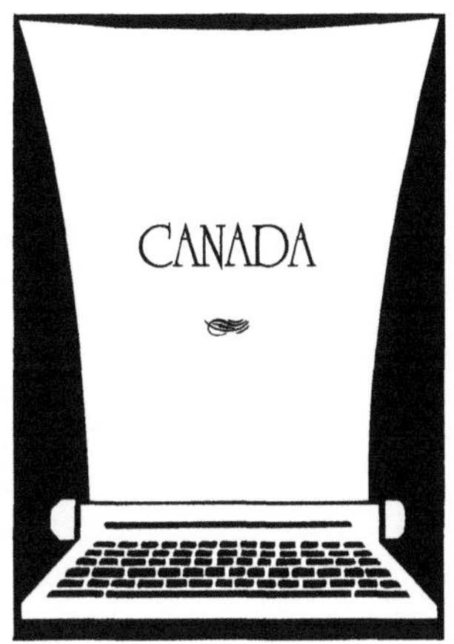
CANADA

Canadian Heritage
Strategic Research and Analysis Directorate
Hull, Québec

Significance

The Strategic Research and Analysis Directorate of Canadian Heritage represents an approach to cultural research that is policy driven. It is unusual among the national organizations considered in this book in the extent to which its work is explicitly involved in international comparisons. Perhaps more than some of the other countries whose research and information systems are considered here, Canada has developed the habit of looking elsewhere for models as well as the habit of participating in international comparative work. This is undoubtedly due to the ever-present realization that Canadian culture draws upon two main European traditions, the British and the French, as well as the traditions of its indigenous peoples and of other immigrant groups.

Description

Canadian Heritage is the national government department responsible for policies and programs related to the arts and heritage, broadcasting, the cultural industries, Canadian identity, multiculturalism, official languages, and sport. In 1993, Canadian Heritage was combined with the Canadian Conservation Institute, the Canadian Heritage Information Network, and the Cultural Property Export Review Board to comprise the government's Canadian Heritage Portfolio in order to consolidate the national policies and programs that seek to maintain Canada's cultural sovereignty and to promote Canadian identity.

This portfolio also includes eight departmental agencies: the Canada Information Office, the Canadian Radio-Television and Telecommunications Commission (an independent regulatory agency), the National Archives of Canada, the National Battlefields Commission, the National Film Board of Canada, the National Library of Canada, Parks Canada, and Status of Women Canada. Ten Crown corporations also operate, more independently, under this portfolio: the Canada Council for the Arts (visual and performing arts), the Canadian Broadcasting Corporation, the Canadian Film Development Corporation (Telefilm Canada), the Canadian Race Relations Foundation, the Canadian Museum of Civilization (including the Canadian War Museum), the Canadian Museum of Nature, the National Gallery of Canada (including the Canadian Museum of Contemporary Photography), the National Museum of Science and Technology (including the National Aviation Museum and the Canada Agriculture Museums), the National Arts Centre, and the National Capital Commission. The Public Service Commission also reports to Parliament through the Minister of Canadian Heritage.

In a government department as expansive as Canadian Heritage, one would expect to find multiple pockets within which research is being conducted, and that is indeed the case. Many of the offices of Canadian Heritage have a researcher or two who are on call to produce research related to the work of that office. This study focuses on one existing office and a new initiative, both of which cross over multiple areas of interest within Canadian Heritage and make up the primary transversal research capability of the agency. But note that both of these must be understood in the context of the ecology of cultural policy research in the Canadian government, which includes the Culture Program of Statistics Canada and the research unit of the Canada Council.

The Strategic Research and Analysis Directorate is the closest thing to an agency-wide research division within Canadian Heritage. When Canadian Heritage was created, the directorate was established to provide a critical mass of social science expertise and research within the department. The idea was that each of the many offices of the department did not need, for example, its own econometrician; one econometrician could be shared through the directorate. Like the *Département des Études et de la Perspective* of the French Ministry of Culture and Communication, its emphasis is on the social and economic aspects of culture, but what distinguishes the Strategic Research and Analysis Directorate from other research divisions is its substantial investment in international comparative research.

The directorate is divided into three groups: the Economic Research Group, the Social Research Group, and the International Comparative Research Group. Each group employs approximately six people, so the balance among the groups is fairly even. The goal of the directorate is to provide the minister with analysis that feeds into the department's strategic management needs. That is to say, the research is typically linked to either cultural policy or agency management concerns.

Recently, the Economic Research Group has focused considerable attention on the economic impact of the arts and culture and tried to develop a set of tools that would allow it to better isolate net effects and true benefits. (This is a sector of cultural policy research that has been plagued with shoddy work, often to the detriment of the government agencies that have commissioned it for political reasons.) In this vein, this group has commissioned the development of a "Socio-Economic Benefits Framework Applied to the Cultural Sector." It is also working on improving the measurement of the percentage of gross domestic product that is attributable to culture.

A major emphasis for the department, and therefore for the directorate, is the use of economic information in advocacy. The department is fond of citing the case of tourism. The tourism agency's budget had eroded over the years even while the government was mounting an effort to build a satellite tourism account as part of the national accounts. It discovered that tourism was an industry that generated on the order of $13 billion to $14 billion Canadian per year. This realization of the magnitude of the sector was parlayed into a new budget for government tourism programs of $50 million Canadian per year plus partnership money from the private sector in about the same amount. Here, the economic impact argument clearly worked (in the sense of freeing additional resources), but the directorate is highly critical of the statistical and economic work that was done because it believes the analysis did not take adequate account of the redistributive nature of much tourism spending (i.e., whether a Canadian citizen makes tourism expenditures in one part of Canada or in another is immaterial from the economic standpoint of the country as a whole).

The role of the International Comparative Research Group is to be ready to look elsewhere at what is happening in a particular policy area and to collect this information in a timely way. Accordingly, it maintains many international contacts. Typically, this group will respond to a request by collecting ten to fifteen relevant documents from other countries and preparing a synthetic document that summarizes its findings and discusses their implications in the Canadian context. The work of this group is, in some ways, defensive. It wants to be able to answer "Yes" when asked if it has checked on what other countries are doing.

The Social Research Group focuses on demographic and socioeconomic research, undertaking research, for example, into the societal implications of globalization, North American integration, the new information and communication technologies, and the changing nature of Canadian society. Like the other groups, it commissions research by outside consultants and academics as needed. This group has expertise in both qualitative and quantitative social research.

The directorate visits the various offices within Canadian Heritage, soliciting requests for research. "In the early days we went around and beat the bushes. . . . People got used to us." An important element in getting the research ball rolling was that the directorate had funds it would use as an incentive for cost sharing. At the beginning, it had $250,000 Canadian in the discretionary pot for cost sharing (over and above the costs of permanent personnel); today, it has $800,000 Canadian. The staff believes it is absolutely necessary to have that research pot to promote research. Nevertheless, the research funds beyond staffing have been limited, and the directorate must partner with a variety of agencies and institutions to carry out the research it would like to do. But, as Director Dick Stanley points out, "If you spend all your time beating the bushes for money, you don't do any research."

Now that the directorate has been able to establish itself within Canadian Heritage, it has a bit freer rein to do projects that it thinks will be of use to the department. Today, about half of its work is in response to the minister's requests, and about half is related to more strategic issues with a longer time horizon. A current example of the latter is a commissioned economic study that will evaluate if cultural goods are strategic goods necessary to society building (above and beyond their economic role). The working hypothesis is that cultural goods are a "symbolic resource that society has to have to keep itself together." Clearly, this is rather experimental and does not respond to any particular ministerial decision making. Yet, because the directorate is able to begin to look further into the future and because the theme of "culture and social cohesion" is in the air, it is free to move in this direction.

The directorate does not operate alone within Canadian Heritage, however. There has been a proliferation of program-related research groups and research capacity throughout the department. As its role moves more toward looking strategically to the future, other capacities have been created with a particular focus on industrial organization in each substantive area of the department. In part this has to do with internal departmental politics; areas that thought they had been perceived as "poor cousins" concluded that they had to build up their own research capacity to get on the policy map. Of course, not all of these efforts have been conducted to the same level of quality, and policy research in some areas is, quite simply, more difficult than it is in others.

The Strategic Research and Analysis Directorate has compiled an impressive repertoire of studies. Its annotated bibliography includes nearly 250 reports, documents, and articles completed over the last ten years on a wide-ranging list of topics.

The directorate maintains a library with some documentation capabilities. It is described as a "fugitive collection" containing whatever arrives in the researchers' in-boxes. As items are added to the collection, they are listed in a newsletter distributed to interested individuals and offices, and there is a computerized catalog, but the collection is limited (though strong on comparative cultural policy) and not well-known even among the other cultural agencies. (The research manager of the Canada Council did not know of the existence of this library until we held a meeting there during my visit to Canadian Heritage.)

Other Initiatives

The Strategic Research and Analysis Directorate is engaged in a number of other, multi-agency initiatives to develop an overall framework for cultural statistics. These initiatives are in response to the recommendation made by the Standing Committee on Canadian Heritage that Canadian Heritage should ensure that "the collection of statistics on cultural activity be of the same quality and timeliness as those now available for other sectors of the Canadian economy."[35]

The ideal would be to develop a "global positioning system" of data that would provide a reference point or framework within which cultural policy could be positioned. Excluding sports (for which a separate framework is being developed), Canadian Heritage is moving toward the UNESCO statistical framework; departments and agencies are being asked to use this framework or explain why not. Canadian Heritage is working with a wide variety of agencies throughout the government at both the national and provincial levels to develop common methodologies and approaches. It is particularly concerned about the proliferation of research done by consultants hired by the government, who, in their view, often produce shoddy work.

To take one example, a Cultural Labor Force Working Group has been formed that includes Canadian Heritage, the Canada Council, Statistics Canada, the Cultural Human Resources Council, the Canadian Artists and Producers Professional Relations Tribunal, Human Resources Development Canada, and the Department of Foreign Affairs and International Trade, as well as some consultants who have been working with these partners. The goals of the working group are to adopt common definitions and categories that can be used across agencies, to provide for the exchange of information, to harmonize information needs, to reconcile data sources, and to maximize existing data collection. It is hoped that this effort will generate reports with key findings and help to determine a research and dissemination strategy.

There is a similar working group in the area of trade and investment, and another group on economic impact has concluded its work.

Assessment

The research record of the Strategic Research and Analysis Directorate is every bit as impressive as the research record of other major cultural policy research centers, but much of its work has been focused on the internal demands of Canadian Heritage. As such, the work of the directorate is very much in line with the recent move for research divisions to focus on research in the service of strategic decision making and policymaking. One consequence of this focus, however, is that the directorate has generally been ineffective or uninterested in disseminating the results of its work to a broader audience. To those who have worked in the field for a long time, it has been nearly invisible, and that is a shame. Moreover, its library and documentation services have not received the visibility that they warrant. There is a capability to provide information and documentation services to the field that has not yet been realized. (This is all the more unfortunate, given that the commitment to the Canada Council's library has been mixed over the years.)

With plans for the creation of a new cultural observatory in Canada (see below), the work of the directorate is likely to remain behind the scenes. It is quite possible that the observatory will become the focal point for much of the research, information, and documentation on cultural policy in Canada.

Interviews and Contacts

Dick Stanley
Director
Strategic Research and Analysis Directorate
Canadian Heritage
25 Eddy St., 12th Floor
Hull, Québec K1A 0M5
Canada

Phone: 1-819-997-1662
Fax: 1-819-997-6765

e-mail: dick_stanley@pch.gc.ca

Also Interviewed

LUC PERRON, Senior Economic Analyst, Economic Research Group, Strategic Research and Analysis Directorate

BRUCE JAMIESON, International Comparative Research Group, Strategic Research and Analysis Directorate

JOHN FOOTE, Manager, Economic Research and Analysis, Strategic Planning and Policy Coordination, Cultural Development

JOSÉE PÉLOQUIN, Industry Analyst, Research, Analysis and Compliance, Publishing Policy and Programs

Other Canadian Heritage Staff Who Participated in Group Meetings

FRANCE TRÉPANIER, Senior Policy Analyst, Arts Development and Programs

ROMA QUAPP, Policy Analyst, Arts Financing and Legislation

ELIZABETH MACKINNON, Arts Policy Branch

ANNE-MARIE MCSWEEN, Copyright Policy

JANE CONDON, Head, Program Policy, Documents and Publications Assistance Program, Cultural Industries Policy

SOPHIE LALIBERTÉ, Industry Analyst, Research, Analysis and Compliance, Publishing Policy and Programs

WEB SITE

http://www.pch.gc.ca/

DOCUMENTS AND PUBLICATIONS CONSULTED

Cultural Industries Sectoral Advisory Group on International Trade, *Canadian Culture in a Global World: New Strategies for Culture and Trade*, February 1999.

Economic Research and Analysis, Strategic and Policy Coordination, Cultural Development, Canadian Heritage, "Cultural Participation Trends: Statistics Canada GSS 1992 and 1998," May 2000.

Government of Canada, *Connecting to the Canadian Experience: Diversity, Creativity and Choice—The Government of Canada's Response to "A Sense of Place—A Sense of Being," the Ninth Report of the Standing Committee on Canadian Heritage* (Ottawa, Canada: Minister of Public Works and Government Services Canada, November 1999).

Outspan Group, "Socio-Economic Benefits Framework: Cultural Sector," discussion paper prepared for the National Arts Center, the National Capital Commission, and the Department of Canadian Heritage, March 1999.

Standing Committee on Canadian Heritage, *A Sense of Place—A Sense of Being: The Evolving Role of the Federal Government in Support of Culture in Canada*, ninth report, June 1999. [http://www.parl.gc.ca/InfoComDoc/36/1/CHER/Studies/Reports/cherrp09-e.htm]

Standing Committee on Canadian Heritage, *The Challenge of Change: A Consideration of the Canadian Book Industry* (Ottawa, Canada: Public Works and Government Services Canada–Publishing, June 2000).

Strategic Research and Analysis, Department of Canadian Heritage, "Annotated Bibliography," 28 July 2000.

The Canada Council for the Arts
Public Affairs, Research and Communications Division
Research Unit
Ottawa, Ontario

More information, more statistics, more interpretation, more ideas.

SHIRLEY THOMSON

Significance

The relatively new Public Affairs, Research and Communications Division of the Canada Council for the Arts is the only one of the institutions considered here to combine explicitly research, planning, advocacy, and communications into one office. The rebirth and reconfiguration of research at the Canada Council, after a distinguished history followed by a relatively fallow period, encapsulates well the changing fortunes of the research function within arts-funding agencies.

Description

From the late 1970s through much of the 1980s the research and evaluation office of the Canada Council had a substantial national and international reputation for the quality and the quantity of research and documentation that it provided on the arts and culture in Canada. Unfortunately, budgetary restrictions and, to a lesser degree, a personality conflict eventually led to a nearly complete dissolution of the council's research efforts including its library and documentation center.

But another important factor—one that should not be minimized—fueled these events as well. As the research and evaluation office achieved a higher and much valued profile throughout the arts field in Canada, the program divisions of the Canada Council began to resent that profile and to question the investment of money in research rather than in direct assistance to artists and arts organizations. This critique became even stronger in response to large-scale research projects that were intended to develop a solid base of statistical information documenting the profile of the arts in Canada; these projects were not seen as particularly useful for the day-to-day decisions of the Canada Council. As has already been seen in other cases, this tension is one that is particularly palpable when the research function is housed within the primary funding agency rather than being structured through an institution that is at a greater distance from the direct funding function because within the primary funding agency the trade-off between research funding and program funding becomes more visible.

Although it never disappeared entirely, the research function was restructured four or five times over this period. Research was still required for speeches and press releases, but little of a more substantive nature was generated. In 1995, the staff of the Canada Council was cut in half (though not the grants budget), and at the same time the data services relating to council clients provided by Statistics Canada went from annual to biennial. At that point, research was moved into the Arts Program Division to become a service to the staff running the council's programs. Research became very program oriented.

In late 1998, Shirley Thomson, director of the Canada Council, reversed this earlier trend and announced that she was planning a "more coordinated approach to research, planning, communications, and advocacy." She was struck by renewed calls from the field for "more information, more statistics, more interpretation, more ideas." In the meantime, the fortunes of the council had changed as well. Parliament came to perceive the council as an increasingly "lean and mean machine" and rewarded its commitment to organizational efficiency by increasing its budget by $25 million Canadian per year for five years.

While some of the newly valued research and information tasks were already being handled in various corners of the organization, it was thought that a new, coordinated approach was necessary, particularly in the face of several new pressures facing the council. What eventually became known as the Public Affairs, Research and Communications Division was formed.

One important factor in the council's decision to revive and reorganize these functions came in response to the view from both inside and outside the organization that the council needed to devote more attention to strategic planning. This was particularly in response to an increasing call for performance measures and indicators against which the work of the council could be assessed. This, in turn, was linked in an important way to activities that were undertaken to tell the story of the work of the Canada Council during its first forty years. Another factor contributing to this reorganization was the sense that the Canada Council needed to become more proactive on behalf of the arts and artists (as well as on its own behalf) with regard to making claims on the public purse. Thus, advocacy became married to research. The reputation of the Canada Council and the quality of the information on which it based its work were both seen as being at stake.

The plans for this new office initially called for three separate streams in its work—research, planning and policy, and public affairs—but in the fall of 2001 the office was reorganized once again to reflect the increasing demand on its work. The Public Affairs, Research and Communications Division now includes five units: public and media relations, outreach (audience and market development), production services (writing and editing), business management (division support, Web design, and Web site maintenance), and research.

The functions of the reconfigured research unit include:

- The analysis of arts and cultural statistics
- The analysis of trends to inform the work of the section heads (the directors of the office dealing with various art forms)
- Audience studies
- Monitoring of domestic arts issues
- Liaison with respect to international trends, issues, and studies, including interaction with the Canadian Commission for UNESCO
- Publication of a journal
- Running a resource center (library and documentation center)
- Commissioning original research

But this list does not really capture the importance that advocacy has assumed in conjunction with the research function. The Canada Council's *Corporate Plan 1999–2000 to 2001–2002* spelled this relationship out much more clearly, and because the advocacy role of research is rarely acknowledged explicitly, it is worth looking at the ideas contained in the *Corporate Plan* in some detail.

Under the corporate priority to foster and promote the study and enjoyment of the arts is the operational objective to "advocate Canadian arts, artists, arts groups and arts-related issues to the Canadian public." The plan then records the strategies that will be used to achieve this, the performance indicators that will be used to measure this, and the impact that the council expects to see. First, the strategies:

- Create a research, analysis, and communications unit at the council
- Collect and interpret data for public use
- Expand the council's prizes and awards programs
- Create and produce a yearly council communications plan
- Create advisory committees when necessary from business and government to strengthen the council's position on public policy issues, management, and marketing
- Develop customized advocacy position papers on arts issues
- Participate in or create public forums for discussion of the arts and arts-related issues (e.g. taxation, globalization, and new communications technologies)
- Maintain and reinforce existing goodwill among the council's contacts
- Expand staff, management, and board contacts with target audiences

The council intends to tap this research/advocacy function to develop a new language to respond to conflict and controversy in arts funding. It maintains that it is searching for new justifications for what it does, a trend that is reflected throughout the cultural policy research world, whether in North America or Europe or elsewhere.

It is clear that, in this new structure for the council, research is to be particularly valued for the role that it can play along the multiple fronts of advocacy. This becomes even clearer when one turns to the impacts that these strategies are expected to have:

- More favorable media reviews, editorials, and other forms of media coverage of the council, council-supported artists, arts organizations, and events
- A higher level of awareness of the council, its mandate, programs, and policies
- A higher level of awareness and interest in the artistic merit, originality, and excellence of the creations and productions of Canadian artists and arts organizations
- A higher level of awareness of public policy issues that impact on the creation and production of the arts in Canada
- A higher level of awareness of council initiatives, programs, mandates, and actions
- An increased number of acknowledgments of the council and an improvement in their form and effectiveness

To be sure, connecting research to advocacy is more easily done in an arm's-length arts council than in the heart of a government ministry. Nevertheless, it is unusual to see this much candor even among arm's-length agencies.

Rebuilding a research and information capability once it has been lost is not easy. For four years or so the council had no resources that it could use to continue collecting information. Thus, significant gaps exist. Nevertheless, the current staff seems committed to the view that research is necessary and that an ability to deliver research well and in a timely fashion will generate a demand for more such research from inside the council as well as from outside.

The reestablishment of the research function has been assisted by the development of a new awards-tracking system that is used to monitor the activities of the council. This system makes it rather easy to assemble most of the documents that the research unit is now producing. Some of the output of the unit is currently in the form of profiles of council funding presented by art sector or by province. Primarily descriptive, such documents further the renewed emphasis on advocacy. The research unit has also taken on the task of providing more detailed analysis of Statistics Canada data that pertain to the cultural sector but that otherwise would not find their way to individuals in the field. The unit also undertakes research projects on different sectors of the arts, such as a recent report on the condition of large performing arts organizations in Canada.

Such documents also provide background for the new Parliamentary Advocacy Program of the council. This program is the council's initiative to inform Parliament on a regular basis about the council's successes and about its activities in the members' provinces and among their constituencies. This initiative has resulted in an increasing level of information requests from Parliament.

The research unit has also taken on the internal task of preparing the council's annual *Report on Performance Indicators* as part of measuring its achievements under the *Corporate Plan*. These performance indicators are intended to measure the performance of the council itself in carrying out its various goals and objectives. This relatively recent effort may be unique among arts councils; at the very least, it is uncommon.

Finally, the research unit expects to be in the position of commissioning research projects from time to time, though it will have to be careful. A recent project is illustrative. In the fall of 1999, the council commissioned a study to ascertain what impact Canada Council individual artist grants have had on their grantees. The study concluded that these grants have a "profound and far-reaching impact on the creative lives and careers of artists." But this result has been seen by the press more as evidence of the council's self-interest (artists benefit from council grants), or as evidence of the fact that anyone would prefer more money more quickly with more flexibility, than as evidence of any real impact of these grants. This experience, the interpretation of which is likely to continue to be debated, nicely illustrates the complexities that arise when advocacy and research become intermingled within an agency with multiple objectives.

Like virtually all of the research offices within arts-funding agencies, the research office of the Canada Council has managed, for the most part, to steer clear of the shoals of evaluation. Except for one year, there has never been an evaluation program at the council. (In that year, two evaluations were completed, but then evaluation completely disappeared once again.) The staff would claim, with justification, that they do accomplish some evaluation, but always by another name. For example, some council programs are now being consciously designed as experiments; information will be kept and performance will be tracked in order to ascertain how the program is operating.

The research unit is cooperating with representatives of a number of federal agencies on the development of a framework for cultural statistics, particularly with respect to the newer themes of trade, labor force development, and consumer spending. Eventually, the hope is that all agencies working in the cultural field will agree to use a common framework or will have a reasonable explanation as to why not. The Cultural Labor Force Working Group, in which the Canada Council participates along with a number of other interested agencies and organizations, is a case in point. The research unit also collaborates with the Department of Canadian Heritage and other partners in commissioning and cofunding studies.

Budget and Personnel

Currently, the base budget of the research unit (not including the other parts of the division) is about $235,000 Canadian per year. This includes salaries for three people (the research manager, a junior research officer, and an access-to-information officer), totaling about $160,000 Canadian. In 2000, the division had an additional $170,000 Canadian for special one-time initiatives, including expenses related to the World Summit of Arts Councils (held in Ottawa at the end of November 2001), the Parliamentary Advocacy Program, and special research. Some advocacy-related projects that are research oriented may be funded through the divisional director's budget.

Assessment

The story of research at the Canada Council is a cautionary tale of the difficulties inherent in integrating a research capacity into an arts-funding agency. This is particularly true as it relates to the arm's-length council model, within which there traditionally has been less of an emphasis on research because of its facilitative funding style, as opposed to the ministry of culture model, within which there has been more of a natural emphasis on explicit policy development and implementation. The fact that research has persisted and has begun to grow in importance once again within the council is a testimony to the critical role that it is assuming in arm's-length public agencies, which are under increasing pressure to establish their credibility, responsibility, and accountability with respect to managing public resources.

Despite the rosy nature of much of this renewed emphasis on research within the Canada Council, the truth is that much of the work is still simply responding to press inquiries and the immediate needs of the director. A true research agenda for the council has not yet been reestablished, though there has been an increasing emphasis on developing a de facto joint research agenda at the federal level through collaboration and the funding of research projects across departments and agencies, particularly with Canadian Heritage. To what extent the research unit will return to the broad research mandate of the 1970s and 1980s remains to be seen, but that breadth may be less important now given the arrival of other governmental actors in Canada, most notably the Strategic Research and Analysis Directorate of Canadian Heritage, which has begun to increase its visibility and influence, and the proposed Canadian Cultural Observatory.

INTERVIEWS AND CONTACTS

CLAIRE MCCAUGHEY
Research Manager
Public Affairs, Research and Communications Division
The Canada Council for the Arts
350 Albert St.
P.O. Box 1047
Ottawa, Ontario K1P 5V8
Canada

Phone: 1-800-263-5588 x 4522; 1-613-566-4414 x 4522
Fax: 1-613-566-4411

e-mail: claire.mccaughey@canadacouncil.ca

Web Site

http://www.canadacouncil.ca

Documents and Publications Consulted

Canada Council for the Arts, Research Unit. Various profile documents:

"Arts Sector Profile #2: Artists in the Labour Force," July 1999.

"Arts Sector Profile #3: Performing Arts Companies Funded by the Canada Council—10 Year Audience Trend," June 1999.

"Profile of Funding to Manitoba, 1998–99," February 2000.

"Profile of Funding to Music, 1998–99," June 2000.

"Corporate Priority II: Dissemination and Communications," extract from *Corporate Plan 1999–2000 to 2001–2002*, The Canada Council for the Arts.

Planning and Research Section, The Canada Council for the Arts, "Corporate Plan 1999–2000: Interim Report on Performance Indicators, 1999–2000," report prepared for the meeting of The Canada Council for the Arts, 9–10 June 2000, May 2000.

"Some Notes for Discussion on the Communications and Research Function at the Canada Council," draft of an internal document, The Canada Council for the Arts, September 1988.

Thomson, Shirley, "A New Structure for the Public Affairs, Research and Communications Division," internal memorandum, The Canada Council for the Arts, 18 October 2001.

Thomson, Shirley, "Research, Planning, Communications and Advocacy," internal memorandum, The Canada Council for the Arts, 20 November 1998.

WME Consulting Associates, "The Impact of Canada Council Individual Artist Grants on Artist Careers: Results of Research on Grant Patterns and Discussion Groups with Individual Artist Grant Recipients," report for The Canada Council for the Arts, March 2000.

Statistics Canada
Culture Statistics Program
Ottawa, Ontario

Significance

The Culture Statistics Program of Statistics Canada, the national statistics agency, represents the model of a separately identified culture office within a broader statistics agency. The Culture Statistics Program has a mandate to collect data on the arts and culture and to mine data from other government agencies (as well as from outside) to present a statistical portrait of the extent and conditions of the arts and culture in Canada.

Description

The work of the Culture Statistics Program of Statistics Canada is built around eleven government surveys that are conducted either annually or biennially. These surveys are designed to provide a census of all the institutional activity in particular fields: heritage institutions; book publishers and exclusive agents; periodical publishing; performing arts; sound recording; music publishing; film, video, and audio-visual production; film, video, and audio-visual distribution and videocassette wholesaling; motion picture laboratory operations and production and post-production services; and motion picture theaters. These surveys are augmented by a number of others that either focus on culture or include data on culture in a broader survey instrument.

Beyond overseeing the implementation of surveys in the fields of culture and heritage, the Culture Statistics Program produces three different types of publications on a regular basis:

- *Canada's Culture, Heritage and Identity: A Statistical Perspective*. This biennial report is a detailed summary of all of the data collected by the Culture Statistics Program, augmented by other data from Statistics Canada and other government agencies. While quite comprehensive, it is often criticized for the time lag involved in its publication. The 1997 edition, which is the most recent version available, is, for the most part, based upon 1994 surveys. ($31 Canadian per issue)

- *Focus on Culture.* This bulletin is produced quarterly and includes a variety of articles discussing the results of recent Statistics Canada studies. It is similar in style to *Développement Culturel*, the newsletter of the research division of the French Ministry of Culture. ($27 Canadian per year)
- *"Shelf Tables."* The Culture Statistics Program generates a set of standard data tabulations when new survey data are released. No discussion or interpretation accompanies these tables, and the only analysis performed is that implied by the decision of which tables to produce. Obviously, the standard set of tables does not exhaust all of the possibilities for analysis in any set of survey data. ($50 Canadian per set) (Note: Customized tables can be prepared on an individual, proprietary basis, but this service is very expensive, as is the purchase of digital data sets, when it is possible at all.)

The issue of access to data is something of a sore point. On the one hand, Statistics Canada is reluctant to release data because of confidentiality concerns. On the other hand, by government policy its activities must be run on a cost-recovery basis, so if it were to sell data sets, they would be extremely expensive. Recently, Statistics Canada undertook a "Data Liberation Project," intended to find ways to make its data more accessible and more economical. One proposal is to sell databases to university culture and arts departments with training on how to use them in order to expand, in a sense, the analytic ability of Statistics Canada. In addition, the Culture Statistics Program of Statistics Canada has just written a $300,000 Canadian proposal to enhance its analytic capabilities at the regional/provincial level. At the moment, provinces can get the data for free through their statistical agencies, but only Québec is taking advantage of this possibility; this is especially the case in the area of culture.

The criticisms of the Culture Statistics Program seem to be the standard ones heard with respect to all government statistics agencies:

- *The production of publications and the dissemination of information are much too slow*, losing much of the value of the data.
- *The categories and concepts used for data collection do not respond well to the changing realities of the field.* With respect to this point, statistical agencies often find themselves

treading the thin line between ensuring comparability over time by retaining methodologies and procedures that may be less and less relevant or applicable, and evolving and redesigning measurement instruments that facilitate a more responsible tracking of changes in the field.

- *The work is not creative.* Indeed, curiosity does not seem to be encouraged. If the Culture Statistics Program were to propose to gather information that it had not collected previously, it would need to go through an arduous and uncertain process and indicate exactly how it would look at the new data before the data collection and analysis would be approved and funded. This is understandable given concerns about the inappropriate use of data by government, but it is difficult to explain to a field that believes it has particular data needs.
- *The program is poor at disseminating information.* Presumably, this critique applies to the difficulty and expense of access to the raw data as well as to the quality, frequency, and reach of information dissemination. Unlike Canadian Heritage or the Canada Council, Statistics Canada would not be proactive about marketing its information to the arts and culture sector; it perceives its job as generating information, and if the world wants it, the world will find it.

Budget and Personnel

The Culture Statistics Program of Statistics Canada has an annual budget of $1.5 million Canadian per year. A staff of approximately fifteen people oversees this work. One group of employees oversees the Culture Surveys. Another group, Research and Communications, mines data on the cultural sector that are generated in the normal operations of Statistics Canada, data collected by other government agencies, and data from outside; summarizes these data; and prepares a relatively fixed set of publications. For example, it would summarize data from the General Social Survey, supplementing it with respect to other data sources on cultural participation. While it claims to respond to demand as well as doing proactive work, the impression is that there is a set way of conducting business that is methodically followed. For the most part, provinces do not have researchers or analysts, so the Cultural Statistics Program partners with them to do profiles of various sorts for the provinces and for some localities. The exception is Québec, which operates its own statistical agency in collaboration with Statistics Canada.

Assessment

The Culture Statistics Program of Statistics Canada provides a constant and predictable flow of data on the arts and culture that might well be envied in other countries. Having these functions under the umbrella of the national statistics agency, which has good reason to be careful and scientifically sound, undoubtedly enhances comparability and accuracy. But this comes at the cost of distancing the data from the ongoing and changing concerns of the sector. By itself, the program would not provide a sufficient source of data and information for cultural policy purposes, but it does play a role in the Canadian cultural policy research and information infrastructure. As such, it illustrates both the advantages and disadvantages of having the national statistics office play a formal role in the collection and distribution of data on the arts and culture.

Interviews and Contacts

Michel Durand
Chief
Research and Communication Section
Education, Culture and Tourism
Statistics Canada
R. H. Coats Building, 17-C
Ottawa, Ontario K1A 0T6
Canada

Phone: 1-613-951-1566
Fax: 1-613-951-9040

Web Site

http://www.statcan.ca/start.html

Documents and Publications Consulted

Statistics Canada, *Canada's Culture, Heritage and Identity: A Statistical Perspective*, 1997 edition (Ottawa, Canada: Statistics Canada, 1997).

Statistics Canada, "Canada's Culture, Heritage and Identity: A Statistical Perspective," internal document summarizing data sources and publications available from Statistics Canada, no date.

Statistics Canada, *Focus on Culture*, quarterly bulletin from the Culture Statistics Program, Vol. 11, No. 4, Winter 1999.

Canadian Heritage
The Canadian Cultural Observatory
Hull, Québec

Data never speak for themselves.

TERRY CHENEY

Significance

The Canadian Cultural Observatory project is a new initiative being developed within the Cultural Development (broadcasting and cultural industries) area of Canadian Heritage. It is yet another of the newly created or proposed cultural observatories. Because this observatory is under development, it is premature to predict what shape it will eventually assume. Indeed, whether it will be housed within Canadian Heritage is uncertain as of this writing. What is of interest here is the fact that the initiative has grown out of a demand for better and more easily available data on broadcasting and the cultural industries, an area of government policy that is receiving increasing attention in many countries and one that has a particular need for high-quality data because of the importance of regulation in that area.

Description

Because it was encountering increasing difficulty in finding pertinent and accurate data on which it could base policy, the Publishing Policy group of Canadian Heritage hired an independent consultant, Terry Cheney, to assess the data that were available and to make recommendations concerning how to improve the collection, quality, and analysis of those data, particularly with respect to the publishing industry. In some ways, the result was not surprising.

What Cheney found was that each sector had its own constellation of data sources including, among others, Statistics Canada, the program office within Canadian Heritage that deals with the sector, and service organizations and associations operating within the sector. In other words, a considerable volume of data is available, but the institutional capability for mining those data is limited. Accordingly, his first conclusion was to focus on using the data sources that already exist.

Still, he found that these sources were incomplete, inconsistent, and of varying quality. His assessment of current needs is telling:

> At the moment not only is there a lack of available instruments to gather data on vital areas, there is an erratic capacity to provide expert advice relating to data which do exist; there are few, if any, academic centres of excellence; consultants are called upon on an ad hoc basis; and there is no federal capacity to analyse and reflect upon culture industry data on a committed ongoing basis, within the Branch, within the Department, or at Statistics Canada. Statistics Canada is not, nor does it pretend to be, a cultural research centre. Absent the resources for the effective application of data found in other areas (health research, education research, forestry research . . .) *the development of statistics on culture has been adrift for many years*. There has been no accumulation of a body of knowledge, limited development of expertise, and little progression in the means of data collection or analysis.[36]
> [Emphasis in original]

When relying on multiple sources, one cannot access the data quickly or efficiently. Moreover, it is difficult to reconcile the various sources because they have not been designed with an eye to coordination and comparability.

Cheney's recommendation was that Canadian Heritage should move toward the creation of a Canadian Cultural Observatory that would take over the data collection, analysis, and dissemination function on a coordinated basis. This recommendation echoed a recommendation that had been made by the Standing Committee on Canadian Heritage and seemed almost inevitable given the proliferation of so-called cultural observatories in other countries and regions.

Cheney's vision was a broad and holistic one; he recommended that Canadian Heritage:

> [I]nitiate a feasibility study on creating a cultural industries "observatory" for Canada to provide long-term, comprehensive, independent information on the sector, to contribute to the development of consistent survey instruments, to develop a comprehensive analytic framework, to provide expert advice, to develop a critical mass of expertise able to address topical issues, and to serve as a breeding ground for developing careers in culture research.

> This observatory could carry out short-term surveys of the industry (capital spending and hiring projections); could take over the surveys of the nonprofit culture sector which is not in need of the strict, and restrictive, confidentiality requirements of Statistics Canada; [and] could provide independent estimates and projections of the universe of activity.[37]

The Assistant Deputy Minister of Cultural Development at Canadian Heritage took the lead and seconded one of his staff members, Michel Normandeau, to work full-time on designing the cultural observatory initiative. Preliminary work is under way with the goal of being online in 2003 with three people worked on the early conceptualization phase. It is envisioned that the observatory will ultimately have twelve employees during the development phase and sixteen employees when it is in full operation. As work on this book progressed, it was announced that Vladimir Skok had been appointed director of the new observatory, succeeding Michel Normandeau.

As he undertook the design of the observatory, Normandeau interviewed a wide variety of potential "clients" (users of the data and services that such an observatory might provide) and traveled around explaining to the field just what a cultural observatory could be. The questions under discussion included: What would be the scope of the field that it would cover? Should it conduct research? Participate in research? Or should it provide a network through which the research results of others could be digested, summarized, interpreted, and disseminated? Could industry be co-opted to play a role? ("If we see that industry is using the information we create, then we must be giving value.") Would the observatory be located within a university? Within Canadian Heritage? Aligned with some other research institute (e.g. the Institute for Research in Public Policy in Toronto)? Or would it become an independent institution on its own?

From the data-quality perspective, it is hoped that an observatory functioning as a separate, if not entirely independent, entity will be able to balance the advantages of private-sector data collection with the advantages of public-sector data collection. To quote Cheney once again, "There is no way Statistics Canada can match the timeliness and price of the private sector in terms of data collection. There is no way the private sector can match the quality and credibility of Statistics Canada, and the potential of being integrated into overall national statistics. In terms of data gathering [the initiative] requires a two-pronged approach."[38]

The demand for this type of coordinated data agency seems to be coming from industry as well as from government. There is a general sense that there are a lot of data out there, but no one is quite sure how to access what is available. Ideally, they should be brought together in, and be retrievable from, one source.

Yet, the proponents of the Cultural Observatory seem to be cognizant of its potential pitfalls, particularly its attractiveness to private interests. One cautionary tale provides a reference point to which its proponents often refer. About ten years ago the Department of Tourism established the Canadian Tourism Research Institute, which was intended to provide documentation and research. The original attempt was to launch it in collaboration with Canadian universities, but this initiative failed. It was then lodged with the Conference Board, a private organization. The result was that it became more of a consulting group that now functions as a profit-making business. Operating within the context of numerous consulting groups with more or less expertise in the tourism area, it has failed to become the consulting group of choice, but, more importantly, its agenda has been shaped by its location on the private-industry side of tourism.

Proponents are also very conscious of the fact that creating an observatory in the age of the Internet has other implications. Because more and more initiatives are online and because the digital transfer of information is becoming easier and easier, there will undoubtedly be competition to a publicly supported observatory initiative. It also means that the potential clientele will be larger. The intent is very much to provide the information services of the observatory through a Web site, bringing it in line with the federal "Government On-line" initiative.

At the same time, the Internet allows for much more specialization in the supply of information, so the proponents of the initiative have to be concerned about the degree to which they must be specialized to be useful. But would that herald a return to compartmentalization in cultural policy research, a tendency that ministerial research divisions, and the idea of an observatory itself, were intended to counter?

The cultural observatory will be positioned to take advantage of the Policy Research Initiative set up in the Canadian federal government in 1997. That broadly based initiative put in place a capability to monitor societal changes that would affect policy. Canadian Heritage has participated in a number of areas, looking at historical trends, making predictions a few years into the future, and conducting literature reviews. Its Strategic Research and Analysis Directorate has been investigating the role of culture in social cohesion and its role in Canada-U.S. relations. The Policy Research Initiative has developed data sets that were not previously available, and the beginnings of a rather substantial literature have been established. But this initiative has done a better job at producing research than at disseminating it. Thus, a role for something like a cultural observatory can be easily imagined.

In the Canadian context there is one important factor that would limit the work of an observatory if it were to operate as a public agency: the requirement that all publications, information, and Web sites be bilingual. Translation costs money and takes time. Interestingly, an observatory that is independent of government would not be subject to the same language requirements.

The recent announcement of the creation of *L'Observatoire de la Culture et des Communications* at the provincial level in Québec has upped the ante for the national government. If there is justification for such an institution at the provincial level, they believe, surely there is justification at the national level.

Assessment

It is much too early to predict how this initiative will fare. As planning and development proceed, there is also an effort under way to find out exactly how the various observatories in place worldwide are structured and how they function. The common terminology does not belie a common model; Canada will have to invent its own.

Michel Normandeau's vision was to provide one-stop shopping for cultural data: "There is so much going on. You want a kind of marketplace that you can go to so you will know that if you have gone there you will have seen all the booths." There is a commitment to proceed despite the tremendous coordination and methodological problems that lie ahead.

Interviews and Contacts

Michel Normandeau
Secretary General
Canada Music Fund Council
Canadian Heritage
(former Director, Canadian Cultural Observatory)
15 Eddy St, 6th floor
Hull, Québec
Canada
K1A 0M5

Phone: 1-819-997-5848
Fax: 1-819 997-5709

e-mail: Michel_Normandeau@pch.gc.ca

VLADIMIR SKOK
Director, Canadian Cultural Observatory
Canadian Heritage
15 Eddy St.
3rd Floor, Room 65
Hull, Québec K1A 0M5
Canada

Phone: 1-819-953-8562
Fax: 1-613-762-6351

e-mail: vladimir_skok@pch.gc.ca

Also Interviewed

YANA HOF, Canadian Cultural Observatory

TERRY CHENEY, T. J. Cheney Research Inc.

WEB SITE

http://www.pch.gc.ca/obs/index_e.cfm

DOCUMENTS AND PUBLICATIONS CONSULTED

Cheney, Terry, "Summing Up . . . Better Data in an E-Culture Age: DGCI Needs for Better Data—A Review and Recommendations," report prepared for Research, Analysis and Compliance, Publishing Policy and Programs, Canadian Heritage, February 2000.

Government of Canada, *Connecting to the Canadian Experience: Diversity, Creativity and Choice—The Government of Canada's Response to "A Sense of Place—A Sense of Being," the Ninth Report of the Standing Committee on Canadian Heritage* (Ottawa, Canada: Minister of Public Works and Government Services Canada, November 1999).

International Relations, Canadian Heritage, "Summary of Questionnaires," report of the results of a survey of cultural observatories prepared for the UNESCO workshop on the creation of an International Network of Observatories on Cultural Policies, 2000.

Standing Committee on Canadian Heritage, *A Sense of Place—A Sense of Being: The Evolving Role of the Federal Government in Support of Culture in Canada*, ninth report, June 1999. [http://www.parl.gc.ca/InfoComDoc/36/1/CHER/Studies/Reports/cherrp09-e.htm]

Telescope: News from the Canadian Cultural Observatory, premier issue, November 2001.

Institut de la Statistique du Québec
L'Observatoire de la Culture et des Communications
Québec City, Québec

[J]e n'ai jamais vu de secteur aussi mal documenté que celui des arts de la scène.

PIERRE-OLIVIER SAIRE
Le Devoir—February 5, 2000

Pour obtenir un portrait complet de notre réalité culturelle et en suivre l'évolution.

AGNÈS MALTAIS

Significance

The Québec *Observatoire de la Culture et des Communications* is another example of the proliferation of "cultural observatories," this one at the provincial level in Canada.

Description

On June 27, 2000, the Québec Minister of Culture and Communications, Agnès Maltais, announced the creation of an *Observatoire de la Culture et des Communications* (OCC). This observatory, a partnership of the provincial Ministry of Culture and Communications, the Council of Arts and Letters of Québec, and the Society for the Development of Cultural Enterprises, will be based within the *Institut de la Statistique du Québec* (ISQ), the provincial statistics agency.

The observatory will gather together in one place the production and release of statistical data that heretofore have been collected and disseminated by various sources. It will be responsible for:

- Establishing and updating a list of the organizations, enterprises, and primary actors active in the fields of culture and communications

- Implementing surveys, gathering data from existing statistical data sources, and establishing consortia for the purchase of data
- Creating several nonconfidential data banks
- Distributing and communicating the information gathered through publications and activities

By creating this unit within the provincial statistics agency, the hope is to increase the reliability of the data in the cultural field, to take advantage of the agency's professionalism, and to gain a level of neutrality. By creating a separately named unit, the intention is that the unit will be able to go beyond the traditional boundaries of the activities of the statistical agency within which it will be located. Its creation is viewed as a way of sustaining the development of expertise in cultural research in the province.

Eight advisory committees represent the different sectors of activity in the fields of culture and communications, the university sector, and local municipalities. Each one of the committees is, in turn, represented on the board of the observatory.

The first year's budget was $940,000 Canadian, and it was supported by four funding partners: the Québec *Ministère de la Culture et des Communications*, the *Conseil des Arts et des Lettres du Québec*, the *Société de Développement des Entreprises Culturelles*, and the *Institut de la Statistique du Québec.*

Although it is not spelled out in the materials describing the new observatory, it is quite possible that its creators see it as linked to the decision by UNESCO to site its new Institute of Statistics in Montreal. This new institute is intended "to strengthen the capacity of [UNESCO] member states to compile and analyze statistical data in the fields of education, science, culture and communications, and to design training and development programs."

Assessment

Although it is too early to tell what direction *L'Observatoire de la Culture et des Communications* will eventually take and what success it will have, it is interesting to note that, at least in the province of Québec, a consensus has developed that it would be better to make policy on the base of a commonly held reservoir of information. Whether a highly integrated agency that seems poised to take on all aspects of the collection, analysis, and dissemination of data and research results will prove to be better than a more disaggregated system with a clear division of labor remains to be seen. Nevertheless, the *Observatoire* has its Web site up and running, and a growing array of statistical data on the cultural life of the province is already available there. The first issue of the quarterly bulletin of the observatory was published in March 2001, and it, too, is available online.

The fact that a cultural observatory had been announced at the provincial level in Québec drew attention at the national level and may well have been an impetus behind the creation of the national Canadian Cultural Observatory (see above).

Interviews and Contacts

Michel Durand
Chief
Research and Communication Section
Education, Culture and Tourism
Statistics Canada
R. H. Coats Building, 17-C
Ottawa, Ontario K1A 0T6
Canada

Phone: 1-613-951-1566
Fax: 1-613-951-9040

Serge Bernier [*not interviewed*]
Institut de la Statistique du Québec
200, chemin Sainte-Foy
Québec, Québec G1R 5T4
Canada

Phone: 1-418-691-2414 x 3137; 1-800-463-4090
Fax: 1-418-643-4129

e-mail: Serge.Bernier@stat.gouv.qc.ca

Web Site

http://www.stat.gouv.qc.ca/observatoire/default_an.htm

Documents and Publications Consulted

Baillargeon, Stéphane, "Observatoire en Vue!" *Le Devoir*, 20 May 2000, p. B8.

"Création de l'Observatoire de la Culture et des Communications," press release, Ministère de la Culture et des Communications, Québec, Canada, 27 June 2000.

Office of the Minister of Foreign Affairs, Media Relations Division, Government of Canada, "Montreal Chosen as Site for UNESCO Institute of Statistics," press release, 26 May 2000.

"Pour la Création d'un Observatoire de la Culture," 16 May 2000.

OTHER
COUNTRIES

Zentrum für Kulturforschung
Bonn, Germany

Significance

Like the *Département des Études et de la Prospective*, the *Zentrum für Kulturforschung* in Bonn, Germany, is one of the oldest and best-known research institutions working in the field of cultural policy. But it is fundamentally different from the *Département des Études* in that it is a private, profit-making firm that provides research, documentation, and information services to the field.

Description

The *Zentrum für Kulturforschung* (ZfKf) was created in 1969 as an offshoot of the German news magazine, *Der Spiegel*. Modeled on American-style think tanks, *SPIEGEL—Institut für Projektstudien*, as it was originally known, was created to engage in empirical studies in areas like the arts and culture that had been traditionally out of bounds for such research. Moreover, the center began with a strong predilection for unconventional research methods, particularly "action research" in which the boundary between objective social science research and arts activism in the field was intentionally blurred. Andreas Wiesand and Karla Fohrbeck were hired to direct the institute.

In 1972, Wiesand and Fohrbeck severed their relationship with *Der Spiegel*, formed a freelance consulting business, the *Zentrum für Kulturforschung*, and began to expand the institute's role to include research for public authorities, artists' organizations, foundations, and the media. In 1989 it was reorganized once again, this time as a real limited society because the government preferred to contract research services from an institutional business structure with which it was familiar. Even so, the structure of ZfKf is mixed, allowing a 25 percent minority interest to be held in public hands (though this has never materialized). Thus, ZfKf is today a private research firm that conducts research in a variety of areas related to the arts and culture.

Because of the federal nature of the German government, in many ways ZfKf has served as a kind of de facto ministerial research center (but without a supervising ministry of culture). Though the ZfKf now has an ongoing cooperative agreement with the Federal Ministry of Education and Science, which pays approximately 50 percent of its annual base budget, it has operated mainly from contract to contract and has not been able to engage in the ongoing basic research that other research centers have been able to undertake in other countries.

Over the last thirty years, ZfKf has:

- Conducted empirical surveys of arts professionals with an emphasis on legal and social issues
- Conducted studies and engaged in advisory tasks with respect to the development of the arts, the cultural infrastructure, and the cultural industries at regional, national, and international levels
- Conducted international comparative studies of arts and media policies and funding
- Designed and convened training programs
- Provided conceptual support to foundations, artists' associations, and research bodies
- Conducted surveys of public participation in cultural life
- Conducted applied anthropological research and cross-cultural studies

During the first ten years of the center, the real focus was on research concerning artists and writers, with work being done for government officials responsible for particular artistic sectors. Issues such as taxation and social security were important. In the 1980s there was an advocacy focus to the work of the center, which accompanied the change toward comparative work, particularly with respect to the cultural industries. During this period the German Arts Council *(Kulturrat)*, a consortium of some 220 member organizations in the arts and media, was founded with Andreas Wiesand as Secretary General. This council was created as a platform through which individuals and organizations in the field could meet with the government in Bonn, apparently operating in the area of advocacy and lobbying. Wiesand is reluctant to characterize this work as "advocacy," preferring the characterization "a portal to government."

In 1993, ZfKf pulled away from the *Kulturrat*, reestablishing to some degree the line of demarcation between advocacy and research. It continued its international comparative work and began a new emphasis on studies and research having to do with German reunification. More recently, contracts with the government have changed in nature once again. The Ministry of Education and Research is particularly interested in questions of training and professionalization, and other ministries are supporting work on the cultural industries. Also, the center is becoming involved in administering programs that previously would have been administered directly by government agencies. For example, ZfKf is organizing a model funding program on behalf of the central government and the *Länder* that will distribute 12 million DM over three years for programs dealing with the confrontation between various artistic fields and new technologies. This will provide much-needed funding, but ZfKf is concerned, and rightfully so, about the possibility of goal displacement.

Over the years, ZfKf has become very involved in European collaborative projects through CIRCLE, the Council of Europe, the European Union, and, most recently, through ERICArts. It assembled and published the *Handbook of Cultural Affairs in Europe*, which has appeared in several editions.

Today, ZfKf operates as a consortium of several interlinked institutional entities. ARCult is the institutional structure responsible for the library and archives of ZfKf, *Archiv für Kulturpolitik*. This library and documentation service comprises more than 15,000 volumes and archival boxes covering some 12,000 categories. When the new company was created, the archives had to be separated (under German law everything that was put into a company had to be valued). Approximately 40 percent of the collection is currently available; the rest is stored off-site. There is an internal computerized catalog, but nothing has been done on this for more than five years. (Because of the difficulty in maintaining and cataloging this collection, Wiesand would consider selling the collection to an interested party willing to set up and maintain a similar center. He estimates that approximately 10,000 books plus the dossier boxes would be of interest.)

ARCult Media is a nonprofit arm set up to run the publishing function of ARCult. There is a substantial flow of publications, since approximately 90 percent of its commissions generate books or reports of more general interest. ARCult Media publishes a newsletter, *Kulturforschung*, containing summaries of the various research projects in which ZfKf has been engaged; it publishes a series of books entitled *Media und Kultur* in which five titles have been published; and it maintains another series, *Kultur und Wissenschaft*, which is used to circulate reports to a broader audience in paperback form.

ARCult Media functions as a tax shelter; "profits," which would otherwise be taxed by the state, are channeled into ARCult Media to pay for its publishing programs. As Wiesand points out, because the demand for this type of publication is relatively limited, the publication function has to be cross-subsidized somehow; otherwise, ZfKf would have to pay others to do it, which would be considerably more expensive.

ZfKf is also developing a surveying service to conduct audience surveys and participation surveys at different levels. Finally, ERICArts (discussed elsewhere in this book) is also currently housed at the offices of ZfKf.

Because ZfKf entered the cultural policy research field quite early, it is part of the first generation of private entrepreneurs, a generation that has behaved rather differently from more recent generations of private entrepreneurs in the field. Partly this comes from the privileged status of having been one of the few to provide these services for many years, but it also comes from its involvement in early, collaborative trans-European projects and consortia where the differences in institutional status meant less than they appear to mean today.

When asked about the new competition from profit-making entrepreneurs, Wiesand does not seem too concerned. He prefers to see the early years as problematic: "We had the problem for twenty years of not having competition, so we could not be compared to others. We did not have the incentive to be better." Potential clients still seek it out, and, generally speaking, ZfKf does not have to run after commissions. This optimism notwithstanding, Wiesand must be concerned about the changing terrain within which ZfKf will have to operate as a private research firm.

Budget and Personnel

Prior to reunification, more funds were available for the sort of work ZfKf wanted to do. But, in Wiesand's words, "The funds dried up when the wall came down." The annual budget for ZfKf is now approximately 800,000 DM per year. About half of this comes from projects proposed to the German government under the ongoing cooperative agreement with the Federal Ministry of Education and Science.

In Germany, as elsewhere, there has been a clear shift toward "value for money" in government contracts. This has been accompanied by another trend—the privatization of the administration of what had previously been public programs. At one time during the transformation of the government, ZfKf received an additional 120,000 DM per year to administer the Fund for Arts Administration, and it is currently receiving approximately 100,000 DM per year for this type of activity.

This income, of course, brings with it the necessity of increasing the staff size. Nevertheless, ZfKf has profited from the tendency to outsource government services by administering and, to some extent, evaluating such programs.

There are six permanent internal staff, two closely related staff members, plus others who are picked up depending on the project load. At any one time, there may be eight to twelve people working under the auspices of ZfKf.

Assessment

The *Zentrum für Kulturforschung* has had a long and distinguished history in the field of cultural policy research. Its work is well-known, and it is in considerable demand. Because it has had to work project by project, it has not had the luxury of developing a continuing reputation in particular subfields. Perhaps this can be attributed to operating as a private firm without guaranteed support to maintain one or another area of specialty.

For economic reasons, ZfKf has found its attention pulled away from research toward a variety of activities to ensure cash flow, and it has tried its hardest to give such projects a research twist. One imagines that it is at some risk as the number of new entrepreneurs and new research centers in the field increases along with the inevitable pressure to spread the work around more evenly. It may be that those who do a better job of marketing and communication will replace those who continue the older style of operation based on strong connections, in-depth knowledge, and commitment. While its profile at the European level has risen, it has had to begin sharing the research attention with others at the national level.

Interviews and Contact

Andreas Wiesand
Director
Zentrum für Kulturforschung
Dahlmannstrasse 26
D-53113 Bonn
Germany

Phone: 011-49-(0)228-242-0996
Fax: 011-49-(0)228-241-318

e-mail: wiesand@ericarts.or

Web Sites

http://www.uni-bonn.de/~uzr604/zfkfe.html
http://www.kulturforschung.de/

Documents and Publications Consulted

KulturForschung, newsletter of ARCult and the Zentrum für Kulturforschung, various issues.

Zentrum für Kulturforschung, "The Centre for Cultural Research 1969–97," 1997(?).

"Zentrum für Kulturforschung," *Circular: Research and Documentation on Cultural Policies*, Nos. 4/5, 1996, pp. 30–31.

The Budapest Observatory: Regional Observatory on Financing Culture in East-Central Europe Budapest, Hungary

Significance

The Regional Observatory on Financing Culture in East-Central Europe (the "Budapest Observatory") is another of the new generation of cultural observatories. It was formed just recently, so there is little to be concluded at this point.

Description

The Budapest Observatory was founded with seed money from UNESCO and given a very particular vocation: to assist those seeking information about the ways that cultural life, cultural activities, and cultural products are being financed in eastern and central European countries. In other words, it was formed to provide a place through which information could be gathered and shared as government cultural policies made the leap from life under Communism to life after Communism. Its goal is to facilitate research, collect and provide information, and establish contacts in a variety of areas including the financing of culture, the design of cultural policy, the drafting of legislation, and the collection of statistics.

Contact

Péter Inkei
Director
The Budapest Observatory
Regional Observatory on Financing Culture in East-Central Europe
H-1251 Budapest, Pf. 27
Hungary

Phone: 011-36-1-487-0162
Fax: 011-36-1-487-0162

e-mail: bo@budobs.org

Web Site

http://www.budobs.org

Part II. Notes

1. At a June 24–26, 2001, workshop at UNESCO in Paris, "Research in the Arts and Cultural Industries: Towards New Policy Alliances," Andreas Wiesand of the *Zentrum für Kulturforschung* estimated that there are now nearly 100 major institutes for cultural policy research in the forty-eight countries of Europe, along with countless other less important ones.

2. The British section includes the somewhat anomalous case of *Cultural Trends*, a journal that plays an important role in the cultural policy research and information infrastructure in the United Kingdom.

3. Julia Lowell of the Rand Corporation has pointed out that perhaps the distinction between evaluation of policy and evaluation of programs is intended, in part, to "remove the onus from the 'grantee' and put it on the 'grantor'" (e-mail correspondence with the author, December 10, 2001). This is an interesting suggestion; it may well be the case. Still, she rightfully points out that it does not solve the logical problem of how one evaluates a policy without evaluating programs.

4. Now in (semi) retirement, Augustin Girard directs this effort.

5. The political travails of this effort deserve a case study of their own. According to Christopher Gordon, the agreement to move forward with the creation of the leadership group to coordinate the development of cultural statistics was reached in 1997 during the U.K. presidency of the European Union. The French, accustomed to thinking about these issues in a more structured way than other countries, had originally put forward their own rationale for a proposed approach to statistics gathering. They even offered to set up and pay for a European Union cultural research unit with the condition that it be located in Paris. The British, joined by several other countries, objected because they thought that the French model was too "statist," giving insufficient recognition to the links between culture, the economy, private industry, and civil society and insufficient attention to the particular problem of collecting statistics in countries with a federal governmental structure. What then ensued was a prolonged period during which the various countries involved debated the appropriate definitional boundaries for the field of culture (as each saw it).

In the end, the decision was taken to continue working incrementally through Eurostat in Luxembourg, adopting, in effect, the "British" solution. A leadership group was formed to coordinate the effort through working groups. This solution meant that countries were able to confirm their interest by signing up to contribute effort in those areas that were most relevant to them. Four working groups were formed: (1) Methodology (coordinated by France and Italy with nine other countries participating); (2) Cultural Employment (coordinated by France with six other countries as members); (3) Expenditure and Financing (coordinated by The Netherlands with seven other members); and (4) Participation in Cultural Activities (coordinated by Italy with four other members). The work of these task forces has now been fed into a coordinated Eurostat effort, and a final report was issued by the leadership group: *Cultural Statistics in the E.U.:*

Final Report of the LEG, Eurostat Working Papers, Population and Social Conditions 3/2000/E/N° 1 (Luxembourg, Belgium: Eurostat, 2000).

6. http://www.culture.gouv.fr/culture/dep/eng/f-cata-eng.htm

7. http://www.culture.fr/documentation/mnemo/pres.htm

8. http://www.culture.gouv.fr/culture/dep/eng/f-docu-eng.htm

9. Benhamou points out that the best economists do not do economic impact studies any longer, believing them to be insufficiently rigorous and uninformative, so the work is being done either by second-rate economists or consultants.

10. Benhamou points out that this has affected the ministry's research division itself in that it is now operating in an environment in which other government agencies working directly in the cultural industries—e.g., the *Centre National de la Cinematographie* and the *Conseil Superior de l'Audiovisuel*—have developed their own research capacity.

11. Boekmanstichting, *Jaarverslag 1999 [Annual Report 1999]/ Beleidsplan 2001-2004 [Policy Plan 2001-2004]* (Amsterdam, The Netherlands: Boekmanstichting, 2000), p. 89.

12. Emanuel Boekman (1889–1940) was one of the first people to carry out research into government policy in the arts. As an Amsterdam alderman, he was responsible for Education and Cultural Affairs in the period leading up World War II. He received his doctorate in 1939 for his dissertation, "The Government and the Arts in the Netherlands."

13. The most recent example of such a reader is Annemoon van Hemel, ed., *A Must or A Muse: Arts and Culture in Education—Policy and Practice in Europe*, Conference Reader for a *Boekmanstichting* conference held in Rotterdam, The Netherlands, September 26–29, 2001.

14. http://www.fitzcarraldo.it/

15. http://www.kulturdokumentation.org

16. These issues are explored in his widely discussed policy document: Frederik van der Ploeg, *Principles on Cultural Policy 2001–2004: Culture as Confrontation* (Zoetermeer, The Netherlands: Ministry of Education, Culture and Science, November 1999).

17. See, for example, the pair of documents: Westat, Inc., *A Sourcebook of Arts Statistics: 1987* (Washington, D.C.: Research Division, National Endowment for the Arts, April 1988), and National Endowment for the Arts, *The Arts in America: A Report to the President and to the Congress* (Washington, D.C.: National Endowment for the Arts, October 1988).

18. More precisely, the history of research and information services described here spans both the research function as it was structured under the former Arts Council of Great Britain and the research function as it has evolved within the newly constituted Arts Council of England. Under the government of John Major, the Arts Council of Great Britain was split into three agencies. The Scottish Arts Council and the Welsh Arts Council (now the Arts Council of Wales), which originally had functioned

as fairly autonomous committees of the Arts Council of Great Britain, became independent agencies that were funded, respectively, through the Scottish and Welsh Offices; and the Arts Council of England was created and funded, rather confusingly, through the new British cultural ministry (originally named the Department of National Heritage and now titled the Department for Culture, Media and Sport).

19. One example of this type of initiative is the arts council's recent participation in the convening of a conference on the creation of a "Culture Bank" that would bring a wide variety of funding mechanisms to bear in the cultural sector as alternatives to the traditional direct-funding arts council model.

20. As an interesting side note, Peter Hewitt attributes this change to two primary factors: the election of a Labour government but, even more importantly, the arrival of national lottery money. The arrival of lottery money in amounts much larger than had been predicted forced many questions to be asked of the traditional funding mechanisms. Hewitt, at least, would argue that combining the old grant-in-aid programs with the new lottery-funded programs together within the arts council was a good decision because it broke loose an organization that had been fossilized.

21. For the most current description of the work of the Research and Development Directorate, see: http://www.artscouncil.org.uk/news/ResDevindex.html

22. http://www.arts-research-digest.com

23. The key document, *Working Together for the Arts: The Arts Council's Detailed Plan for Future Support of the Arts in England* (London, England: Arts Council of England, 18 July 2001), can be found, along with various ancillary documents, on the Arts Council of England's Web site: http://www.artscouncil.org.uk/towards/index.html

24. To be sure, this proposal would create an organization whose regional offices better correspond to the current governmentally defined regions in England rather than basing them on anachronistic World War II Civil Defense regions.

25. I am grateful to Julia Lowell of the Rand Corporation who called this point to my attention.

26. With the culture function having been devolved to the Scottish Parliament and the Welsh Assembly, the picture becomes rather complicated. Although the Department for Culture, Media and Sport appears to be a national ministry, it actually has direct influence over these matters only so far as England is concerned. This federalization of the culture portfolio means that the infrastructure for cultural policy research and information is likely to become only more complicated in Great Britain.

27. In this regard, Paul Allin and Stephen Creigh-Tyte both believe that the advent of the National Lottery has fueled the proliferation of "appalling consultants" because of the perceived role that they can play in getting lottery bids through the system. Each proposal has to be a "qualified bid" meeting certain technical requirements, and organizations

hire consultants to prepare their bids for them. Individuals and firms have also been commissioned by the lottery distributing agencies to assess the various bids and assist in making funding decisions because the distributing agencies have not had sufficient staff to appraise the bids themselves.

28. Creative Industries Task Force, *Creative Industries Mapping Document, 1998* (London, England: Department for Media, Culture and Sport, 1998) [http://www.culture.gov.uk/creative/creative_industries.html]; and Ministerial Creative Industries Strategy Group, *Creative Industries Mapping Document, 2001* (London, England: Department for Media, Culture and Sport, 2001) [http://www.culture.gov.uk/creative/creative_ industries.html].

29. Quoted in Phyllida Shaw, "Sources of Cultural Statistics: The UK and the Republic of Ireland—Statistics: A Matter of Trust," *Arts Research Digest*, Issue 13, Summer 1998, p. i.

30. Christopher Gordon points out that the fact that the research and information capacities of the arts council were originally so closely allied with regional concerns may have been one of the important factors in marginalizing the research function within the arts council. The discipline-based art form offices perceived this regional emphasis as a threat to their own traditional strengths: discipline-based support programs that viewed grantees through a discipline-based lens of artistic quality rather than through what were perceived as extraneous socio-demographic factors such as regional distribution.

31. Using a standard definition of culture and considering a four-year budget period, a report commissioned by the European Commission concluded that 7.7 percent of the money that the European Union has spent on cultural programs had actually come from budget items identified as cultural, 9.6 percent had come from general E.U. programs, and 82.7 percent had come from its structural funds. Bates and Wacker SC, *Community Support for Culture* (Brussels, Belgium: European Commission, June 1993).

32. Christopher Gordon has also suggested that another reason that the contracts went to the large multinational management/accounting firms was that they were accustomed to scouring the *Official Journal of the European Communities* to look for projects that were being put out for tender. Moreover, British firms, he would argue, suffered from a conservative Europhobic viewpoint, which kept them from looking for these types of opportunities.

33. For a list of the official Cultural Contact Points, see: http://europa.eu.int/comm/culture/contact-point_en.html.

34. Sara Selwood, ed., *The U.K. Cultural Sector: Profile and Policy Issues* (London, England: Policy Studies Institute, 2001).

35. Standing Committee on Canadian Heritage, *A Sense of Place—A Sense of Being: The Evolving Role of the Federal Government in Support of Culture in Canada*, ninth report, June 1999. [http://www.parl.gc.ca/InfoComDoc/36/1/CHER/Studies/Reports/cherrp09-e.htm]

36. Terry Cheney, "Summing Up . . . Better Data in an e-Culture Age: DGCI Needs for Better Data—A Review and Recommendations," report prepared for Research, Analysis and Compliance, Publishing Policy and Programs, Canadian Heritage, February 2000, p. 20.

37. Terry Cheney, "Summing Up . . . ," p. 24.

38. Terry Cheney, "Summing Up . . . ," p. 20.

III

Research and Documentation Consortia

INTRODUCTION

Research and documentation consortia, another important component of the cultural policy research and information infrastructure, can provide a desirable level of collaboration by achieving economies of scale through the sharing of information and the development of common research frameworks and methodologies. Often these consortia provide the venue for the development of truly comparative (cross-national) research projects, which have a critical and growing role to play in cultural policy analysis as countries begin to turn to one another more frequently in search of policy and program models that might be adapted for their own purposes.

This section considers six such consortia. The first three are linked to the cultural work of the Council of Europe: Cultural Information and Research Centres Liaison in Europe (CIRCLE), which has derived much of its support from the Council of Europe and has functioned as a cultural policy monitoring and research group acting on behalf of the Council; the European Research Institute for Comparative Cultural Policy and the Arts (ERICArts), with strong roots in the CIRCLE network but with its own ambitions to create an independent European cultural research institute; and the Council of Europe's own Program for the Evaluation of National Cultural Policies, conducted in large part with the assistance of CIRCLE. Two initiatives linked to the cultural work of UNESCO are then discussed, beginning with its own Cultural Policies for Development Unit and then turning to Culturelink, the Network of Networks for Research and Cooperation in Cultural Development, an initiative funded by UNESCO. Finally, I consider one example of a consortium created by a group of academic and government researchers with a set of common cultural policy interests: the Canadian Cultural Research Network.

Despite their advantages, consortia are also subject to a great deal of criticism. A number of researchers in the field fear that the activities undertaken by the rapidly proliferating number of consortia are drawing energy and attention away from their primary work—to provide research and information services to the field of culture—toward a variety of nonproductive administrative and network-maintenance tasks. With a few notable exceptions, the promise of providing truly comparative research is still more of a goal than a reality. In part, this is because it is quite difficult to design and implement well-designed comparative research projects in the cultural field because of the variation in national conceptions (and definitions) of culture as well as the variation in the structure of cultural policy and cultural support systems. While making comparative research more interesting than country-by-country or case-by-case research, this heterogeneity also makes it considerably more difficult.[1]

Although (with the exception of *Cultural Trends* and *Boekmancahier*, both discussed in Part II) they are not covered in this book, professional journals can also be thought of as a form of research and information consortium, bringing quality research from a variety of countries together under one cover. Such journals currently include, for example, the *Journal of Cultural Economics*; the *International Journal of Cultural Policy*; the *International Journal of Arts Management*; the *Journal of Arts Management, Law and Society*; *Media International Australia* (incorporating *Cultural Policy*); *Nordisk Kulturpolitisk Tidskrift* (the *Nordic Journal of Cultural Policy*); and *Economia della Cultura* (the journal of the Italian Association for Cultural Economics).[2] But here, too, lies a problem. None of these journals does a very good job at bridging the gap between the field of research and the field of practice, a challenge that remains to be confronted by the research and information infrastructure in a meaningful and effective manner.

CIRCLE
Cultural Information and Research Centres Liaison in Europe
Amsterdam, the Netherlands

Significance

CIRCLE, Cultural Information and Research Centres Liaison in Europe, is the oldest network of institutions and individuals working in cultural policy research, information, and documentation. Created at a time when the field was quite small and it was conceivable to gather all of the key individuals in Europe around the table several times a year, CIRCLE has had to weather a number of changes in the field. It illustrates well the tension between researchers, documentation specialists, and administrators, as well as the tension between the non-profit side of the research infrastructure, the governmental side of the research infrastructure, and the growing profit-making side of the research infrastructure. Originally structured as a network that relied on the volunteer efforts of individuals who took on CIRCLE responsibilities in addition to their usual job responsibilities (typically with the support of the institutions that employed them), it has had to cope continually with the burnout and exhaustion that accompanies that way of doing business.

Background

Though some would trace the roots of CIRCLE as far back as to trans-European meetings in the early 1970s, the first formal roots can be found in a 1980 proposal for the creation of an "Association for Cultural Research and Documentation" made by Andreas Wiesand at the request of the Council of Europe.[3] By 1985 the organization had become formalized, adopting the acronym CIRCLE, with ten different national institutions present (though including only two of the original six who had participated in 1980).[4]

Augustin Girard, in a highly personal account of the history of CIRCLE, has characterized its early roots:

> Who then were the founders of CIRCLE? They were not high-ranking civil servants or outstanding academics, neither were they learned researchers nor seasoned documentalists. They were, above all, "militants," in the sense of militants for education for all, for peace, for culture. In other words they were "believers" rather than "knowers," people who have suddenly found a vocation that gives meaning to their lives, almost as if they have no choice. What then did these founders believe in? What did they have in common?
>
> - They innocently but obstinately believed that documentation has a vital role to play in any type of research or action system.
> - Although not scientists themselves, they were aware of that which is scientific, believing that facts should take precedence over ideology. They believed that the social science discoveries are highly effective (in policymaking) because of the social science deliberately empirical approach.
> - These people had both a deep-rooted wish to see cultural policies modernised and rationalised and an extremely humble capacity for copying.
> - Their passionate interest in cultural cooperation was such that they took considerable administrative and financial risks: [T]hey put pressure on their employers to give them adequate time and material means.[5]

One way of interpreting this is to say that CIRCLE was actually interested in a form of advocacy. This is clearly revealed in Wiesand's proposed statute for the organization that eventually became CIRCLE. Among the research, documentation, and cooperation goals spelled out there, one also finds:

> Supporting an improvement of the working conditions and the freedom of expression for artists, writers, and other cultural workers, while promoting a better use of their talents for the development of society as a whole and for the safeguarding of cultural diversity all over the world."[6]

As a reflection of what is happening in the cultural field, these words could have been written yesterday as well as twenty years ago. As a reflection of what is happening in the cultural policy research field, they may be more dated.

When it was created, CIRCLE was one of very few networks in the cultural field. (Now there are many.) For those who were involved, it was the first structured opportunity to sit around the table and share with one another what was happening (and not happening) in cultural research at the national level. The Council of Europe, which supported the creation of CIRCLE, saw it as a collaborative research group that would also function as the Council of Europe's eyes and ears on evolving cultural policy trends, a kind of early warning system, functioning much like the more recent national and regional cultural observatories are expected to function.

Because of their positions, the early members of CIRCLE each had a reasonably synthetic overview of the situation in their country. Some represented their ministry's (or arts council's) research divisions, others represented the primary cultural policy documentation and information center in that country, and still others represented the main research institution doing cultural policy work in that country. Over time, a sense of different levels of membership evolved, with "formalized members" recognized by their national authorities.

CIRCLE's central method of working has been focused around its roundtables (table 1). The essential idea is that a theme is selected, the individual members of CIRCLE are then asked to prepare a dossier summarizing how that theme is played out in their own country, and these national reports then provide the background material for a roundtable meeting to which a number of speakers are invited to present papers. Typically the roundtable is followed by the publication of a book summarizing the proceedings.[7]

While succeeding at pulling together a considerable amount of information without substantial expenditure, these roundtable efforts have suffered from the fact that everyone is volunteering their labor, completing their CIRCLE work on top of their other responsibilities, and the fact that CIRCLE has been surprisingly reluctant to insist on comparability across the national dossiers. Thus, the results have been mixed. It is clear that when CIRCLE has insisted on comparability, as has been the case with the several editions of the *Handbook of Cultural Affairs in Europe*, projects have taken far longer than expected.

CIRCLE has also made a major contribution with respect to the Council of Europe's Program of Evaluations of National Cultural Policies (discussed below).

Table 1

CIRCLE Roundtables, Workshops, and Conferences

Year	Topic	Venue
1987	New Measures for Financing the Arts and Culture	Survey only No meeting
1988	The State, Market, and Culture	Budapest
1989	Employment in the Arts and Regional Development	Dublin
1991	Participation in Cultural Life: Current Trends and Future Strategies	Moscow
1993	The Single Market and the Maastricht Treaty on the Arts and Media in EC and non-EC States (CIRCLE Seminar)	Venice
1993	Human Rights and Cultural Policies in a Changing Europe: The Right to Participate in Cultural Life	Helsinki
1994	The Distribution of Roles and Changing Nature of Relations between Governments and Arts Councils, Organizations and Foundations	Budapest
1995	Preparation of the European Report on Culture and Development	Barcelona
1996	New Frontiers for Employment in Europe: The Heritage, the Arts, and Communication as a Laboratory for Ideas	Spoleto
1997	Privatization/Désétatisation and Culture	Amsterdam
1999	Beyond Cultural Diplomacy—International Cultural Cooperation Policies: Whose Agenda Is It Anyway?	Cracow
2000	Making Connections: Culture and Social Cohesion in the New Millennium	Edmonton
2000	New Alliances: Civil Society, Social Cohesion, and Culture	Vienna
2001	Workshop Session on Applied Culture Research Methodologies	Moscow
2001	A Must or a Muse—Arts and Culture in Education: Policy and Practice in Europe	Rotterdam
2001	Culture, Civil Society, and Volunteerism	Newcastle

Networks such as CIRCLE depend to a considerable degree on the people who step in to coordinate and motivate them. In the early years, Rod Fisher, the International Affairs Manager of the Arts Council of Great Britain, was ideally suited to run the secretariat because his official job was to monitor, maintain, and encourage international (European) collaboration. Next, the French *Département des Études et de la Prospective* (DEP) took over the secretariat, bringing a more centralized manner of managing the affairs of the organization and injecting quite a bit of French content into its proceedings. (DEP has retained the publication of CIRCLE's newsletter, *Circular*, which is one of the more useful publications in the field though now heavily weighted toward reporting on the work of DEP. Its current circulation is approximately 3,000 copies three times per year. Contents are published in English and French with a third European language for the lead article.)

Eduard Delgado, who had returned from the Council of Europe to Barcelona to found what is now known as the INTERARTS Foundation: European Observatory for Cultural Research and International Cultural Co-operation, then took over the secretariat. This phase was marked by a widespread perception that certain members of CIRCLE were being favored over others, not a surprising problem for a network that relies on one of its members to provide the secretariat; such a situation is ripe for conflicts of interest. (Note that the logical solution to this problem—for the Council of Europe to have provided a permanent secretariat—has never been the operational model for CIRCLE.) INTERARTS was then succeeded as the home of the CIRCLE secretariat by the *Boekmanstichting*, which, because of its role as a library and documentation center and as a place for encounters, placed its own mark on CIRCLE, turning it more toward documentation activities through its RECAP and CRIE projects.[8] Recently, Péter Inkei, director of the Regional Observatory on Financing Culture in East-Central Europe, became Secretary General, though most administrative matters are still being handled out of the *Boekmanstichting* in Amsterdam.

During the 1990s, a number of pressures and changes affected the mission and functioning of CIRCLE:

- A number of the stalwart members have found it difficult to maintain a high level of involvement in CIRCLE, especially since their employment situation has changed. This change has been most striking for Rod Fisher, whose function at the Arts Council of Great Britain was privatized and contracted out to a new firm that he created, the International Arts Bureau (now International Intelligence on Culture).
- CIRCLE has always been closely tied to the Council of Europe's Program of Evaluations of National Cultural Policies, providing much of the pool of expert examiners. As the number of countries under evaluation increased, it was necessary to open up the pool of examiners to others outside of the inner cadre of CIRCLE.

- As the number of observatories, research centers, and information centers has grown, there has been increasing demand to abandon the "one representative per country" policy in favor of a broader association with institutional and individual memberships.
- This trend has been further accelerated by financial necessity, since the guaranteed subsidy from the Council of Europe has declined dramatically.
- The rise of the European Union and its forays into the funding of cultural projects, particularly through noncultural programs, has brought onto the scene a coterie of consultants and researchers who are more closely allied with Brussels than with Strasbourg and who are making claims on participation.
- And, finally, the differences between the researchers, the documentation people, and the administrative people that were evident from the inception of CIRCLE have been accentuated by the creation of ERICArts, originally conceived as a subset of CIRCLE but now functioning quite independently (see discussion below).

Cas Smithuijsen is quite sanguine on this last point: "CIRCLE used to be a researchers' club. In the end the researchers' club will be taken over by ERICArts and what will remain of CIRCLE will be a contact club. . . . For the time being, CIRCLE is still important as a way of making contacts." Not surprisingly, Andreas Wiesand sees this differently; he foresees an inevitable split between those whose vocation is research and those whose vocation is information and documentation. While he would like to see the two function in cooperation with one another, he is prepared to separate them if the resulting research can be strengthened.[9]

The statutes of CIRCLE have recently been rewritten to accommodate individual members—some foresee that in a few years it will be member-driven like the Association of Cultural Economics International or the Canadian Cultural Research Network—as well as to make it easier to apply for support from the European Union. (This restructuring was also done with the hope that membership dues would provide a source of much-needed income.) Now that membership is opening up, new members are coming more from the ranks of civil servants and other people interested in international cultural policy, but it is no longer driven as much by international organizations. Yet individual membership fees have not provided the level of financial support that had been expected.

CIRCLE has expanded to include representatives from central and eastern Europe, but in welcoming members who are at an earlier point in the development of their information, data gathering, and research systems, it must be concerned about a change in the nature of the work and a diminution in the quality of the work that can be produced collectively.

The fact that CIRCLE was reorganized under Dutch law has proven to be an impediment for the French DEP, which has had to withdraw temporarily from CIRCLE because French law prevents a French governmental agency from belonging to an institution that is organized under the law of another country. Steps are being taken to reorganize CIRCLE a second time, this time under French law, and perhaps to move the secretariat permanently to Paris.

While its main protagonists think that there is still a need for one venue through which information can be gathered and evaluated and that the annual conferences and roundtables are still useful, there is increasing competition, not the least of which may be coming from a new network created by the Council of Europe, the Forum of European Cultural Networks (*Forum des Réseaux Culturels Europeens*).[10] The Forum may be taking on much of the cultural policy monitoring role formerly assumed by CIRCLE.

In 1998, Kathrin Merkle, head of the Cultural Policies Research and Development Unit of the Council of Europe, spoke of CIRCLE "as a partner of the Council of Europe. . . . [A]lthough CIRCLE is just one of many networks supported by the Council of Europe, it is *the* privileged partner in cultural policy research since it has inspired and accompanied the work of the Cultural Action and Policy Division for many years and will hopefully do so in the future." But others wonder whether the Council of Europe now sees CIRCLE more as a threat than as a partner, foreseeing the time at which the council will simply stop its subsidy of CIRCLE. The Dutch Ministry of Education, Culture and Science has provided a grant to the *Boekmanstichting* to hire a coordinator for CIRCLE, and Diane Dodd is now managing CIRCLE's activities from her base as an independent consultant working near Barcelona. Thus, the Dutch currently pay more of CIRCLE's ongoing operating expenses than does the Council of Europe.

Carla Bodo, former director of research at the Observatory for the Performing Arts of the Italian Ministry of Culture, has suggested that CIRCLE's main strength has been in its ability to stay at the "cutting edge" of the debate on cultural policy, detecting in advance the important issues and taking them on through their roundtables. She believes that it has been less successful at monitoring changes after these issues have been debated.

Assessment

It is clear that whatever happens, CIRCLE cannot continue to function drawing on the volunteer labor of its members. Several of the founding members have recently retired from the board, and the Council of Europe's support for CIRCLE is being reduced. At the same time, the ecology of research and information centers is rapidly expanding. CIRCLE is no longer the first among few. Indeed, it may find it difficult to maintain its preeminence among many such organizations.

Some are raising the question as to whether there is a need for CIRCLE any longer. It was designed to bring people together, and it worked, but it does not have the political connections it used to have, nor, perhaps, the *raison d'être*. The gradual shift away from the Council of Europe to the European Union as a seat of influence and a source of money will certainly influence the role that CIRCLE can play, though it is not clear that the European Union will ever become a major funder in the cultural sphere in the way that some of its member countries hope, particularly those who continue to face large expenditures for the preservation and conservation of their cultural heritage (one of the chronic cultural funding problems in Europe).

CIRCLE has had a tremendous impact on the field of cultural policy research and on the international exchange of information in that field. Whether it will continue to make a unique set of contributions or be swallowed up in the evolving mix of institutions remains to be seen. Its contribution deserves to be celebrated and its evolution managed.

INTERVIEWS AND CONTACTS

CAS SMITHUIJSEN
former Secretary General, CIRCLE
Boekmanstichting
Herengracht 415
1017 BP Amsterdam
The Netherlands

Phone: 011-31-(0)20-624-3736
Fax: 011-31-(0)20-638-5239

e-mail: secretariaat@boekman.nl

PÉTER INKEI
Secretary General, CIRCLE
Director, Regional Observatory on Financing Culture
in East-Central Europe
H-1251 Budapest, Pf. 27
Hungary

Phone: 011-36-1-487-0162
Fax: 011-36-1-487-0162

e-mail: bo@budobs.org

DOROTA ILCZUK [*not interviewed*]
President, CIRCLE
Institute of Public Affairs
Jagiellonian University
Rynek Glówny 8
31-042 Kraków
Poland

Phone: 011-48-12-411-4784
Fax: 011-48-12-422-5892

e-mail: dilczuk@post.pl

DIANE DODD [*not interviewed*]
Coordinator, CIRCLE
C/Cadí 9,
Urb. Castellà d'Indies
E-08396 Sant Cebrià de Vallalta (Barcelona)
Spain

Phone: 011-34-(0)93 763 0162
Fax: 011-34-(0) 93 763 1053

e-mail: circle@eresmas.net

WEB SITE

http://www.boekman.nl/circle

DOCUMENTS AND PUBLICATIONS CONSULTED

"CIRCLE—Past, Present and Future," Draft Report, CIRCLE Round Table '98, 4 December 1998, Strasbourg, France.

"CIRCLE—Past, Present and Future," Minutes of CIRCLE Annual Meeting '98, 5 December 1998, Strasbourg, France.

Circular: Research and Documentation on Cultural Policies, newsletter of CIRCLE, various issues.

Council of Europe, "A Framework for CIRCLE," Document DECS/AC (85) 21, 1985.

Girard, Augustin, "Thirty Years," *Circular: Research and Documentation on Cultural Policies,* No. 10, July 1999, p. 3.

Smithuijsen, Cas, "The Need for a European Liaison for Cultural Policy Resources," in Boekmanstichting, *RECAP: Resources for Cultural Policy in Europe* (Amsterdam, The Netherlands: The Boekman Foundation, 1999).

Zentrum für Kulturforschung, "Proposal for a Statute of the Association for Cultural Research and Documentation (ACREDO)," Bonn, Germany, 1980.

ERICArts
European Research Institute for Comparative Cultural Policy and the Arts
Bonn, Germany

Significance

ERICArts began as a way to focus the CIRCLE network more effectively on the delivery of high-quality comparative research. The eventual goal is to create a permanent research institute or center with its own staff of researchers who would then be able to focus strictly on research. The story of ERICArts is a story of the difficulties in maintaining two different sensibilities, one inclined toward information and documentation and one inclined toward research, together in the same organization. It is also a story of what happens when funding realities and research design come into conflict with one another.

Background

The original notion for ERICArts was hatched in 1991 on a bus ride during the Council of Europe's review of the national cultural policy of Austria. There had been a sense that it was always the same people in CIRCLE who were doing that program's work but that those individuals were not necessarily the best individuals to be conducting comparative research because they were not trained as social science researchers. Why not do it the "right" way by creating an entity focused on research that could draw on a pool of trained researchers?

The initial proposal was to create three arms within CIRCLE: documentation, statistics, and research. The third arm would have had to be beefed up because of the lack of real researchers in CIRCLE at the time. But this idea was consistently rejected. In December of 1993 a decision was made to create ERICArts, the European Research Institute for Comparative Cultural Policy and the Arts, as a separate entity rather than as a division of CIRCLE. Even so, about 90 percent of CIRCLE members at that time were actually involved in the initiative. Yet, some CIRCLE members were quite opposed to the creation of ERICArts, whether inside or outside of CIRCLE. For these members it was quite inconceivable that something that had been so important to them could be run and could succeed independently without state influence and without the support of the Council of Europe.

In order to avoid taking administrators and documentation specialists into this new organization, a set of membership criteria was established. For example, one had to have had five years of comparative research experience. Moreover, a distinction was created between associate members and real members. The membership list has taken on considerable importance because it is to this list that ERICArts turns first to see if any new project can be staffed from among the membership. In many cases, the politics of funding have necessitated turning to other organizations to involve them in ERICArts' projects.

To differentiate itself from CIRCLE and from the many other cross-national organizations that have sprung up in the last ten or fifteen years, ERICArts stresses that it is not a network; legally, it is an association. The membership is made up of working researchers.

Despite its problematic history with CIRCLE, the protagonists of ERICArts insist that they would be interested in restoring ties to CIRCLE and perhaps setting CIRCLE up as a sort of "Friends Of" organization to ERICArts or creating a real European professional association of cultural researchers.

The driving concept of ERICArts has always been the creation of a stand-alone research institute with its own facility and a secretariat of six to seven researchers. The secretariat would search for funding, develop projects, and conduct research. It would have a state-of-the-art documentation center taking advantage of high-end technology. The focus would be on applied research, and the coverage would be European with links developed to the European Union and the Council of Europe.

Since 1993, the originators of this idea have worked to secure funding for the original model, but without success. They believe they have come close several times, particularly with a proposal that was linked to the movement of the German government from Bonn to Berlin. They have also explored procuring European industrial development money to establish ERICArts as an independent business as part of a regional development strategy that would be focused on scientific research. The question of finally forming an institute was taken up once again in early 2002 (see below).

In 1996, the members of ERICArts met in Turin. At that meeting they decided that they would have to start with projects and wait for institutional funding (general operating support). The idea was simple: Do something first, then maybe the rest will come later.

Since the beginning, ERICArts has had a close relationship to the *Zentrum für Kulturforschung*, Andreas Wiesand's private research firm. While continuing his work at a national level through ZfKf, he was also attempting to launch ERICArts. In 1997, Danielle Cliche was hired as an independent contractor to be the project advisor and only employee of ERICArts. Her post was cross-subsidized out of existing ZfKf projects. Her job is to conceptualize projects, look for project funding, look for the experts necessary to complete these projects, and to keep in mind a sense of European results at the end.

One of the first projects undertaken by ERICArts in its own right was "Women in the Arts and Media Professions: European Comparisons." A conference on this theme was held in Bonn in 1997, and then ERICArts wrote an application to the European Commission for a two-and-a-half-year project on this theme that involved fifteen partners throughout Europe.

Collaboration of the sort that is represented by ERICArts is, in some ways, being driven by the realities of European funding. The European Union will provide only partial funding for a project; in each case there must be a national partner cofinancing the project (in this case, the German Ministry of Women's Affairs). Beyond the national partner, there have to be national research partners from other member countries; some E.U. programs specify the minimum number of countries to be involved.

ERICArts would prefer not to work in a national way (each country with its own researcher and its own report), but at the present time E.U. funding more or less forces that. It would prefer to develop cross-disciplinary teams of researchers trained in comparative work. On the women's project, ERICArts received eight totally different reports despite a simple methodology with strict definitions and strict categories. Another complaint that ERICArts has of the E.U. is that, in some ways, its bureaucracy seems more interested in the administration of the project than in the results. (Every three months a progress report of fifteen to twenty pages must be filed.)

The arrival of what might eventually prove to be relatively large-scale funding through the European Union has clearly initiated a new phase in the evolution of cultural policy research in Europe. During the 1980s the focus of much of this work was CIRCLE. Part of the networking culture of the 1980s, everyone worked for free (with the blessing of their respective employers), and everyone was more or less content with the feeling that they were making a difference. The second phase, a "limbo" phase, began when those who had participated freely earlier were no longer able to do so as their jobs and functions were privatized. In this new job reality, the volunteerism of the earlier phase was no longer possible. When the European Union arrived as the new cash cow of Europe, cultural policy research and information organizations had to reorient themselves toward Brussels and to operate in an increasingly competitive environment, which seemed to work to the advantage of a new generation of profit-making consultants. This resulted in a lot of hostility; people who had once been friends and collaborators were no longer.

The founders of ERICArts hoped that they would be able to affect this situation by dealing with people professionally, particularly by paying them for their work, but they have found it difficult to train researchers in the new Euro-reality. When a contract is signed, there are deliverables and dates; with the E.U. the deliverables must meet the contractual due date or the money is lost. It has been very difficult to deliver this message to ERICArts' researchers, who have delivered some work as much as a year late. The researchers in the field do not regard the administrative minutiae as their problem.

To ERICArts this experience is reminiscent of the problems experienced in the old pure networking context: low responsibility, no accountability. If anything, this has solidified its conviction that the goal should be to have researchers working together in one institute.

A second recent project undertaken by ERICArts also illustrates the institutional tensions within which cultural policy research takes place. Looking over the collected materials from its Program for the Evaluation of National Cultural Policies, the new director of the Cultural Policy and Action Division of the Council of Europe decided that it would be desirable to have a more usable synthesis of the accumulated material. The idea was to create a compendium of cultural policies that could be updated easily on an ongoing basis. The first idea was to have CIRCLE complete the compendium, as CIRCLE had been funded by and had worked closely with the Council. CIRCLE made a proposal that would focus on providing information with no analysis, a proposal that was rejected. The Council of Europe then turned to ERICArts, which proposed a decentralized approach within a common framework, an approach that would lead to a loose-leaf binder and a Web site with summaries and updates.[11] Selected to do the work, ERICArts soon realized that the results were too static; instead, it returned with a new approach that would focus on policy issues and trends over the past five years. A framework was developed, and ERICArts coordinated the project working through a number of national partners, made up of government officials, researchers, CIRCLE members, and ERICArts associates. In a way, the fact that ERICArts was chosen over CIRCLE may have ended their relationship, with ERICArts becoming something of an outcast.[12]

Other projects have also proven problematic. In Wiesand's words, ERICArts finds itself "doing projects for funders who do not know what they want and do not understand how to work and who have not worked in the cultural sector. Trying to administer European projects is almost impossible."

But several projects have brought ERICArts closer to the way in which it would like to operate. One was a conference, "Reconstructing Cultural Productivity in the Balkans," and the variety of activities related to it. This project was undertaken with an eye toward revitalizing artistic and cultural ties within the Balkans and toward transnational cooperation in the face of the onslaught of outside advisors. Dimitrije Vujadinovic of the nongovernmental organization Blue Dragon approached ERICArts for assistance. ERICArts first tried to get the European Union to designate one percent of its Stability Pact budget for reconstructing the artistic life of the Balkans; failing that, it organized the conference with financial support from the Finnish, German, and Austrian governments. In some ways this model is what ERICArts had hoped for all along. A member had an idea, brought it to the central ERICArts office, and they worked together to make it happen. A number of derivative projects have been launched from this initiative, but note that these have all been actual cultural projects, not research.

Another major initiative for ERICArts has been its involvement in the European Food Project. This project combines agricultural policy with cultural heritage concerns. ERICArts began its involvement in this project with the Bread Project, has continued with the Olive Project, and hopes to continue through a project on the fish trade. Consider the Olive Project, which began with a proposal to the European Commission through its RAPHAEL Program (which focuses on cultural heritage) for a project on the production and consumption of olive oil. The proposal included everything from the cultural dimensions of agricultural production to government policies toward the industry. A conference held in Crete hosted local producers and politicians, as well as researchers and policymakers. This project has uncovered interesting results, including the fact that Finland is the leading exporter of olive oil (to Russia); unfortunately, Italy was not represented at the conference, despite the fact that it is the largest market for olive oil. Generally, the seminars and conferences have worked smoothly, even though the nature of these projects is such that it is necessary to seek out and coordinate a wide variety of partners.

ERICArts aims to tread a middle ground here. There is a predisposition toward research in action, and its board would very much like ERICArts to get back to direct interaction with artists, working with the main protagonists themselves to generate experience and data rather than working with secondary data. (The true model for this is ZfKf, particularly its earlier years, which is not surprising given the ties between the two organizations.) Accordingly, ERICArts would like to develop a project on artists' rights, working with artists rather than working with lawyers and collecting societies.

The result of this approach is that ERICArts is not looking to attract mainline researchers. Its focus will remain on applied research.

Assessment

The dream of a stand-alone research institute with its own facilities and its own resources operating throughout Europe is still very much alive. The board continues searching for "sponsors" to cover the basic institutional costs for the ERICArts concept, but that has proven difficult. In many ways the model for ERICArts is the Getty Conservation Institute, where good work is being done (and which does not have to be concerned primarily about facilities or financial support). Eventually, the dream might even be expanded to include regional offices looking for their own projects, with their own sources of money, but it is difficult to envision exactly how this would happen given the current proliferation of efforts outlined elsewhere in this book.

How the relationship between ERICArts and CIRCLE will ultimately work out remains to be seen. The two organizations are beginning to separate; Ritva Mitchell, who until quite recently was the president of both organizations, has stepped down as president of CIRCLE. Whatever else happens, it is likely that the documentation and information functions of CIRCLE will be more highly separated from the research functions of ERICArts. It may be that both groups will be unwilling to let go entirely, and many individuals will continue to function as part of both efforts.

For the moment, ERICArts survives from project to project, finding that it often has to depart from the areas of research in which it would like to focus to maintain sufficient cash flow. It would not have been able to survive this long, even in its abbreviated, project-based form, without its relationship to ZfKf. In large part, ZfKf has carried the overhead for ERICArts (though more recently ERICArts has been able to reciprocate, assisting ZfKf through its own difficult financial moments). But the time is coming soon when a decision will have to be made whether to go the next step and form the institute that ERICArts was always intended to be, rather than continuing to operate as a consortium project by project. Toward this end, in January 2002 a General

Assembly of ERICArts voted to dissolve the ERICArts association under German law in order to prepare the way for a foundation structure as a successor body and, eventually, for the creation of a true institute.

Interviews and Contacts

Andreas Wiesand
Secretary General
European Research Institute for Comparative Cultural Policy
and the Arts
Dahlmannstrasse 26
D-53113 Bonn
Germany

Phone: 011-49-(0)228-242-0996
Fax: 011-49-(0)228-241-318

e-mail: wiesand@ericarts.org

Ritva Mitchell [*not interviewed*]
President, ERICArts
Arts Council of Finland
Maneesikatu 7
P.O. Box 293
FIN-00171 Helsinki
Finland

Phone: 011-358-9-1341-7362
Fax: 011-358-9-1341-7060

e-mail: ekvit@saunalahti.fi

Danielle Cliche
Project Advisor
European Research Institute for Comparative Cultural Policy
and the Arts
Dahlmannstrasse 26
D-53113 Bonn
Germany

Phone: 011-49-(0)228-242-0996
Fax: 011-49-(0)228-241-318

e-mail: cliche@ericarts.org

Web Site

http://www.ericarts.org

Documents and Publications Consulted

Council of Europe/ERICArts, *Cultural Policies in Europe: A Compendium of Basic Facts and Trends* (Bonn, Germany: ARCult Media, 2000).

ERICArts, *Bulletin*, various issues, 1997–2000.

ERICArts, ICUSEM, FINN-EKVITT, "Final Report: ELEA—Producing and Consuming Olive Oil: A Contribution to European Culinary Cultural Heritage," May 1999.

Council of Europe
Cultural Policy and Action Department
Program for the Evaluation of National Cultural Policies
Strasbourg, France

Significance

Over the years, the Council of Europe has engaged in a number of European projects on cultural policy. Rather than trying to establish an ongoing research and information function, the council tends to work thematically, picking emerging issues and trends for cross-national investigation. This section focuses on the Program for the Evaluation of National Cultural Policies. What is significant here is the understanding that a commitment to research does not have to be structured through freestanding research institutions; it can also be structured around coordinated research programs (or projects). It is of interest to track the impact that such a program can have on efforts to build a more substantial, ongoing research focus in cultural policy and the contribution that it can make to the cultural policy research and information infrastructure.

The Council of Europe

The work of the Council of Europe can be characterized in a number of ways. In the view of Raymond Weber, the former director of Culture and Cultural Heritage, the Council of Europe has four main areas of activity:

- It acts as an informal observatory, or a monitoring center, concerned with several policy areas. In this role it takes a look at the European situation in a particular field, analyzes it, and assesses it. Often this work is conducted through the creation of public forums. At the present time, two topics are of particular interest in the cultural sector: the withdrawal of the state from the cultural sector, and cultural diversity.

- It acts as a "repository of values," promoting a consideration of human rights, democracy, and the rule of law. It is concerned with the ethics of cooperation.
- It serves as a testing ground on which new ideas can be played out. In the cultural field, it is currently focusing on culture and social links and culture and civil society.
- It acts as a cooperative agency, particularly with respect to assistance to the countries of southeast Europe.

Thus, the Council of Europe offers a viewpoint that is distanced a bit from the everyday workings of national policy and national politics, a viewpoint that can offer a more comparative and, perhaps, more objective perspective, but a viewpoint that is affected by that distance.

The Program for the Evaluation of National Cultural Policies[13]

A program to evaluate national cultural policies was first put on the table of the Council of Europe by the Swedish Ministry of Culture and Education. It was interested in seeing whether the OECD's (Organisation for Economic Co-operation and Development) program of evaluating national education policies could be adapted to, and implemented in, the cultural field. At a 1985 seminar in Sweden, the basic parameters of such a program were laid out.[14]

After a country formally requested to enter the program and was accepted, it would follow four steps (with a fifth added more recently):

1. The preparation of a National Report by a team designated by the country whose policy is under review. This report would set out the "official" view of the national authorities with respect to their policies on the arts and culture. The ministry or government office in charge of cultural affairs must endorse it.
2. The naming of an international team of "examiners" or "experts" who, acting in their individual capacity rather than as representatives of any organization or institution, would visit the country, conduct interviews, and supplement the National Report with the collection of additional documentation.

3. The preparation of an Examiners' Report with recommendations and further questions. This report would compile the conclusions of the examiners' evaluation made in response to, and in dialogue with, the National Report.
4. The presentation of the two reports at a hearing (Review Meeting) before the Culture Committee in Strasbourg, which would include the Minister of Culture of the country under review, other staff involved in that country's national cultural policy, and the examiners.
5. A National Seminar held in the country itself, accompanied by the publication of the two reports in both English and French and often in the local language of the country under evaluation. (This last step was begun several years ago with the completion of the reports on Slovenia.)

It is important to note that this style of program had benefits for all of the actors within the Council of Europe system. For the country whose policy was to be evaluated, it would provide an opportunity to benefit from an outside consideration of, and reflection upon, its policies. It would also provide an impetus to put in place documentation mechanisms and to develop indicators that previously had been unavailable. For the member states as a group, the program would result in the collection of information on cultural policy objectives and practices in each of the countries evaluated, information that previously had been available only on an anecdotal basis; it would highlight innovations that might be transferable; it would analyze the successes and failures of the measures implemented, not so much to serve as an overall evaluation of that country's success (or failure) but as an indicator of promising practices; and it would provide a mechanism through which information gathering and evaluation methods in cultural policy would gradually be improved. It would allow the Council of Europe to provide a service to its members while also collecting important research information, to develop measurement tools and guidance to facilitate international comparison of cultural policies, and it would provide a basis on which to build future cultural cooperation.

While stopping well short of insisting on a common template for evaluation,[15] the Council of Europe did identify six broad policy themes that it hoped would be addressed in both the National and the Examiners' Reports during the review process:

- ❒ Decentralization
- ❒ Support for creativity
- ❒ Cultural identity and diversity

- Access and participation
- Cultural minorities and fundamental rights
- The creative industries

These areas, reflecting the traditional concerns of the Council of Europe, became a way for the council to give a bit of its imprint to the process. These evaluations were not to be slightly disguised attempts to increase the public resources invested by member states in culture. The focus was kept firmly on efficiency and effectiveness in policy delivery—on "value for money," to use a phrase currently popular in European cultural policy.

France and Sweden, two of the biggest promoters of this program, were the first two countries to have their cultural policies evaluated. To date, seventeen national evaluations have been completed,[16] four are under way,[17] and six other candidates are on the waiting list.[18] France has recently inquired as to whether it could be afforded the opportunity for a second evaluation to focus on what it believes are rather substantial changes in its cultural policy during the intervening fifteen years.

The costs of each national evaluation have typically been shared by the Council of Europe and the country under review. Generally, the country under review has been responsible for compiling or commissioning the National Report plus a summary; translating the National Report into French or English and translating the Examiners' Report into the national language (and possibly publishing both reports); paying the daily living expenses of the examiners during their visits to the country, their travel within the country, and any interpretation costs during these visits; and paying travel and daily expenses for the country's delegation to the hearing before the Culture Committee (and any additional translation expenses incurred at this meeting). The Council of Europe has assumed responsibility for travel and daily living expenses of the president and the rapporteur of the panel of examiners for a first visit to the country under review, travel and a per diem for two visits by the group of examiners to the country under review, fees for the rapporteur (the rapporteur was the only member of the board of examiners to be paid for his or her services), and expenses related to the participation of the experts in the hearing at the Culture Committee. As the budget of the Council of Europe has become tighter, the payment scheme has become more mixed, complicating the relationship between the country under review and the examiners.

In a number of cases, the evaluations resulted in rather concrete results. National legislation was adopted in some countries, thereby changing the profile of cultural policy. A variety of healthy debates arose around the findings of the two reports: In both Austria and

Portugal, centers for cultural policy research were created as part of the process of researching and writing the National Report, and these centers have been left as legacies of the process. In the Dutch case, Theodoor Adams, director of the Cultural Policy Directorate in the Dutch Ministry of Education, Culture, and Science, was so pleased with his country's participation in the national evaluation and his own participation as an examiner in other evaluations that he undertook the preparation of a second National Report that would document changes in Dutch cultural policy since the publication of the first one (even though the second one would be exposed only to public opinion and not a panel of examiners).

The comparative intent of this program is open to some debate. Original documents clearly indicate that the program's designers hoped that it would provide an opportunity to evolve methodologies for the collection of comparable data. Yet, the extent to which a country perceives that it is going to be compared to others must affect its decision to participate. So there is pressure to present the program as offering a service to one country at a time. Perhaps this is why Raymond Weber has stated flatly that it was never the intent of this project to be comparative.

His remarks notwithstanding, it was always the hope of some of the key individuals who designed the program that a common set of methodologies and measures would be developed under the auspices of the program. See, for example, Augustin Girard's 1992 report on cultural indicators or Ritva Mitchell's 1996 articles on the use of these evaluations for making comparisons.[19] The seventeen completed national cultural policy evaluations and the countless other documents generated during the evaluation process comprise a rich database of information on cultural policy that deserves to be tapped, and the Council of Europe is beginning to do so. A couple of publications have led the way, though they make it quite clear that the dream of complete comparability has not been achieved, and they end up comparing the *studies* more than they compare the *policies*:

- *A Comparative Study* by John Myerscough (with Christopher Gordon and William Dufton), which documents and assesses the overall program of evaluations.
- Two books published in the Council of Europe's series of training handbooks for cultural managers. The first, *Cultural Policies in Europe: A Comparative Approach*, explicitly compares the results of the first eight national evaluations along a number of dimensions. The second, *Cultural Policies in Europe: Method and Practice of Evaluation*, uses the national evaluations as a way of extracting lessons for further evaluation of cultural policies.

More recently, the council has been building a Cultural Policies Research and Development Unit. Its job is to undertake research and projects on issues of interest in comparative policy, to publish a variety of publications that begin to explore the comparative implications and lessons of this body of work, and to form an information and documentation center on cultural policies at the Council of Europe. This unit was established not as an in-house research unit but as a service activity to respond to the increasing demand for information from the council by the newly admitted member states; the need to process, digest, follow up on, and better communicate the work and projects of the Culture Committee; and the need to introduce efficiencies into the information and documentation process.

As the Program for the Evaluation of National Cultural Policies evolved, Europe changed, particularly through the emergence of new democracies (and new members of the Council of Europe) in central and eastern Europe. The program, which had originally been conceived as an evaluation of an existing, more-or-less stable set of policies, found itself, instead, being called upon to carry out "policy therapy" and, eventually, to design new cultural policies. The examiners increasingly believed that the countries they were looking at should be helped, not just assessed.

Recently, another factor has entered into this equation. As countries from central and eastern Europe request the opportunity to participate in the evaluation project, their emphasis has tended to be on the cultural heritage and the cultural infrastructure (capital facilities). This emphasis is a reflection of the fact that, in these countries, the state had until very recently been relieved of much of the financial burden for the support of contemporary art by massive infusions of funds from the Soros Foundation. The Soros Foundation, however, has now begun to move out of the cultural sphere, and these countries are finding themselves struggling with an even larger policy dilemma.

These changes have necessitated a realignment and redesign of the Council of Europe's cultural policy programs. The Program for the Evaluation of National Cultural Policies has, itself, been separated into three linked programs. The first, Evaluation of National Cultural Policies, is a continuation of the existing program. The second, Transversal Cultural Policy Review, has introduced a comparative thematic approach to the program.[20] These reviews are conducted across a single policy theme and are offered to groups of countries that express an interest in focusing on and evaluating this aspect of their national cultural policies. These projects are still based on cross-cultural peer review, national reports, site visits, country information notes, a final report, and possible follow-up activities. To date, two transversal studies have been launched: National Cultural Institutions in Transition: *Désétatisation* and Privatization[21] and Cultural Policy and Cultural

Diversity.[22] The third program, Evaluation of Sectorial Cultural Policies, is also offered to groups of countries and considers policies in particular cultural sectors across countries. The first Sectorial Cultural Policy Review is in the area of book publishing and marketing.[23] The design of both the transversal and the sector-specific reviews allows countries to join the review process as they become interested in the topic area.

In 1988, the Council of Europe launched another project with a particular emphasis on cultural exchange and cooperation among the countries of southeast Europe. The MOSAIC program (Managing an Open and Strategic Approach in Culture) intersects with each of the cultural policy evaluation programs outlined above by sponsoring a wide variety of debates, seminars, workshops, training programs, technical assistance, and publications. At the moment these activities are financed by voluntary contributions from other member states. A strength of this program is the Council of Europe's access to experts, an access that the European Union has not yet developed as fully.

Building on the Program for the Evaluation of National Cultural Policies, a number of other publications have begun to flow from the Research and Development Unit:

- Simon Mundy, a British arts management consultant and arts journalist, was commissioned to write a "personal analysis" of the points and recommendations that emerged from the national evaluations. This has been published as *Cultural Policy: A Short Guide.*
- A *Compendium* of basic facts and trends in cultural policies in Europe, based on the national evaluations, but also including other countries that have not been through the evaluation process, was commissioned from ERICArts (with updates provided by a variety of local partners). Summaries for twenty countries are currently available in a loose-leaf notebook form. Cultural policy profiles for other countries are to be provided as inserts as they become available. These policy summaries are also available online, and the Web site is updated as further profiles become available.[24] The compilers of this collection stress that the intention of this project was to "explicitly avoid making any judgements or conduct comparisons between respective national cultural policies, but rather to provide the basic informational tools that, in yet another step, allows [*sic*] one to engage in further analytical work at one's discretion—in conjunction, of course, with additional or original sources."[25] Once again, comparison is being facilitated even while being accompanied by a protestation that comparison is not the intent.

Significantly, the Web site has been constructed to facilitate comparison; users can now employ a variety of menu options to generate custom-made tables that allow direct comparison of selected aspects of cultural policy for a set of specified countries.

- Finally, moving a step away from the evaluations themselves, the Research and Development Unit has begun publishing a series of *Policy Notes*, small booklets on particular issues in cultural policy.

The documentation center of the Cultural Policies Research and Development Unit is slowly being built up on the base of the cultural material that had formerly been centralized in the Education and Culture Division of the Council of Europe. The center is called upon to distribute information to Council of Europe staff, the Culture Committee, and external research institutes. Unfortunately, there is no budget for buying books. Financial resources are borrowed from other budgets. To receive periodicals, the documentation center proposes exchanges for Council of Europe documents, and it has begun to formalize this through a network of corresponding partners with whom it has signed contracts to share information. This is partly a legacy of the old collection policy, which was simply to collect materials that Council of Europe staff no longer wanted but were willing to contribute. The documentation center is also intending to build a database of experts who can be consulted on various topics. It provides two periodical publications: *Current Contents*, which summarizes the contents of various periodicals and journals, and *New Acquisitions*, which summarizes new materials added to its library.

Assessment

Quite a lot has been written on the country-by-country successes (and failures) of the Program for the Evaluation of National Cultural Policies.[26] Much of this discussion has focused on the methodology of this very complex process of assessment. The politics of the program have also attracted attention, particularly as the program turned to countries from central and eastern Europe, where cultural policies are still highly politically motivated. Some think that the quality of the examiners' work has declined as the council has turned to relying more heavily on the corps of private arts consultants and less heavily on those who were active in the early days of CIRCLE. Some are also critical of the quality of the debate that occurs in the Culture Committee at the end of the evaluation process, suggesting that it can all too easily become captive to political considerations that are extraneous to the realities of the cultural policy under consideration.

The critiques of this program are often couched in the context of a more general critique of the work of the Council of Europe. For example, Sara Selwood, building on her review and critique of the *Policy Notes*, comes to the following conclusion:

> Given that [the Culture Committee of the Council of Europe] has no direct relationship with—indeed, is at some distance from, the majority of cultural policymakers, providers or practitioners it seeks to influence—on what grounds is it likely to be relevant to them? To what extent has the Cultural Co-operation Committee . . . balanced their own act in respect to the dilemmas which lie at their own hearts: the fact that they simultaneously want to develop awareness of cultural diversity, while stressing the significance of common values; and, that they seek to influence a geographically extensive cultural milieu on the basis of what seems to be a fairly closed shop?[27]

But there is also a consensus that the program has resulted in an unparalleled compilation of, and reflection upon, the cultural policies in the participating countries. The process of preparing the National Reports, conducting site visits, preparing the Examiners' Reports, and holding the review meetings and debates has afforded an opportunity for the assessment of national cultural policies that otherwise would not have occurred, and it has done so for some seventeen countries. That some countries took less advantage of the opportunity than others can hardly be blamed on the program itself.

What is more interesting for the current study, however, is the model of a collaborative research project playing an important role in the development of the research and information infrastructure. The experience of the Program for the Evaluation of National Cultural Policies suggests that it might be worth considering project models as well as institutional models when setting out to change the world of cultural policy research. That this model has continued for some fifteen years, albeit in an evolving form, and that UNESCO has considered adapting this model for evaluations in non-Council of Europe countries,[28] are both testimonies to its value.

Other Programs of the Council of Europe

This section's focus on the Program for the Evaluation of National Cultural Policies should not be interpreted as minimizing the other cultural programs of the Council of Europe.

The council has evolved a method of working that is structured around time-limited projects intended to last three to five years. Through a variety of programs, the council would explore a topical area with an eye to eventually spinning off an institution that would continue to deal with a set of related issues in the long term. In this vein, the council sees itself as doing exploratory work to influence policies. A typical Council of Europe project would end its five-year run with final publications, a set of recommendations, and a "Common Framework" for policy in whatever field was under consideration.

The current book program is functioning in exactly this way, with a focus on promoting four measures: enforcing copyright; reducing the Value Added Tax (VAT) rate for electronic publishing (once a book is on the Internet, it becomes a service rather than a product and is thus taxed at a higher rate, effectively making the preferential rate disappear); requiring legal deposit of electronic publishing; and revising all legislation in the field to assist publishers in moving toward a more flexible, print-on-demand basis.

Although it is no longer in a position to give considerable direct operating support to outside agencies, in some cases the council does still create field projects, whose success it then "analyzes" in order to pass information along to its member states. In other words, it develops experiments or models and then communicates the essential ideas to the field (though there are some who question the council's effectiveness at dissemination). The Culture and Neighbourhoods Project and the Culture and Regions Project have both operated in this way. Concerning these council-generated projects, the staff is quite firm: "We do not *evaluate* these projects; we *analyze* them. We do not fund researchers; we do action research." Typically, a "Reflection Group" is created to monitor and reflect upon what is happening in each such program.

The Heritage Program is illustrative in that it combines these modes of operation. Its two main aspects are (1) the development of guidelines, advice, and a sounding board with respect to heritage policies and strategies, and (2) projects, technical assistance, and multilateral cooperation through networks—the European Foundation for Heritage Skills, the new European Heritage Network Project, and the Heritage Discovery Network. In the words of its director, "We create networks for transversal, intersectoral work."

The council has also established a Forum for Cultural Networks (*Forum des Réseaux Culturels Europeens*), which it convenes on a regular basis in Strasbourg each time around a particular theme (e.g., culture and the prevention of conflict in Southeast Europe, ethics in cultural policy, and so on). This forum functions as a mechanism to inform the Council of Europe of trends and directions in cultural policy and cultural practices among its member countries. Seen in this way, this forum may replace some of the value that the Council has derived from supporting CIRCLE.

Interviews and Contacts

Raymond Weber
former Director
Directorate of Culture and Cultural Heritage
Council of Europe

Vera Boltho
Director
Cultural Policy and Action Department
Council of Europe
F-67075 Strasbourg Cedex
France

Phone: 011-33-(0)3-88-41-21-73
Fax: 011-33-(0)3-88-41-37-82

e-mail: vera.boltho@coe.fr

Laura Mäkelä
Head of the MOSAIC Project
Cultural Policy and Action Department
Council of Europe
F-67075 Strasbourg Cedex
France

Phone: 011-33-(0)3-88-41-28-31
Fax: 011-33-(0)3-88-41-37-82

e-mail: laura.makela@coe.int

Also Interviewed

Michela Cecchini, Head, Division on Education for Democratic Citizenship and Human Rights Education

Daniel Thérond, Principal Administrative Officer, Cultural Heritage Department

Giuseppe Vitiello, Programme Advisor, Content, Books and Archives

Evelyne Porri, Cultural Policies Research and Development Unit, Cultural Policy and Action Department

Web Site

http://www.coe.int/T/E/Cultural_Co-operation/Culture/Cultural_policies/

Documents and Publications Consulted

Cultural Policies Research and Development Unit, *Policy Notes* (Strasbourg, France: Council of Europe Publishing, various dates):

- Everitt, Anthony, *The Governance of Culture: Approaches to Integrated Cultural Planning and Policies*
- Feist, Andy, *Cultural Employment in Europe*
- Fisher, Rod, and Roger Fox, *Culture and Civil Society: New Relationships with the Third Sector*
- Heiskanen, Ilkka, *Decentralisation: Trends in European Cultural Policies*
- Matarrasso, François, and Charles Landry, *Balancing Act: 21 Strategic Dilemmas in Cultural Policy*
- Rellstab, Ursula, *Culture—A Way Forward (Culture and Neighbourhoods: An Action-Research Project in Urban Europe)*
- Robinson, Ken, *Culture, Creativity and the Young: Developing Public Policy*
- Rouet, François, *VAT and Book Policy: Impacts and Issues*

Cultural Policy and Action Division, Directorate of Culture and Cultural Heritage, "European Programme of Reviews of National Cultural Policies—National, Transversal, Sectorial," DECS/Cult-Gen (2000) 01 (Strasbourg, France: Council for Cultural Co-operation, Culture Committee, Council of Europe, May 2000).

d'Angelo, Mario, and Paul Vespérini, "Comparability—A Light on the Horizon," *Circular: Research and Documentation on Cultural Policies*, CIRCLE Newsletter, No. 12, July 2000.

d'Angelo, Mario, and Paul Vespérini, *Cultural Policies in Europe: A Comparative Approach* (Strasbourg, France: Council of Europe Publishing, 1998).

d'Angelo, Mario, and Paul Vespérini, *Cultural Policies in Europe: Method and Practice of Evaluation* (Strasbourg, France: Council of Europe Publishing, 1999).

ERICArts and Council of Europe, *Cultural Policies in Europe: A Compendium of Basic Facts and Trends* (Bonn, Germany: Council of Europe/ERICArts in cooperation with ARCult Media Verlagsbuchhandlung für Kultur & Wissenschaft, 2000).
[http://www.culturalpolicies.net]

Girard, Augustin, "Cultural Indicators," provisional document, DECS-Cult (92) 6 (Strasbourg, France: Council for Cultural Co-operation, Council of Europe, 1992).

Gordon, Christopher, "Cultural Policy Reviews: Some General and Methodological Reflections on the Council of Europe's Programme of Reviews in Member States (1985–1999)," paper commissioned by UNESCO, published in *Culturelink* 30, Vol. 11, April 2000, pp. 173–201; reprinted in Christopher Gordon and Simon Mundy, *European Perspectives on Cultural Policy* (Paris, France: UNESCO Publishing, 2001).

Methods for Evaluation of National Cultural Policies, Report from a seminar in Stockholm, Sweden, April 16–18, 1985 (Stockholm, Sweden: Swedish Ministry of Education and Cultural Affairs, 1986).

Mitchell, Ritva, "The Appraisal of National Cultural Policies, a Council of Europe Programme—The Dilemma of Cross-National Comparisons (first part)," *Circular: Research and Documentation on Cultural Policies*, CIRCLE Newsletter, No. 3, 1996.

Mitchell, Ritva, "The Appraisal of National Cultural Policies, a Council of Europe Programme—Comparability of Results: Several Basic Questions (second part)," *Circular: Research and Documentation on Cultural Policies*, CIRCLE Newsletter, Nos. 4/5, 1996.

"MOSAIC (Managing an Open and Strategic Approach in Culture)," brochure, Council of Europe, 2000.

Mundy, Simon, *Cultural Policy: A Short Guide* (Strasbourg, France: Council of Europe Publishing, May 2000).

Mundy, Simon, "Requirements for a Sustainable Cultural Policy in Western Europe, North America and Australasia," in Christopher Gordon and Simon Mundy, *European Perspectives on Cultural Policy* (Paris, France: UNESCO Publishing, 2001).

Myerscough, John, with Christopher Gordon and William Dufton, *Comparative Study: European Programme of National Cultural Policy Reviews*, DECS-Cult/CP (97) 2 (Strasbourg, France: Culture Committee, Council of Europe, 1997).

Selwood, Sara, "Book Review: Policy Notes 1–5, Cultural Policies Research and Development Unit, Council of Europe Publishing, Strasbourg," *The International Journal of Cultural Policy*, Vol. 6, No. 2, 2000, pp. 317–321.

Wangermeé, Robert, *Evaluation of National Cultural Policies: Guidelines for the Preparation of National Reports*, DECS-Cult/CP (93) 3 (Strasbourg, France: Council for Cultural Co-operation, 4 August 1992).

UNESCO Cultural Policies for Development Unit International Network of Observatories in Cultural Policies Paris, France

Significance

Through its Cultural Policies for Development Unit (CPDU), UNESCO is making tentative steps to return to a field in which it was quite active in the 1970s and 1980s, particularly through the publication of its series, *Studies and Documents on Cultural Policies*. That series ultimately resulted in the publication of booklets documenting the then existing cultural policies in some sixty member countries. For about fifteen years this collection, despite the lack of comparability from document to document (i.e., from country to country), provided the only available information on comparative cultural policies. In particular, the CPDU is charged with consolidating a number of the recommendations to come out of the *Report of the World Commission on Culture and Development*. Among other projects, it is currently actively considering the various roles that it might play in the cultural policy research and information infrastructure.

Description

The Cultural Policies for Development Unit was created to support the work of the World Commission on Culture and Development. With that work completed, it is now developing project ideas to reestablish its claim on cultural policy and assure its institutional survival. As of this writing, three projects have emerged:

- Creation of an International Network of Observatories in Cultural Policies
- Adoption of the Council of Europe's Program of National Cultural Policy Evaluations and the application of it to member countries of UNESCO
- Development of an international compendium of cultural policies (through Culturelink, discussed further below)

The unit is also exploring the possibility of reviving UNESCO's earlier efforts to develop cross-national cultural statistics.

The CPDU says that it is undertaking a three-pronged set of activities:

- Research and analysis, including the construction of cultural indicators
- Clearinghouse and awareness-building work to share this knowledge
- Capacity building to apply that knowledge to local needs and situations

It is significant that in the materials of this initiative, culture is discussed as a transversal initiative rather than as a sectoral initiative. This reflects the general trend toward considering culture as instrumental in a number of other socioeconomic areas. (It also reflects a bit of imperialism on the part of culture units that wish to assert increased importance.)

In Stockholm in 1998, the Intergovernmental Conference on Cultural Policies for Development adopted an Action Plan that included the recommendation that the Director-General of UNESCO "encourage the establishment of networks for research and information on cultural policies for development, including study of the establishment of an observatory of cultural policies." The key here was that cultural policies would be integrated into development policies and play a role in sustainable development. What is particularly interesting is that this represents, in some sense, a return to the roots of the oldest research unit, the *Département des Études et de la Prospective* of the French Ministry of Culture and Communication, whose work in the early years came out of a movement toward cultural development, but with a new emphasis on cultural pluralism and cultural citizenship.

At the present time, the Cultural Policies for Development Unit of UNESCO has backed off the idea of creating a single overarching observatory. In part, this is due to the recognition that a number of observatories of varying stripes are already in existence; there is a strong predisposition not to sap the energies of these emerging agencies. UNESCO has turned, instead, to the idea of creating an International Network of Observatories in Cultural Policies.[29]

An initial meeting was held in Hannover, Germany on September 19–20, 2000, at which UNESCO brought together representatives from many of the existing observatories in order to consider what type of network might be necessary, desirable, and feasible.

What UNESCO seems to have had in mind is remarkably broad (and global):

> There is a need for shared work in order to develop the instruments and indicators necessary for analyzing and monitoring not only the evolution of complex cultural processes but also the relevance of cultural policies designed to address them. There is a need for comparative data collection and analysis on cultural change in the context of current globalizing processes in the socio-economic and technological arenas. Sharing experience could also facilitate the creation and the strengthening of observatories and similar institutions in less privileged regions and countries. Co-operation and exchange of information between and among such institutions [observatories] would appear to be essential to building a worldwide *cultural information infrastructure*. [Emphasis in original] [30]

To its credit, UNESCO does seem to recognize some of the pitfalls of a network of such organizations. A network would have to be built on the sharing of information that makes up its own "intellectual capital"—its own distinctiveness—but these observatories are operating in a "marketplace for knowledge services," which requires clients to commission work and which is increasingly based on competition, particularly with the arrival of explicitly profit-making entrepreneurs into the mix. As of this writing, UNESCO's plans to create an African Observatory of Cultural Policies appear to be going forward,[31] but the implementation of the network has been delayed for further study of its viability and necessity.

The efforts of the CPDU will not necessarily be limited to the creation of this network. It has also been discussing adapting the Council of Europe's model of national cultural policy evaluations and offering a similar service to countries that are members of UNESCO but outside of the Council of Europe. No action has been taken yet in this regard.

It also appears that UNESCO is considering taking up the question of cultural statistics once again. In the 1980s, a major UNESCO initiative along these lines collapsed because of the variations in national definitions and administrative structures and the difficulty of providing the depth and detail of information that UNESCO deemed necessary.

Finally, one must also note that transnational organizations are picking up on the application of research and information to national needs and situations at the same time as ministries of culture and arts councils are decentralizing their decision making, if not devolving cultural policy entirely, to the local and regional levels. Thus, there are two contrasting calls for research capability: one for building that capability at the local level (indeed, this is the impulse out of which many of the existing cultural observatories have been initiated) and the other for building that capability at the transnational level (the Council of Europe, the European Union, UNESCO). These transnational agencies slip easily into the rhetoric of "monitoring" activities and "reporting" on them, but there is a real fear in the field, which cannot be neglected, that monitoring could turn into control in one form or another as recommended models surface and as approved policies are promulgated.

The Cultural Policies for Development Unit also recognizes, and rightfully so, that a major problem in the field is the "poverty of the links between researchers and policymakers in most countries, which is one of the main reasons why the knowledge base for cultural policymaking is so inadequate." Amen.

Interviews and Contacts

Y. R. Isar
former Director
Cultural Policies for Development Unit
UNESCO

Katérina Stenou
Director
Division of Cultural Policies
UNESCO
7, Place de Fontenoy
75732 Paris 07 SP
France

Phone: 011-33-(0)1-45-68-43-03
Fax: 011-33-(0)1-45-68-55-97

e-mail: k.stenou@unesco.org

Web Site

http://www.unesco.org/culture/development/

Documents and Publications Consulted

"Annotated Agenda: Workshop—Towards an International Network of Observatories on Cultural Policies," draft, Cultural Policies for Development Unit, UNESCO, August 2000.

Delgado, Eduard, draft paper commissioned by UNESCO, "UNESCO World Observatory of Cultural Policies: SCANARTS," 1999(?).

Gordon, Christopher, "Cultural Policy Reviews: Some General and Methodological Reflections on the Council of Europe's Programme of Reviews in Member States (1985–1999)," paper commissioned by UNESCO, published in *Culturelink* 30, Vol. 11, April 2000, pp. 173–201; reprinted in Christopher Gordon and Simon Mundy, *European Perspectives on Cultural Policy* (Paris, France: UNESCO Publishing, 2001).

International Relations, Canadian Heritage, "Summary of Questionnaires," report of the results of a survey of cultural observatories prepared for the UNESCO Workshop on the creation of an international network of observatories on cultural policies, 2000.

Our Creative Diversity: Report of the World Commission on Culture and Development (Paris, France: World Commission on Culture and development, 1995).

"Towards an International Network of Observatories (and Similar Bodies) Devoted to Cultural Policies," Description of an International Workshop, Cultural Policies for Development Unit, UNESCO, 7 July 2000.

Culturelink
Network of Networks for Research and Cooperation in Cultural Development, Institute for International Relations
Zagreb, Croatia

Significance

Culturelink is representative of the trend to create networks of networks in an effort to bring some rationality to the field. Its main function is to facilitate communication among its member networks and to bring the work of these networks to the attention of the broader community of researchers and practitioners.

Description

Culturelink was established jointly by UNESCO and the Council of Europe to promote cultural development and international cooperation. Its official title is the Network of Networks for Research and Cooperation in Cultural Development. Culturelink sees its task as threefold: (1) the exchange of information through its journal *Culturelink*, (2) the establishment and development of databases, and (3) international research in the field of cultural development and cooperation.

Although Culturelink has organized some conferences and begun some documentation work, its primary output is its journal. This journal is basically a compendium of descriptions of organizations operating in the field and announcements of various publications, seminars, and conferences. For the most part, material that is sent into the journal is simply repackaged and redistributed. The journal probably provides more of a valuable service for central and eastern

Europe because it brings together and disseminates information that central and eastern Europeans would not otherwise easily receive. It also provides, to a limited extent, an outlet for the writing of researchers who have difficulty gaining access to other professional publishing venues. On occasion, the journal publishes the papers presented at conferences, seminars, or meetings in the field.

Culturelink has been funded by UNESCO to compile an International Compendium of Cultural Policies, which is available on its Web site.[32] This compendium, while including more countries than the compendium prepared for the Council of Europe by ERICArts, is regarded by some as being a less useful source of comparative information than the database assembled for the Council of Europe by ERICArts. This example illustrates the duplication of effort that accompanies the uncoordinated proliferation of organizations in the field.

Contact

Biserka Cvjetičanin [*not interviewed*]
Network Coordinator
CULTURELINK/IMO
Ul. Lj. F. Vukotinovića 2
P.O. Box 303
10000 Zagreb
Croatia

Phone: 011-385-1-48-26-522
Fax: 011-385-1-48-28-361

e-mail: clink@mairmo.irmo.hr

Web Site

http://www.culturelink.org

Documents and Publications Consulted

Various issues of *Culturelink*, the journal of the Network of Networks for Research and Cooperation in Cultural Development, Institute for International Relations, Zagreb, Croatia.

Canadian Cultural Research Network
Centre for Cultural Management
University of Waterloo
Waterloo, Ontario, Canada

Significance

The Canadian Cultural Research Network is an example of independent researchers banding together in a network with the hope of collectively encouraging increased research on cultural policy in Canada. The idea has its roots in the tradition of academic social science societies ("learned societies"). In this sense, it is similar to the national associations that have spun off, for example, from the Association of Cultural Economics International.

Background

In the mid-1990s, a steering committee composed of individuals with an interest in promoting cultural research from the academic community, the private sector, and the federal government developed a proposal for a Canadian Cultural Research Network (CCRN). In the spring of 1996, the committee undertook a survey of cultural researchers throughout the country to determine interest in such a network and to identify specific needs. The survey revealed significant interest in a network and a widespread desire to contribute to its establishment.

In CCRN's view,

> Canada's cultural sector is facing a radically changing operating environment. Reduced government funding, changing demographics, [and] new media and information technologies present

> the sector with major challenges. With fewer resources, governments are seeking new roles and new collaborative strategies. The need for applied research and scholarship into the challenges facing the sector, both short-term and longer term, has never been greater. By extension, the sharing of information and research within Canada and the development of a national cultural research community with strong links to policy development is [*sic*] critical. The establishment of a national networking mechanism also facilitates collaboration with networks in other countries/regions.[33]

To date, the network has focused on the sharing of information. CCRN is interested in encouraging research, but it does not have a budget of its own. It would like to generate research from its members, and, for the moment, seems to have focused on identifying opportunities for cultural policy researchers to conduct their work under the auspices of existing research programs. For example, CCRN has called its members' attention to the research themes announced by the Social Sciences and Humanities Research Council, suggesting that SSHRC might be interested in proposals that fit its strategic research themes:

- ❒ Challenges and Opportunities in a Knowledge-Based Economy
- ❒ Exploring Social Cohesion in a Globalizing Era
- ❒ Society, Culture, and the Health of Canadians

As part of the first meeting of the CCRN board in Toronto in January 1999, a one-day research forum, *Cultural Policies and Cultural Practices: Exploring the Links Between Culture and Social Change*, identified four themes that it thought linked the SSRHC strategic themes with priority cultural research issues identified at the founding CCRN colloquium:

- ❒ Redefining the Public Interest in Culture in a Pluralistic Society
- ❒ Cultural Sovereignty and Globalization
- ❒ The Social, Cultural, and Economic Implications of Interactivity
- ❒ The Contribution of the Arts and Heritage to Healthy Communities

A project to develop a cultural policy thesaurus has apparently been launched, and a couple of conferences, one in conjunction with CIRCLE, have been held.

Assessment

At the present time, CCRN, like most networks operating in the field of cultural policy research and information, does not seem to have a strong *raison d'être*. Beyond a general desire to contribute to the cultural policy debate and the specific desire to get research contracts, there is little to motivate its activities. In part, CCRN is a response to the fact that the commissioning of cultural policy research is perceived by researchers to be haphazard at best. Yet, it is unclear how much the proliferation of networks such as this one has helped to make the field of cultural policy research more predictable and more attractive a place in which to invest one's academic career.

In the view of some, it has been difficult to attract key researchers to this network because they are more attached to their own professional societies (e.g., the Association of Cultural Economics International).

Interviews and Contacts

William D. Poole, Director [*not interviewed*]
Centre for Cultural Management
144 Hagey Hall
University of Waterloo
Waterloo, Ontario N2L 3G1
Canada
Phone: 1-519-888-4567 x 5057
Fax: 1-519-746-3956
e-mail: ccm@watarts.uwaterloo.ca

John Foote
Manager, Economic Research and Analysis
Strategic Planning and Policy Coordination
Cultural Development
Canadian Heritage
Phone: 1-819-997-0326
e-mail: John_Foote@pch.gc.ca

Web Site

http://www.arts.uwaterloo.ca/ccm/ccrn

Documents and Publications Consulted

Foote, John A., "Cultural Consumption and Participation," paper presented at the CIRCLE-CCRN Roundtable, Edmonton, Alberta, Canada, 27–28 May 2000.

Foote, John A., "New Cultural Policy Research Directions," paper presented at the CCRN Colloquium/Social Sciences and Humanities Conference, Edmonton, Alberta, Canada, 28–29 May 2000.

Part III. Notes

1. For a fuller discussion of the issues involved in comparative cultural policy research, see J. Mark Schuster, "Thoughts on the Art and Practice of Comparative Cultural Research," in Ineke van Hamersveld and Niki van der Wielen (eds.), *Cultural Research in Europe* (Amsterdam, The Netherlands: Boekmanstichting, 1996).

2. *Poetics* is also making a concerted effort to report policy-relevant research, but it is not as far developed in this direction as the other journals are.

3. This proposal, in turn, emerged from Wiesand's document, "Proposals for the Creation of a Network of Centres for Cultural Documentation Research and Development," DECS/DC (80) 19.

4. In the late 1980s, a central European group, EUROCIRCON—The European Culture Impact Research Consortium, was formed in Budapest with a similar interest in assessing the impact of the cultural dimensions of the new Europe. Like CIRCLE, it was made up of member institutes. It presented some competition to CIRCLE, but with the fall of governments in Eastern Europe this initiative disappeared. (Today there is a new cultural observatory in Budapest, discussed on page 193.)

5. Augustin Girard, "Thirty Years," *Circular: Research and Documentation on Cultural Policies*, No. 10, July 1999, p. 3.

6. Zentrum für Kulturforschung, "Proposal for a Statute of the Association for Cultural Research and Documentation (ACREDO)," Bonn, Germany, 1980.

7. A list of the main CIRCLE publications can be found at http://www.boekman.nl/circle/pub_arch.htm

8. As the research for this book proceeded, the Boekmanstichting's CRIE project was gradually being replaced with a new program of CIRCLE: Cultural Policy Research Online (CPRO). The intent is to develop a truly international online database of ongoing cultural policy research projects.

9. For a retelling of the history of CIRCLE from a documentation point of view, see Cas Smithuijsen, "The Need for a European Liaison for Cultural Policy Resources," in Boekmanstichting, *RECAP: Resources for Cultural Policy in Europe* (Amsterdam, The Netherlands: The Boekman Foundation, 1999). For a retelling that focuses more on the research side, see Augustin Girard, "Thirty Years," *Circular: Research and Documentation on Cultural Policies*, No. 10, July 1999, p. 3.

10. http://www.interarts.net/web_forum/01/01.htm

11. http://www.culturalpolicies.net

12. The Compendium is not too far removed from another project, the *Handbook of Cultural Affairs in Europe*, which is a directory of key names and addresses in cultural policy in the various European countries.

Originally developed by Andreas Wiesand with the Council of Europe, it became a CIRCLE project. Over the years it has become more of a ZfKf project.

13. At some point during its history, the name of this program seems to have been changed from the Program for the Evaluation of National Cultural Policies to the European Program of National Cultural Policy Reviews. One wonders if the word "evaluation" had become problematic.

14. The deliberations of this meeting are summarized in *Methods for Evaluation of National Cultural Policies*, Report from a seminar in Stockholm, Sweden, April 16–18, 1985 (Stockholm, Sweden: Swedish Ministry of Education and Cultural Affairs, 1986).

15. After the first few national evaluations were completed, a set of common guidelines was developed for future evaluations: Robert Wangermeé, *Evaluation of National Cultural Policies: Guidelines for the Preparation of National Reports*, DECS-Cult/CP (93)3 (Strasbourg, France: Council for Cultural Co-operation, 4 August 1992).

16. In chronological order: France, Sweden, Austria, the Netherlands, Finland, Italy, Estonia, Russian Federation, Slovenia, Latvia, Lithuania, Bulgaria, Croatia, Portugal, Romania, Albania, and Armenia.

17. Andorra, Moldova, the Slovak Republic, and Turkey.

18. Azerbaijan, Bosnia-Herzegovina, Cyprus, "The Former Yugoslav Republic of Macedonia," Georgia, and Malta.

19. Augustin Girard, "Cultural Indicators," provisional document, DECS-Cult (92) 6 (Strasbourg: Council for Cultural Co-operation, Council of Europe, 1992); Ritva Mitchell, "The Appraisal of National Cultural Policies, a Council of Europe Programme—The Dilemma of Cross-National Comparisons (first part)," *Circular: Research and Documentation on Cultural Policies*, CIRCLE Newsletter, No. 3, 1996; and Ritva Mitchell, "The Appraisal of National Cultural Policies, a Council of Europe Programme—Comparability of Results: Several Basic Questions (second part)," *Circular: Research and Documentation on Cultural Policies*, CIRCLE Newsletter, Nos. 4/5, 1996.

20. For a more detailed description of this program, see http://www.coe.int/T/E/Cultural_Co-operation/Culture/Cultural_policies/Comparative_reviews/

21. Included in this study were Cyprus, Finland, Lower Saxony (Germany), Hungary, the Netherlands, and Poland.

22. Included in this study were Austria, Canada, Belgium (French Community), Bulgaria, Luxembourg, Switzerland, and the United Kingdom.

23. Included in this study were Bulgaria, Romania, Albania, Estonia, Lithuania, Moldova, Latvia, and the Slovak Republic.

24. http://www.culturalpolicies.net

25. ERICArts and Council of Europe, *Cultural Policies in Europe: A Compendium of Basic Facts and Trends* (Bonn, Germany: Council of Eu-

rope/ERICArts in co-operation with ARCult Media Verlagsbuchhandlung für Kultur & Wissenschaft, 2000), p. III.

26. See, for example, John Myerscough et al., *Comparative Study: European Programme of National Cultural Policy Reviews,* DECS-Cult/CP (97) 2 (Strasbourg, France: Culture Committee, Council of Europe, 1997); Christopher Gordon, "Cultural Policy Reviews: Some General and Methodological Reflections on the Council of Europe's Programme of Reviews in Member States (1985-1999)," paper commissioned by UNESCO, published in *Culturelink* 30, Vol. 11, April 2000, pp. 173-201, reprinted in Christopher Gordon and Simon Mundy, *European Perspectives on Cultural Policy* (Paris: UNESCO Publishing, 2001); Ritva Mitchell, "The Appraisal of National Cultural Policies, a Council of Europe Programme—The Dilemma of Cross-National Comparisons (first part)," *Circular: Research and Documentation on Cultural Policies*, CIRCLE Newsletter, No. 3, 1996; and Ritva Mitchell, "The Appraisal of National Cultural Policies, a Council of Europe Programme—Comparability of Results: Several Basic Questions (second part)," *Circular: Research and Documentation on Cultural Policies*, CIRCLE Newsletter, Nos. 4/5, 1996.

27. Sara Selwood, "Book Review: Policy Notes 1–5, Cultural Policies Research and Development Unit, Council of Europe Publishing, Strasbourg," *The International Journal of Cultural Policy*, Vol. 6, No. 2, 2000, pp. 319–320.

28. As of this writing, this initiative appears to be dormant.

29. This initiative developed to the point of setting up a Web site: http://www.unesco.org/culture/development/observatories/index.shtml

30. "Towards an 'International Network of Observatories (and Similar Bodies) Devoted to Cultural Policies," Description of an International Workshop, Cultural Policies for Development Unit, UNESCO, 7 July 2000.

31. http://www.unesco.org/culture/development/observatories/html_eng/news2.shtml

32. http://mirror-us.unesco.org/culturelink/culpol/index.html

33. http://www.arts.uwaterloo.ca/ccm/ccrn/ccrn_IA1-3.html

APPENDIX

The Research and Information Infrastructure for Cultural Policy: A Consideration of Models for the United States

by

Ruth Ann Stewart

and

Catherine C. Galley

DISCUSSION AND POLICY RECOMMENDATIONS FROM MEETING CONVENED DECEMBER 7, 2001

—

CENTER FOR URBAN POLICY RESEARCH
EDWARD J. BLOUSTEIN SCHOOL OF PLANNING AND PUBLIC POLICY
RUTGERS, THE STATE UNIVERSITY OF NEW JERSEY
NEW BRUNSWICK, NEW JERSEY

Supported by

THE PEW CHARITABLE TRUSTS

Ruth Ann Stewart *is research professor of cultural policy at the Center for Urban Policy Research at Rutgers University's Edward J. Bloustein School of Planning and Public Policy. She is the former Assistant Librarian of Congress for national education and cultural programs.*

Catherine C. Galley *is postdoctoral associate at the Center for Urban Policy Research at Rutgers University's Edward J. Bloustein School of Planning and Public Policy. In the fall of 2002, Dr. Galley will be assistant professor of architecture at Texas Tech University.*

INTRODUCTION

On December 7, 2001, eighteen key members of the cultural policy community gathered at Rutgers University in New Brunswick, New Jersey, for a one-day meeting held under the auspices of Rutgers' Center for Urban Policy Research. Ruth Ann Stewart, research professor at the Edward J. Bloustein School of Planning and Public Policy at Rutgers, organized the meeting with funding provided by The Pew Charitable Trusts. Participants in the meeting represented a broad cross section of organizations and institutions in the field of cultural policy, including think tanks, foundations, service organizations, universities, business, and government agencies. Participants were selected for their experience and expert knowledge about the nonprofit and commercial arts sectors and their potential need for research and information.

The meeting took as its starting point a draft version of the present book by J. Mark Schuster, professor of urban cultural policy at the Massachusetts Institute of Technology. His draft report, "Informing Cultural Policy: A Consideration of Models for the Information and Research Infrastructure," became the platform on which the daylong discussion of the arts and cultural policy research and information system in the United States was based. Formal presentations were made by Christopher Gordon, former head of the English Regional Arts Board, who also served as moderator; Augustin Girard, president of the Comité d'Histoire of the French Ministry of Culture and former head of the research division of the French Ministry of Culture and Communication; and Vladimir Skok, program manager of the new Canadian Cultural Observatory. They presented their views of the strengths and weaknesses of the long established cultural policy research and information systems in Great Britain and France and of the newly emerging approach to cultural policy research and information in Canada.

Participants were charged with examining a system that is little understood and generally characterized as fragmentary and ad hoc. They concluded that, while it was useful for them to examine the cultural policy data systems of other Western countries, the singular nature of the American arts and culture sector ultimately required the use of a different approach. Despite the short time available for covering so much territory, the assembled group rose to the challenge and concluded the day with a series of recommendations for strategies and next steps toward the development and advancement of an organized system for maintaining and disseminating information relevant to good decision making about the arts and culture in the United States.

OVERVIEW

In contrast to the situation in other industrialized Western countries, the arts and culture in the United States are primarily a decentralized, private-sector enterprise. Similarly, the U.S. approach to cultural policy research and information is fragmentary and largely ad hoc by comparison. These observations set the framework for consideration of a number of questions raised throughout the day. The current system was dissected at the national, state, and local levels; impediments to the current development of the research and information infrastructure were examined; promising efforts were noted; and funding models were discussed. The concept of a decentralized system was reaffirmed as consistent with the decentralized nature of the U.S. cultural sector and the local dimension of American culture. Although no radical proposals emerged from the discussion, the group's thoughtful definition and analysis of the cultural policy research and information landscape, as well as its recommendations for possible strategies and next steps, have measurably advanced the debate.

Issues of Supply and Demand

Cultural policy information is a commodity and, as such, it is subject to the constraints of demand in considering recommendations for developing a better supply of research and information. An information system is sustainable only if there is demand for that information. Because information suppliers focus more on process, and information users are more concerned with outcomes, the system can serve as a mediator and translator to bridge the gap between the two cultures. Participants argued that organized data exchange and personal interaction between not only the suppliers and the demanders but also within their respective groups would promote the development of a "common intelligence" or language to advance the likelihood of an effective and valued cultural policy infrastructure.

The participants agreed that further analysis is needed to better understand how issues of supply and demand must be taken into account in the development of a research and information infrastructure in the United States. The discussion began with the following questions.

What is the nature of the demand for cultural policy research and information in the United States?

In the United States, the predominant demand for policy data comes not from government agencies or decision makers, as in other Western countries, but from the private sector. Corporations and investors consume economic policy data while benefits planners and insurers are the chief users of health-policy data. In the arts, private and nonprofit arts organizations constitute the primary demand for policy data. (Arts organizations also generate their own research and information and thus can represent supply as well as demand.)

The potential user group for good arts and cultural research data is thought to be quite large, but it is difficult to assess the actual level of this highly segmented demand; far too little is known about the individual components. (Demand by the advocacy community for economic impact information is a recent possible exception.) Furthermore, demand can appear in many guises and may be met in ways that neither address a policy purpose nor follow a systematic and rigorous research process. Questions were raised as to whether actual demand is over- or underestimated.

The following groups were identified, with certain caveats, as among the most likely, as well as desirable, constituencies that would demand good and systematic cultural policy data:

- *Arts administrators*. A growing number of individuals are being trained in arts administration, public policy, or nonprofit management programs, and are utilizing new information to introduce new practices. However, the majority of U.S. art administrators have little or no exposure to formal training in arts administration and even less to cultural policy. The few cultural policy courses offered tend to be narrowly focused on the latest news from the National Endowment for the Arts and are almost totally lacking in international perspective. It was argued that practitioner demand now or in the near future is overestimated. Practitioners are underpaid, overworked, understaffed, and skeptical as to how rigorous data research and interpretation could assist them in their jobs. It was also argued that a better information base could ultimately improve administrative practice, as has been the experience in France.
- *Agency staff*. With good information and communication, policy-related activities carried out by separate agencies and even departments within the same agency that perform parallel, if separately budgeted, cultural functions could be synchronized. Such activities include preservation; economic development; tourism; parks and recreation; and the cultural industries. Experience has shown that collaborations can move policy at the state level.

- *Service organizations.* Market pressures are creating a growing awareness among advocacy groups of the importance of research-based information for advancing their interests both nationally and at the local level.
- *Journalists.* Professional journalists value reliable and accessible data sources. As the gatekeepers for much that the public understands and appreciates about the issues, journalists are key to the development and maintenance of a strong information infrastructure.
- *Elected officials.* Individually and collectively, elected officials directly affect cultural policy. In contrast to other Western countries, demand in the United States for cultural policy information is not a well-established public tradition. Elected officials tend to be indifferent to pure scholarly research and show little interest in supporting the production of good-quality data. Politicians are predisposed to depend on the press and often "pirate" what journalists produce. In recent times, however, some expectations have emerged at the local level that arts and cultural groups should be able to provide the kinds of policy-relevant information marshaled by other community interests, such as sports teams and environmental groups.
- *Commercial industries.* Books, magazines, newspapers, musical recordings, film and videos, multimedia products, and emerging digital industries make up an important cultural subsector that generates large amounts of proprietary research and information. It is not clear the extent to which the cultural industries or their professional associations would be interested in a reliable cultural policy information structure.
- *Grant seekers.* Practitioners and artists are high users of the funding-data supply. As public-arts funding declines at the national level while proliferating at the state and local levels, a system that delivers broader and deeper information will be in even greater demand.
- *Arts funders.* The priorities of this pivotal demand group have major implications for the research and information agenda in terms of both its consumption of data and the type of research it selects to fund. Few foundations, and even fewer government agencies, currently recognize policy research as an important funding priority.
- *Scholars.* There is a sense that scholars doing research in the field of cultural policy have the most interest in reliable cultural policy data. However, researchers, and by extension

the research system, are handicapped by the limited support they receive to work with cultural data on a regular basis, to develop new primary data, to disseminate their findings, or to mentor current or potential young scholars in the field.

What is the current supply of cultural policy research and information in the United States?

It was argued that there is an abundant, though idiosyncratic, supply of cultural policy information, but the data and the ability to document, track, and coordinate the supply have severe limitations. Specific items of concern are set forth below.

- The data are disorganized and scattered. It is difficult to make coherent and purposeful sense of the information and identify good practices and ideas.
- Many cultural policy reports and documents are ephemeral and out of circulation—the so-called gray literature—and therefore difficult to capture.
- Consistent classification of the existing and emerging research and information is lacking, making it difficult to locate it, keep track of it, and disseminate it.
- The data are generated by disconnected "silos" of research activities that are separated and defined by different art disciplines (e.g., performing arts, visual arts), by academic disciplines (e.g., economics, sociology, political science), or by policy issue (e.g., arts funding, intellectual property, preservation). This "siloization" is further compounded by the proliferation of networks of individuals with narrowly focused common interests.
- The data are unreliable and incompatible, making it difficult to verify the numbers or even know their origins. It was argued that information provided by advocacy groups is of questionable value, such as in the case of economic impact studies funded by state arts councils.
- Interpretation is lacking, forestalling the observation of emerging patterns that is basic to good policy analysis and limiting the growth of demand for further data.
- The research and analysis process lacks transparency and is not responsive to emerging markets and issues.

- Research is limited in scope and focus. Basic, across-the-board data are lacking. Most research takes place at the local level and focuses almost exclusively on the nonprofit sector.
- Unlike other Western countries, the United States lacks informed policy analysis of the cultural industries.
- Some of the better data are costly, proprietary, or otherwise inaccessible, especially those produced by the arts industries and the creative unions. Some nonprofit service organizations are also limiting the distribution of their data.
- The research agenda is being shortchanged by the shift in emphasis away from issues to program implementation and its consequences.
- Communication within the cultural sector itself, as well as between information suppliers and research users, is poor. A common language (i.e., "common intelligence") is lacking.
- A set of core information for the field has yet to be determined.
- General agreement on the working definition of cultural policy is lacking.

Which comes first, supply or demand?

There was no clear agreement among the participants as to whether demand must be created first. Perhaps demand would follow if there were sufficient work on the supply side. Some argued that because the United States lacks a consensus about culture as a public good, and by extension cultural policy research, demand would have to precede supply. Others argued that supply would create its own demand. Regardless, it was agreed that the lack of a comprehensive network of suppliers inhibits the creation of enough supply to either meet or stimulate consistent demand.

Encouraging Developments

Although the American approach to cultural policy research and information can rightfully be characterized as scattershot, examination of even long-established systems in other Western countries makes it clear that there are no ideal models to follow. It is encouraging, however, to note a number of promising efforts with positive structural implications for the beginnings of a viable system in the United States.

- *Americans for the Arts* is conducting a profile project to identify support sources for nonprofit arts organizations in ten communities.
- *The Center for Arts and Culture* is a first effort at the creation of a think tank in the arts and culture. It has established the *Cultural Policy Listserv* and a network of cultural policy researchers, administrators, and educators.
- *Cultural Policy and the Arts National Data Archive (CPANDA)* is the first U.S. digital archive of research data on the arts and culture to address the chronic lack of interpretation in arts and cultural policy research. This project will also make these data available to researchers in other interested fields (political science, sociology, and economics) for secondary analyses. Based at Princeton University under a three-year grant from The Pew Charitable Trusts, CPANDA will provide online storage, information retrieval, selective data access, and downloading capabilities.
- *The Foundation Center* has been a longtime supplier of information on private foundation grantmaking and on funding trends in the arts and culture.
- *The National Arts Journalism Program*, based at Columbia University's Graduate School of Journalism, administers fellowships for mid-career and senior journalists in the fields of arts and culture. It serves as a forum for exploring the intersection of journalism and cultural policy issues.
- *The National Information Network for Artists*, based at the New York Foundation for the Arts, was created in response to artists' demand for more information about grants and other resources that could help them pursue their artistic endeavors.
- *The National Endowment for the Arts (NEA)* and *The Urban Institute* are working to create a unified database of artists and arts organizations that expands on aggregate data provided in the U.S. Census.
- *Social Theory, Policy and the Arts* and the *Association of Cultural Economics International* provide annual arts and cultural policy forums that promote multidisciplinary exchange between scholars and researchers from around the country and the world. A biennial *International Conference on Cultural Policy Research* has also been launched.
- *The University of Chicago's Cultural Policy Center* at The Irving B. Harris Graduate School of Public Policy Studies is currently mapping the cultural landscape of Washington State based on methodology adapted from the Council of Europe.

- *A weekly newspaper on the arts*, along the lines of *The Chronicle of Philanthropy*, is being market-tested with a grant from The Pew Charitable Trusts and several other foundations.
- *Think tanks*, such as the Urban Institute and RAND Corporation, are weighing into the cultural policy field with major research and data-generating projects.
- *State arts agencies* have developed a good information exchange network using common denominators for statistical data collection that capitalizes on the research performed within their respective states.
- *Interest in research is growing at the local level* as a result of the experience with economic impact analyses. Though of dubious quality, these studies have raised awareness in the cultural sector of the need for better information based on real policy demand. Arts and cultural groups are realizing that it is crucial to provide the kinds of information that other community interest groups use to influence public officials.
- *International Federation of Arts Councils and Culture Agencies (IFACCA)* is newly established to promote cooperation and information dissemination at the global level. IFACCA mediates an e-mail network called *D'Art*. The National Endowment for the Arts is a charter member of IFACCA.

In short, the diversity of information generated by the highly pluralistic arts and cultural community is a major strength of the cultural policy system in the United States even as it now exists. But much more can be accomplished.

How is a research and information system to be supported in the United States?

With few exceptions, the major cost of cultural policy data and dissemination in the United States is not likely to be borne by government. Although the participants thought it premature to identify potential funders, a few suggestions and some fresh thinking did surface as to who might be among the stakeholders within the public, private, and philanthropic sectors.

Public sector. Although there are likely to be any number of federal-level players, the discussion limited itself to the NEA. It was argued that the federal government should assume the expense of doing the compiling, interpreting, and disseminating of the core data that are essential to the cultural policy field. The investment of public resources in such activities is justified because of the many users both inside and outside the cultural policy field who will benefit, despite the cost associated with such work. Without such support, there will be very little national-level data on the arts. Participants believe it is critical to the development and maintenance of a sound cultural policy infrastructure for the federal government to continue to view the production of trend information in the arts and culture as an important public service. Future discussion should look at the government's role at the regional, state, and local levels.

For a number of years, state arts agencies have supported data collection that has been fairly well standardized across the country. Additional state (and local) support for building on this effort may be forthcoming.

Participants and presenters from outside the United States also viewed the international cultural community as being stakeholders in the success of the American research and information system. Reciprocal arrangements and partnerships at the international level could have direct benefits.

Private sector. Demographic changes have the potential for creating new funding streams for research. As baby boomers age, they often change careers and assume new interests, especially the arts and culture. Certain interests in the business sector could be courted to become subscribers to a cultural-information service that would provide data about the emerging "40-something" market. Foundations and venture philanthropists could be approached for start-up funding and to underwrite the necessary market research. The CPANDA project funded by The Pew Charitable Trusts at Princeton University is a prototype of such an enterprise.

Philanthropic sector. Participants noted that foundations provide proportionally less support for research in the arts than research in other fields. The largest share of arts funding goes to capital expenditures and general support. While The Pew Charitable Trusts has increased its public profile through a major investment in research, small family foundations—the fastest-growing foundation subsector—are the least likely to fund research of any kind. A very small percentage of total foundation funding is directed to arts research. This situation is unlikely to change without a total reorientation and reeducation of foundation program officers.

It was suggested that cultural policy research could be marketed as an innovative and creative philanthropic venture to successful businesspeople looking for new personal challenges. In addition, many small companies want to give back to their communities and are seeking an avenue for bringing their names before a broader audience.

Recommendations

While it is clear that information providers must endeavor to arrive at a better understanding of what is inhibiting the emergence of a more coherent American cultural policy infrastructure, the participants believe that enough is now known to at least begin to develop recommendations for remedial action. These recommendations will inform a plan for the future growth and development of a system that will be trusted and valued by researchers and decision makers alike.

- The large amount of highly dispersed data that already exists should be sorted out and rendered usable. (The NEA and Urban Institute unified database project is an example of such an effort already under way, as is CPANDA.)
- The research and analysis infrastructure should probably remain decentralized but with built-in provisions for communication, interaction, and comparative analysis.
- The databases generated by the new infrastructure should be centralized to ensure coherence and reliability, and made available through digital means. (There was no consensus as to whether a new entity should be created or some existing entity leveraged to assume this function.)
- The infrastructure should undergo periodic review.
- A number of independent but multilateral research centers of excellence—characterized by Augustin Girard as "common intelligence units"—should be developed to bridge the data gap between the academy and decision makers.
- Information providers should formulate a marketing strategy to stimulate demand based on a better working knowledge and understanding of the highly segmented and pluralistic constituency, both current and potential, for arts and culture information in the United States.
- Cultural activities should be synchronized within and across agencies and departments at the federal, state, and local government levels.

- A common language and set of definitional understandings should be a central element of the development of the research and information infrastructure.
- Grants, prizes, and other incentives should be created to encourage doctoral students and young assistant professors to pursue research in the field of cultural policy and to legitimate cultural policy as an academic field.
- The research agenda should include broad-based research and focus on issues as well as programmatic outcomes.
- More-specific links should be developed with the commercial arts and culture, possibly even through the formation of a cultural industries association, as a way of expediting both the supply of, and demand for, research.
- Foundations should be educated about, and program officers reoriented to, the importance of arts-policy research and the dearth of current funding available to develop good data in support of informed policy decision making.
- Communication and broad information dissemination should be facilitated for multiple purposes and multiple audiences, especially beyond the academy. A major target should be advisors and consultants to both private and public decision makers.
- Vehicles should be developed for disseminating timely, accessible, and trustworthy information. Some models of reference include:
    - Monographs, such as *The Nonprofit Sector: A Research Handbook* (Yale University Press, 1989)
    - A quarterly journal, perhaps an American (or international) version of *Cultural Trends*
    - A weekly cultural newsreader similar to *The Chronicle of Philanthropy*
    - Online research and information networks such as the Center for Arts and Culture's *Cultural Policy Network* and its *Cultural Policy Listserv*, or IFACCA's *D'Art*
- The reach of the U.S. system should be extended to encompass cultural policy research at the international level, including participation in global forums and support for cultural infrastructure issues in underdeveloped countries. Finally, the United States should rejoin UNESCO.

PARTICIPANTS

KELLY BARSDATE
Director of Research, Policy, and Evaluation
National Assembly of State Arts Agencies
Washington, D.C.

TOM BRADSHAW
Director, Research Division
National Endowment for the Arts
Washington, D.C.

SHELLEY FEIST
Program Associate
The Pew Charitable Trusts
Philadelphia, Pennsylvania

SARAH GARDNER
Executive Director
International Federation of Arts Councils and Culture Agencies (IFACCA)
Sydney, Australia

AUGUSTIN GIRARD (PRESENTER)
Président
Comité d'Histoire du Ministère de la Culture
Paris, France

CHRISTOPHER GORDON (MODERATOR)
Consultant
Former head, English Regional Arts Board
Winchester, Hampshire
England

JOAN JEFFRI
President, Association of Arts Administration Educators
Director, Program in Arts Administration
Teachers College
Columbia University
New York, New York

JULIA LOWELL
Economist
RAND Corporation
Santa Monica, California

Lawrence McGill
Director, Research and Planning
Cultural Policy and the Arts National Data Archive
Center for Arts and Cultural Policy Studies
Princeton University
Princeton, New Jersey

Edward Pauly
Director of Evaluation
Wallace-Reader's Digest Fund
New York, New York

Loren Renz
Vice President for Research
The Foundation Center
New York, New York

Lawrence Rothfield
Faculty Director
Cultural Policy Program
Harris Graduate School of Public Policy Studies
University of Chicago
Chicago, Illinois

J. Mark Schuster (Meeting Consultant/Book Author)
Professor of Urban Cultural Policy
Massachusetts Institute of Technology
Cambridge, Massachusetts

Bruce Seaman
President, Association of Cultural Economics International
Professor, Georgia State University
Atlanta, Georgia

Vladimir Skok (Presenter)
Program Manager
Canadian Cultural Observatory
Canadian Heritage
Hull, Québec
Canada

Ruth Ann Stewart (Meeting Organizer/Appendix Author)
Research Professor
Center for Urban Policy Research
Edward J. Bloustein School of Planning and Public Policy
Rutgers, The State University of New Jersey
New Brunswick, New Jersey

Harold L. Vogel
Wall Street Entertainment and Media Analyst
Bronx, New York

Margaret J. Wyszomirski
Professor
Graduate Program in Arts Policy
Ohio State University
Columbus, Ohio

Acknowledgments

The organization and success of the CUPR-Rutgers meeting was greatly assisted by Danielle Graves, Mary Jane Hicks, Donita Devance-Manzini, William Marosy, Renée Dougé, and Brenden Cheney. Special thanks to Gregory Perry and the staff of the Jane Voorhees Zimmerli Art Museum at Rutgers University.

INDEX

C

D

E

F

O

P

Q

R

S

T

For Product Safety Concerns and Information please contact our EU
representative GPSR@taylorandfrancis.com
Taylor & Francis Verlag GmbH, Kaufingerstraße 24, 80331 München, Germany

www.ingramcontent.com/pod-product-compliance
Ingram Content Group UK Ltd.
Pitfield, Milton Keynes, MK11 3LW, UK
UKHW011456240425
457818UK00021B/854